The Complete Introduction to
Laser Racing

"*The Complete Introduction to Laser Racing is indeed a very comprehensive book on sailing. It covers all the areas that a competitive sailor must look into to reach the top. Although it is called an 'introduction,' it contains insightful details that will help the experienced sailor as well. Ben has once again done us proud by using his training as an elite sailor, medical doctor, sport scientist and coach to expertly pool together the knowledge of an impressive and diverse team of contributors and reviewers in a book that is useful not only to Laser sailors but to all dinghy sailors.*"

Ng Ser Miang
Member, International Olympic Committee
Chairman, Singapore Sports Council
former Vice President, International Sailing Federation

Editor and Author
Ben Tan

Content Contributors
Michael Blackburn
Rod Dawson
Nick Adamson
Steve Cockerill
Jacqueline Ellis
Takao Otani
Trisha Leahy
Angela Calder
Gary Slater

Foreword by
Peter Fricker and Trevor Millar

THE COMPLETE INTRODUCTION TO LASER RACING

Reprinted 2001

The trademark  is the property of Performance Sailcraft Europe Ltd, Performance Sailcraft Japan Ltd, Performance Sailcraft Australia Ltd, and Vanguard Sailboats Inc.

Published by
Singapore Sports Council
15 Stadium Road
National Stadium
Singapore 397718
Facsimile: 65-345 2541
Email: ssc_pr@ssc.gov.sg

Distributed by
Constant Wind Pte Ltd
12 Changi South Lane
Bodynits Building
Singapore 486353
Phone: 65-445 5108
Facsimile: 65-448 1551
Email: constantwind@pacific.net.sg

Designed and produced by FSTOP Pte Ltd
Designer Josie Quak

Cover photograph by The Straits Times

Proudly sponsored by Singapore Pools (Private) Limited

ISBN 9971-88-759-2
Printed in Singapore

FOREWORD

I was first acquainted with Ben Tan when he arrived as a postgraduate student undertaking the Master's Degree in Sports Medicine at the Australian Institute of Sport and the University of Canberra in 1997.

Ben, not surprisingly, shone as a student and produced some of his research during his time with us that has led to publication in international refereed journals on the subject of strength development and conditioning.

Ben's reputation as an elite sailor goes without saying and he is now in the happy situation of working in the field of sports medicine and heading up the Sports Science Department of the Singapore Sports Council.

This book has been the result of an extraordinary effort by a very talented team of contributors, many of whom are known to me. It is eminently readable and beautifully illustrated and leaves no question unanswered for the novice who wishes to take up Laser sailing and racing.

As an amateur sailor at an extremely recreational level I was pleased to find that the technical terms are kept simple and I found the tips that have been enclosed throughout the book most useful. These tips really provide an extra dimension to an extremely practical manual.

This book deserves success because it is a reflection of the authors' experience and expertise, and particularly so of the Editor.

Professor Peter Fricker OAM MBBS FASMF FACSM FACSP
Director of Medical Services, Department of Sports Medicine, Australian Institute of Sport
Member, Medical Commission, Australian Olympic Committee
Chairman, Medical Commission, Australian Commonwealth Games Association

Ben Tan and I first met about fifteen years ago when I was the UK Team Coach. He spent two months training with us and I was very impressed with his determination and dedication to the sport.

He was able to manage a campaign for both the Asian Games and the Atlanta Olympics. At the same time he became a medical doctor. As a coach I have always viewed the Medical profession as being too difficult for most sailors to balance with a sailing campaign.

This makes Ben a very unique individual, having undertaken both of these successfully. This book is another example of his success and how he can set his mind to anything he undertakes.

I am very honoured to be asked to write this foreword as the book includes a large and international team of contributors and reviewers. It is a good in-depth book and is a mixture of what you need to get started and a bit more. I would have no inhibitions about recommending this book to up and coming sportsmen or women.

Trevor Millar
Managing Director, SailCoach Associates Ltd

CONTENTS

ACKNOWLEDGEMENTS

Without the support and patience of Alison, my wife, I would never have been able to sustain the mammoth task of putting together this book. I am also grateful to Mr Peter H L Lim, writer, media consultant, and former Editor-in-Chief of The Straits Times Group, for convincing me of the worth of this project and for agreeing to take on an advisory role.

The content contributors and reviewers readily and wholeheartedly offered their invaluable time and expertise to produce this book. This is in spite of the approaching 2000 Olympics in Sydney, which the sailors are campaigning for, and the coaches and sport scientists are preparing their athletes for. It is heartening to see so many who will sacrifice their time to help newer sailors.

Besides those mentioned in the credits, many other individuals also helped to make this publication a reality. They include Dr Edmund Wong, Dr Eileen Tan, and Dr Tay Miah Hiang for their contributions to the sections on ophthalmology, dermatology, and general medicine respectively, Mr Tan Yew Kier for proofreading, COL (RET) Kwan Yue Yeong, Mr Robert Tan, Mr Koh Hock Seng, Mr Ho Kah Soon, Ms Maureen Goh, physiologist Rashid Aziz, Laser sailor Stanley Tan, 470 helm Tan Wearn Haw, coach Khor Chek Leong, coach Tony Tan, and nurse Sng Soh Ging.

The Singapore Sports Council has been a great supporter of sailing in Singapore, through the publication of this book and through its collaboration with the Singapore Sailing Federation in sailing programmes throughout the Island.

Funding from Singapore Pools has made this book very affordable to the sailing fraternity, especially to the young sailors actively racing in the Laser Standard, Laser Radial, Topper, Optimist, 420, and other classes. Their contribution has also made it possible for the publisher to donate S$3.00 to the Singapore Sailing Federation for every copy of the first print sold. This will no doubt help in the running of training programmes like that of the Laser Youth Development Squad.

Editor
June 2000

"The Complete Introduction to Laser Racing ... is first class and an excellent resource. The content, layout and typesetting make for easy and informative reading and the graphics and photos are great!"

Angela Calder
Recovery and Performance Consultant, Australian Institute of Sport

CONTRIBUTORS

Editor

Ben Tan competed for more than 20 years, starting from the Optimist and progressing on to the Lark, Fireball, 470, and finally the Laser. He won the Asian Fireball Championships at age 17, but his best sailing years was in the Laser class where he won the 1994 Asian Games Gold Medal and four consecutive Southeast Asian Games Gold Medals. He finished 37th at his very first Laser World Championships in 1989 and competed in five other World Championships thereafter. Ben's ISAF World Ranking was well within the top 50, and he finished mid-fleet in the 1996 Olympics in Savannah. For his achievements in sailing, he was thrice awarded the title of Sportsman of the Year in Singapore, as well as the Singapore Youth Award, the Public Service Star, and Public Service Medal.

Ben graduated in 1991 with a medical degree and obtained his Masters in Sports Medicine in 1997 from the Australian Institute of Sport. He is presently a sports physician at the Sports Medicine and Research Centre, Singapore Sports Council. Besides treating athletes, he also heads the Sports Science Department. Among his published research is the paper *"Manipulating Resistance Training Program Variables to Optimize Maximum Strength in Men: A Review"* in the Journal of Strength and Conditioning Research. Ben's training gives him a well-rounded and balanced knowledge of the sport sciences. His success in both his career and sailing would not be possible without an appreciation of effective and time-saving training strategies in both sporting and academic pursuits.

Ben is presently a member of the Medical Commission of the International Sailing Federation, and he previously served on the Training and Development Committee. He coaches the nation's top single-handed sailors and the National Laser Youth Development Squad, whose sailors are typical of those that this book is aimed at helping.

Content Contributors

Nick Adamson was the US representative at the 1996 Olympics in Savannah. He has won many major championships, including the US National Championship, the North American Championship, and the US Olympic Trials. Nick started sailing at the age of 11 and he is the product of the competitive inter-collegiate racing circuit. A United States Youth Champion and Collegiate All-American, Nick graduated with a mechanical engineering degree from the University of California at Irvine. Since the Olympics, Nick has coached at numerous Laser Clinics. One of the most disciplined and focused sailors around, Nick is an excellent role model for budding sailors.

Michael Blackburn is the 2000 Olympic Laser Bronze Medallist. He finished fourth in the Laser class at the 1996 Olympics and second in the 2000 Laser Worlds, and has consistently ranked amongst the top few sailors in the World, including a number two spot on the ISAF World Ranking. He is known for his effective training programmes, and for his strict adherence to his programmes. Michael has a firm foundation in the scientific method, which he uses to his advantage during training and racing. He was named Australian Institute of Sport Student of the Year in 1990, and has a PhD from the University of Queensland for his work in the field of sports physiology and psychology. He drew on his 20 years' sailing experience, and the cutting edge of sports science to write an excellent book, "*Sail Fit: Sailing Fitness & Training,*" in 1997.

Angela Calder has several university degrees, including a Bachelor of Applied Science in Sports Coaching, and is a Recovery and Performance Consultant at the Australian Institute of Sport. She works with athletes and coaches to help them plan and integrate all aspects of their training and competition. Other than acting as an advisor and consultant to over 50 sports, including sailing, Angela is also a popular speaker who has been invited to speak to the International Coaching School in Victoria, Canada, the Hong Kong Sports Institute, the Welsh Institute of Sport, and the New Zealand Sport Science and Coaching Foundation.

Steve Cockerill, a seasoned and well-known campaigner in both the Laser Standard and Europe Dinghy, is the former Laser Inland National Champion and Europe Dinghy National Champion in the United Kingdom. His experience and versatility are evident as Steve is also the current UK National Champion in the Laser Radial and RS 300 classes. He is currently the UK Olympic Development Coach, and is also the coach to Min Dezille, Belgium's Europe Dinghy representative. Other sailors can also benefit from Steve's attention to detail and insight through the numerous sailing articles he has written for various print and on-line media including *Yachts & Yachting* and *www.roostersailing.com*. Steve is also popularly known as the creator of the tangle-free Polilite® rope that is widely used as a Laser mainsheet by top sailors, including the Gold, Silver, and Bronze Medallists at 2000 Laser Worlds and pre-Olympics.

Rod Dawson, from New Zealand, is a very fast all-round sailor who hikes with the typical Kiwi flat-out technique, as do his compatriots Nik Burfoot and Hamish Pepper. Rod comfortably won the Asia Pacific Championships in 1991, and has also won national regattas in several countries. Rod's dedication and consistent form makes him one of the favourites to win the 2000 New Zealand Olympic Trials.

Jacqueline Ellis has been a dominant force in the Laser Radial class for many years, having won her first Women's World Laser Radial Championship in 1988 and most recently in 1996. In between, she has a formidable string of top five results at World level and eight Australian Championship wins. With her long-time involvement in the Radial, as well as her impressive performances, Jacqueline has a lot to share with other male and female Radial sailors.

Trisha Leahy is a sport psychologist at the Australian Institute of Sport where she is currently working with many of Australia's elite athletes, including the Australian Olympic Sailing Team, in their preparations for the 2000 Sydney Olympics. Originally from Ireland, Trisha, who speaks fluent Cantonese, spent 14 years in Hong Kong. During her six years at the Hong Kong Sports Institute, she provided psychological services to national team athletes including the Hong Kong sailing team. She also worked very closely with the 1996 Olympic Boardsailing Gold Medallist, Lee Lai Shan. As well as having extensive applied experience in elite sport, Trisha has published and presented her research at numerous international conferences. She recently won a prestigious International Olympic Committee award for research excellence in the field of behavioural sciences. Trisha, whose degrees already include a Bachelor of Arts, Master of Arts, and Master of Philosophy, is currently in the final phase of a PhD research programme.

Takao Otani has been involved in the Laser class since 1973 as a competitor, a coach, and a boat builder. Takao started as the secretary for the Class in Japan, and ended up building Lasers as he could not find a good builder. A respected and familiar face at races all over the world, Takao has worked tirelessly and sincerely to promote the Class, always with the sailors' interest at heart.

Gary Slater (Bachelor of Science, Graduate Diploma in Nutrition & Dietetics) is a sport dietician currently working with the Singapore Sports Council. Prior to this, he spent a number of years working with Australia's elite athletes at the Australian Institute of Sport and a number of professional sporting teams. Gary's personal involvement in a number of competitive sports ensures he has a real awareness of the nutritional challenges faced by athletes. His focus - "While the optimal nutrition for an athlete must meet his or her increased nutrient requirements, it must also offer convenience, enjoyment, and individuality, being based on the individual's needs and preferences."

REVIEWERS

Sharifah Shwikar Aljunied graduated from the University of Sydney with a Bachelor of Health Science (Physiotherapy), and is currently the Chief Physiotherapist at the Sports Medicine and Research Centre, Singapore Sports Council. Shwikar has been practicing for 5 years, rehabilitating athletes from diverse backgrounds, and is also a key member of the Singapore Physiotherapy Association.

Pia Bay is a sport physiologist from the top Danish sports organization, Team Denmark, where she works with developmental and elite sailors. Amongst other research, she has investigated the work and injury profiles of the Danish Olympic Sailing Team, as well as the knee injuries in Optimist sailors. Pia also serves on the ISAF Training and Development Committee.

Saratha Bhai Krishnan has a Bachelor of Science (Physiotherapy) from Australia, and seven years' experience as a sport physiotherapist. Saratha's dedication in the field of professional and recreational sports rehabilitation has made her one of the most popular sport physiotherapists amongst peers and athletes in Singapore. Formerly the Chief Physiotherapist of Singapore Sports Council's Sports Medicine and Research Centre, Saratha currently works in a successful private sports medicine centre.

Tullio Giraldi is a Professor of Pharmacology at the Faculty of Medicine and the Director of the Department of Biomedical Sciences, University of Trieste, Italy. Professor Giraldi has a keen interest in the area of doping in sailing, as evident in his appointment as a member of the Anti Doping Commission of the Italian Sailing Federation. He also contributes to the sport as an active member of the ISAF Training and Development Committee.

Patrick Goh, a sports physician of 15 years' experience, is the Deputy Director of Sports Medicine at the Sports Medicine and Research Centre, Singapore Sports Council. Dr Goh is a past president of the Sports Medicine Association (Singapore), and has been the secretary of the Singapore National Olympic Council's Anti Doping In Sports Commission since its inception in 1996.

Lock Hong Kit, who was certified as an ISAF Race Officer in 1990, is an experienced International Sailing Judge and the most qualified Race Officer in Singapore. He is the Race Officer of first choice for all major local and regional regattas held in Singapore. Hong Kit was also the National Sailing Coach from 1984 to 1989. As a sailor, he has competed in many classes, including the Laser. He has a long list of sailing achievements including Gold Medals at the 1973 and 1983 Southeast Asian Games.

Alexandre Nikolaev hails from Moscow, Russia, and has travelled the world competing in Laser Standard and Radial events. In the past few years he accumulated an impressive string of results, finishing second in the highly competitive Apprentice category of the 2000 Laser Masters World Championships and the 1999 Laser European Championships. He demonstrated his versatility in the Radial category of the Laser Masters World Championships by finishing second in 1999, third in 1997, and second in 1996. Prior to sailing Lasers, Alexandre was one of the top OK Dinghy youth sailors in Russia.

James O'Callaghan is a top Laser coach who has been involved with the Class for 10 years. Prominent sailors currently under his wing include the winner of the 1998 Youth Worlds and Sydney 2000 Olympians. He was the Producer and Director of the highly successful *LaserCoach 2000* Interactive CD-ROM by the leading coaching company, SailCoach Associates.

Jacob Palm, from Denmark, is a top Optimist and Europe Dinghy coach. His sailors have won both the team and individual Gold medals in the Optimist class at the Asian Games, Asian Sailing Championships, and Association of Southeast Asian Nation Championships. Jacob's credentials as a sailor are equally impressive. He started sailing the Optimist in 1981 at the age of six, and went on to sail the Europe Dinghy as a member of the Danish National Team. In 1992, he was the Danish Youth Champion in the OK Dinghy as well as the Pirat Dinghy.

Teh Kong Chuan is a sports physician with more than 20 years' experience in the field. Dr Teh is the Director of the Sports Medicine and Fitness Division, Singapore Sports Council, and also the President of the Sports Medicine Association of Singapore. Under him, the Division takes care of all the sports medicine and sports science needs of Singapore's elite athletes, including sailors.

Edgar Tham, a Certified Sports Counselor (USA), is the leading sport psychologist in Singapore. He heads a team of psychologists at the Centre for Mental Training, Sports Medicine and Research Centre, Singapore Sports Council, where he counsels top athletes and coaches. The author of *"In the Zone: The Mindset for Peak Performance in Sport,"* Edgar's creative resource materials and teaching methods have contributed to the rapid advancement and acceptance of sport psychology in Singapore. His success with top athletes, including Olympians, has made his services much sought after by those in the academic and business circles as well.

Todd Vladich studied at the University of Western Australia, where he earned a degree in Bachelor of Physical and Health Education with Honours, investigating the effects of creatine supplementation on competitive swimming performance. He is a qualified Level 2 Strength and Conditioning Coach and Weightlifting Coach. As the Head Strength and Conditioning Coach at the Singapore Sports Council, he prepares athletes for major events, including the Olympics, the Asian Games, and the Southeast Asian Games. Prior to this, he was working at the Australian Institute of Sport, Canberra, where he coached athletes preparing for the 2000 Olympics. Todd himself competed in the sport of weightlifting for 8 years and was ranked second in Australia.

Meteorological Service Singapore is linked to other national meteorological centres in the region through the Global Telecommunication System of the World Meteorological Organisation. It provides official weather information and forecasts for aviation, shipping, and the public.

PREFACE

Thousands of individuals sail or have sailed the Laser, competitively and recreationally. The Class offers intense competition at all levels, posing both physical and mental challenges. Acquiring the necessary skills, fitness, and knowledge to race what must be one of the world's most demanding and competitive classes can be a daunting task for newcomers.

Good books have been written on preparation, tuning, and technique specific to the Laser. There are also countless books on various elements of sailing like tactics, sails, wind strategy, weather, boat speed, etc. Books on the sports science disciplines help athletes, though few of these were written specifically for the sailor. Despite the wide range of books available, no one source can adequately answer the multifaceted requirements of Laser sailing. *The Complete Introduction to Laser Racing* grew out of this realization, and aims to provide the busy Laser sailor with the most complete and comprehensive guide of its kind.

The knowledge and experience of world-class sailors, top coaches, and expert sport scientists were pooled together, resulting in 15 chapters and over 260 illustrations that cover the whole spectrum of Laser racing, from boat preparation to boat speed, to tactics, to the sports science disciplines. It took 10 content contributors and 13 reviewers, each a specialist in his or her respective field, to provide the comprehensive coverage. Written with the novice and intermediate sailor in mind, there is sufficient detail to benefit even the most experienced of sailors.

The sports sciences - sport nutrition, strength and conditioning, exercise physiology, sport psychology, and sports medicine - are covered comprehensively as the majority of sailors do not have easy access to a sport scientist. A practical approach is adopted so that sailors will have no difficulty putting into practice important sailing and scientific principles.

The wide appeal of the Laser has also attracted young sailors and women sailors to the Laser Radial. These groups have not been forgotten as aspects of the sport relating to the Radial rig, the young, and women athletes are discussed by experts within prominent boxed texts.

Prominent sailors and coaches from other classes were invited to review areas that are generic to all boats, including wind patterns and strategy, currents, tactics, and the sport science disciplines. This is to ensure that other than Laser sailors, those sailing Optimists, Europe Dinghies, double-handers, keelboats, and other classes will find these chapters useful as well.

With this succinct, complete, and practical manual on Laser racing, the team of contributors and reviewers hope to equip readers with the knowledge and tools necessary to realize their potential in the sport, while enjoying one of sailing's most successful classes, the Laser.

"Ben Tan says: 'Being able to pass boats at the marks involves not only superior boat handling,
but also a sound knowledge of the racing rules and a war chest of tactical tricks'.
Ben's new book gives you this war chest, structured for easy learning and fast checking-back.
It also nourishes your mind and body."

Peter H L Lim
Round-the-World racing sailor, writer and media consultant
Former Editor-in-Chief of The Straits Times Group

Chapter 1

Laser, the Competitive Sailor's Choice

content by **Takao Otani**

*T*here are many classes of boats in the world, and sailors select boats to sail for various reasons, be it comfort, speed, convenience, physical demands, looks, etc. This book introduces the reader to racing, and since you are reading this book, we will assume that you want to compete. For all racing sailors, the most important criteria for selecting a class is fair and strong competition. This is exactly what the Laser offers.

2000 Laser World Championships, Cancun, Mexico.

A TEST OF ABILITY, NOT EQUIPMENT

One evening after a race, some sailors gathered at the bar of a sailing club, lamenting over the rising cost of yacht racing. That was when the idea of a low-cost, thousand-dollar boat struck. (Even back in the 70's a thousand dollars was cheap for a boat.) They wanted to reduce costs by specifying a standard boat and fittings so that no one could spend on better equipment even if they had the money. That eventually led to the birth of the Laser in 1971, the strict one-design class created by Bruce Kirby.

Your boat is, therefore, identical to the World Champion's. The one-design philosophy spares sailors from having to invest time and money on the boat. Instead, performance is improved by investing in you, the sailor, through training and racing. Money that could have been spent on carbon fibre masts and Kevlar® sails can instead be spent on a trip to a regional regatta, giving you an experience that will outlast the most expensive equipment. When you compete, you are testing your ability against the elements and against that of other sailors.

All authorized Laser builders in the world adhere strictly to manufacturing controls so as to ensure uniformity in the structure of every single Laser that is built and sold. The International Sailing Federation (ISAF) building plaque that is permanently fixed to the rear of the cockpit is an assurance by the ISAF and the International Laser Class Association (ILCA) that the builders have contractually complied with the exact specifications laid down in the Construction Manual.

> *"Where boats are evenly matched in the matter of speed and draught, it is the quality of the piloting that wins the race."*
> Mark Twain

AMPLE RACING OPPORTUNITIES

To start racing, there is no need for elaborate sailing gear and no need to find crew members. Laser races are organized at every level, from club races, to national championships, to regional championships (Asia Pacific, Europe, Middle East, North American, and South American), to World level (Laser Worlds, ISAF Worlds, and Olympics). Ultimately, every athlete's dream is to compete in the Olympics, and the Laser is one of only nine sailing classes to offer you this chance.

With its full-time staff, the ILCA maintains this well-organized racing structure and protects the interest of Laser sailors the world over.

A WORLDWIDE EVENT

An important feature of a competitive class is that it should be sailed internationally, on every corner of the globe. Indeed, the ubiquitous Laser is sailed in over 80 countries. More than 170,000 boats have been built and the number swells by nearly 4,000 a year. When you race the Laser, you can take pride in the fact that there are many others around the world sailing the same boat as you. In the 1996 Olympics, more countries competed in the Laser class than in any other discipline, including the track and field events!

RACING THE LASER THROUGH THE YEARS

The Laser is a class that will allow you to compete for the greater part of your life, so that there is more time to improve your skills and also more time to reap the rewards from all that training and hard work. The Class offers racing to sailors of almost all ages, from youth (under 19), to senior, and to masters (over 35) categories. The Laser 4.7 (crew 35-55 kg) and Laser Radial (crew 55-70 kg) make it possible for those fresh out of the Optimist class to hop onto the boat.

The Laser is the single-handed class for the ISAF World Youth Championships. At the senior level, the Laser World Championship is one of the most competitive and most prestigious regattas around, where sailors have to pre-qualify at the district level. The 2000 Laser

Worlds had a record 50-nation entry. At the masters level, the 1999 Masters World Championships saw 239 competitors from 22 countries participating. The oldest competitor was 76.

Its smaller cousin, the Laser Radial has become so popular around the World that it is now evolving into a class of its own, with lots of competitive regattas attracting youth, lightweight sailors, and women sailors.

Fans of the Laser Radial.

THE BREEDING GROUND FOR CHAMPIONS

1999 Laser World Champion and 2000 Olympic Gold Medallist, Ben Ainslie, was awarded the coveted Sailor of the Year Award by ISAF, ahead of candidates from other classes. If you decide to switch out of the Class, the skills acquired while serving an apprenticeship in the Laser will go a long way in helping you succeed in your next boat. Many big names in the America's Cup 2000 like Russell Coutts (NZL), Dean Barker (NZL), Torben Grael (BRA), Paul Cayard (USA), and Ed Baird (USA) were Laser sailors, and so were many Gold Medallists in other Olympic and International classes.

Laser legends Robert Scheidt (left), the four-time World Champion and Olympic Champion, and Ben Ainslie (right), 1999 Laser World Champion and 2000 Olympic Gold Medallist.

CONVENIENCE

Last, but not least, the boat design itself has played a big part in the Laser's success. It is easy to transport (the flat deck was designed with car-topping in mind), easy to maintain, easy to rig up, and easy on your pocket! Breakages are relatively uncommon, even in the breeziest of races.

Enjoy the competition!

Chapter 2

Preparing the Laser

content by **Steve Cockerill** and **Jacqueline Ellis**

*T*he Laser is a simple and durable boat - with a little preparation, it can be made much easier and more enjoyable to sail. The Fundamental Rule of this one-design prohibits any addition or alteration to the boat unless specifically authorised by the Class rules. Thus, apart from the basic preparation, sailors can spend more time improving their skills and fitness, and less time fiddling with the boat.

HULL AND HULL FITTINGS

Hull

In the past, you would not allow yourself to be too excited about receiving your new boat until you find a dry hull at the end of its first sail. A new hull rarely leaks these days. If it does, check the centreboard casing, gunwale, and fittings for leaks by applying soapy water around these areas and blowing air through the transom drain hole (seal the air bleed hole at the front end of the cockpit first). Re-seal all fittings with silicone sealant.

The mast steps of newer hulls are now more consistent but to be on the safe side, ensure that the distance from the top of the bottom section to the hull on port and starboard are equal. The distance from the top of the bottom section to the transom reflects the mast rake, and this affects leech tension. You may wish to compare this distance against that of a fast hull to ensure that yours is not too far off.

The use of slowly soluble applications on the hull to reduce surface drag is prohibited, and so is refinishing the hull. What is legal - and a lot more time-saving – is washing the hull with detergent (e.g. dishwashing liquid) to keep it clean and grease-free. Do not go stealing soap from the club shower as body soaps may leave emollients behind. Smooth out scratches with fine wet-and-dry sand paper, using filler if the scratch is deep.

When storing the hull, do not subject any part of the hull's bottom to pressure. If storing on a trolley, get one that supports the hull from under the gunwale.

Mainsheet Cam Cleats

If you are new to the Laser, you will probably be relying on these cleats, at least initially. Hence the importance of good-quality cleats that do not allow the mainsheet to slip through and yet be cleated and uncleated easily. Position the cleats forward enough so that they do not get in the way when hiking (*fig. 2.1*), but within the edges of the wooden backing plates under the deck. (*See measurement diagrams in the Laser Handbook for the position of these plates.*)

Fig 2.1 *Mainsheet cam cleat position. Note the tape around the supporting spring for the mainsheet block and the marking on the mainsheet block.*

Mainsheet Block

A good mainsheet block is one that runs smoothly and has a reliable ratchet that can be switched on to make upwind sailing easier, and switched off to improve the feel during off-wind sailing. If you prefer to sail without the ratchet on throughout the race, then silicone (or tape) the switch in the "off" position to prevent it from turning on accidentally.

To avoid pulling the wrong end of the mainsheet when sheeting in from the block, mark the side of the block where the tail end of the mainsheet exits with either a permanent marker or coloured tape (*fig. 2.1*). Also wind some duct tape around the spring supporting the block to prevent the mainsheet from getting caught in the spring (*fig. 2.1*) or replace the spring with a tennis ball cut in half.

Hiking Strap

A padded hiking strap that has an acrylic fabric on its cover offers more grip when hiking from the toes, thus improving hiking performance. Some prefer a fixed-length hiking strap while others use adjustable ones (*fig. 2.2*). To keep the hiking strap further above the cockpit floor so that you do not miss it and fly off the boat after a tack, attach the shockcord to the traveller cleat (*fig. 2.3*).

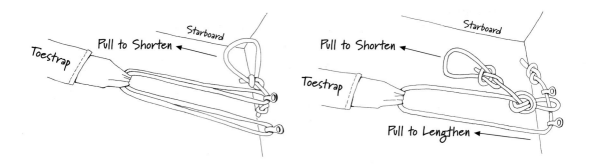

Fig 2.2 Adjustable hiking straps are tightened for the reach and loosened for the upwind leg. Both systems rely on friction, so use 6 mm lines. 1.6 m lines are adequate for both systems.

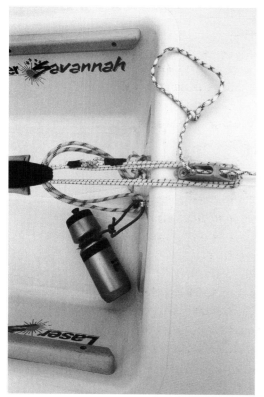

Fig 2.3 Attach the hiking strap shockcord to the traveller cleat. The 750 ml water bottle is attached to the hiking strap eyestrap.

For added security, it is a good idea to fix the forward end of the strap to both the centreboard friction attachment plate and the mainsheet block plastic pressure plate the next time you change your straps.

Self-bailer

To reduce drag and improve suction, seal the gap between the edge of the bailer and the hull with silicone sealant. Also, fill the central screw hole with silicone until it is flush with the surface.

Mast Step

If you launch off a sandy beach, be careful not to get any sand in the mast step. The end cap of the bottom mast section has specially designed grooves to hold the grit, so do change it when it has worn down.

FOILS

Surface Finish

Unlike the hull, surface refinishing is allowed for the foils (i.e. centreboard and rudder), provided the original shape, thickness, and inherent characteristics are not altered. So what is the fastest surface? There are two schools of thought. The first believes a microscopically rough surface will trap a thin layer of water next to the surface, thereby ensuring that friction only acts between the trapped layer and the adjacent layer of water. Friction between two layers of water is less than that between the foil surface and water. Sharks, which have rough skin, seem to demonstrate that roughness and speed can coexist. To trap a layer of water on the surface, proponents sand their foils with grade 400 wet-and-dry sandpaper, rubbing across the direction of water flow or in a circular motion. When water is poured over the finished surface, an even spread is good while beading is bad.

The other school of thought contends that a smooth and polished surface is faster. There is research to back this up, and this view is more widely accepted. Here, the recommendation is to sand the foils with grade 1,000-1,200 wet-and-dry sandpaper, taking care to sand in the direction of the water flow. In either case, use a sanding block for a better finish.

If undecided, do not worry. Drag is more significant in the presence of laminar flow and high speeds. Other than at the leading edge, the flow around the foils tends to be turbulent. And since Lasers are not that fast (compared to skiffs), the difference in drag between the two surface finishes is hardly noticeable in the Class.

The foil's trailing edge needs special attention, especially that of the centreboard. When the boat planes, a centreboard with an uneven or irregular trailing edge acts a bit like a flag flapping from side to side as water flows off one side and then the other. This causes vibration and humming, slowing the boat down. A warped edge from excessive heat, as when left in the car or under the boat cover on hot days, needs to be straightened out. Soften the warped portion by heating with a hairdryer, and clamp it between two flat wooden plates. An irregular edge with finer irregularities should be sanded down evenly on both sides, and then squared off (or put an angle to encourage the water to go off the back edge from the same side all the time). Do not sharpen the trailing edge.

Fig 2.4 The erect centreboard handle stops the vang tail from dragging in the water.

Centreboard

The tension in the centreboard elastic should be high enough to hold the centreboard up fully when sailing downwind. If not, shorten the elastic. Also, adjust the centreboard friction plate to help it stay fully down while beating. Change it regularly for a secure centreboard. If the plastic centreboard stopper has come loose, ensure that the two sides are correctly oriented and then press them firmly together until they click in. "Glue" with silicone sealant to prevent them from coming loose again.

Fix a rope handle to the centreboard. The erect handle (fig. 2.4) can be used to hold the boom vang tail, preventing it from dragging in the water. Alternatively, tie a 1 m long vang tail to the centreboard handle and keep the excess rope near the mainsheet cleat for accessibility.

Rudder

To keep the rudder blade in the "up" position when getting in and out of the water, and to reduce play, the rudder bolt needs to be tightened. Remove the rudder bolt, shave about 1 mm off the inside ends of the two plastic bushings, and reassemble. File down the exposed tip of the bolt to prevent accidental scratching of the centreboard when the foils are stored or carried together. Alternatively, replace the supplied bolt and bushings with a 9.5 mm diameter bolt.

Fig 2.5 Purchase system for the rudder downhaul. The supplied line has sufficient length to do this.

To keep the rudder fully down when in the water (one that is not fully down will make the helm feel heavy), use a 3:1 purchase system for the rudder downhaul (fig. 2.5) and tension the downhaul firmly before cleating. A taut downhaul will hold the tiller firmly in the rudder stock, so the retaining pin is redundant. Remove the pin so that the mainsheet does not catch on it when gybing.

Washers are allowed between the rudder pintles and gudgeon. This prevents wear of the gudgeon and gives a smoother feel. If your tiller rubs against the deck at the transom, washers are the solution.

Tiller

Simple as this "stick" may be, a good one makes a difference. Lightweight carbon fibre tillers are strong and give a better feel. Those that are low and flat in cross-section – yet strong at the same time - keep the traveller blocks as far to the sides as possible and allow them to slide across when tacking or gybing (*fig. 2.6*). Ensure a snug fit between the tiller and the rudder stock to eliminate play and improve feedback from the helm.

Fig 2.6   Carbon fibre tiller with a flat profile. The traveller block rides over the tiller easily when tacking and there is ample clearance over the traveller clam cleat.

Tiller Extension

Tiller extensions come in various lengths, diameters, and materials. The carbon fibre ones are the lightest. Though strong, they can still break. If carbon is wrapped around the extension as well as along its length, then failure is very much less likely. Twill, as this is called, is unfortunately expensive.

When hiking flat out, your hand should be at your chest level while holding the tiller extension. If the extension is too long, it will get in the way when tacking; if too short, pointing while hiking out will not be possible. Buy a long extension, and then cut it to the length that suits you. Do check the tiller extension's universal joint regularly for cracks in the rubber.

Jacqui's Tips *for* RADIAL SAILORS

"Radial sailors need to pay special attention to the diameter of the tiller extension. As they are most often women, young kids and smaller-stature sailors, the tiller extension supplied with the boat or those commonly seen in the full rig is too big in diameter. I always found the 'standard' tiller extension too difficult to hold on to and it made steering very difficult. It proved particularly difficult when I was sheeting in using the hand-over-hand method. I went to a smaller diameter extension, with a longer foam grip (I actually cut down a B14 tiller extension) and this worked really well. With the longer foam grip, I could hold onto the extension closer to where it joined the tiller, and this provided a better grip in those windy downwind conditions."

Jacqueline Ellis

MAST

The top section is, unfortunately, prone to a permanent bend, especially when capsizing to windward at speed. After a windy day, check for this by sighting down the top end while rotating it (*fig. 2.7*). As it is illegal to race with a permanent bend, it will have to be straightened (*fig. 2.8*).

Fig 2.7 Inspecting for permanent bend. Rest the bottom end of the top section over the opening of the mast step and rotate it.

Fig 2.8 Straightening a bent top section. Fit the top section into the bottom section and rest both ends on firm supports. Press the convex side firmly downwards. Check to see if the bend has been corrected before trying again with slightly more force.

If the bend is slight, rotate the top section by 180° such that the bend faces forward, and go out sailing in light wind. Rotate it 180° each time a backward bend develops. Bending the top section back and forth like this work hardens it. On windy days, however, sail with the arrows on the top and bottom section aligned (this ensures the rivet for the plastic collar faces aft) to reduce the risk of snapping the top section at the rivet. Another alternative is to end-for-end the top section by switching the fittings around.

When putting the top and bottom sections together, a snug fit keeps the bend at the joint smooth. If not, a larger than usual crease will form between the clew of the sail and the middle of the luff where the joint is. To obtain a snug fit, apply non-compressible tape (e.g. packing tape) around the collar and end cap of the top section before sliding it into the bottom section.

SAIL

Battens
Make sure that the batten end caps are well glued on. Otherwise you will be spending hours struggling to remove a cap that has been left behind and stuck in the batten pocket.

Telltales
One pair of telltales is all that most sailors have time to pay attention to on the course. The most popular position is that shown in *fig. 2.9*. Wool is a popular material, although it sticks to the sail when wet. However, this can be prevented by rubbing some candle wax onto the sail around the telltale.

Fig 2.9 *The telltales, the forward corner of the sail window, and the corner of sail label should form an equilateral or isosceles triangle.*

Storage
Naturally, you would want to keep your boat's "engine" in good shape. The Laser sail is made from resin-impregnated Dacron® sailcloth, and the more creases and folds there are on the sail, the softer the material becomes. Allowing the sail to flap excessively while on shore is one sure way to thrash the sail; improper storage is another. After rinsing off the salt and drying it,

the sail is best stored by rolling it around a PVC pipe that is aligned along the same axis as the foot. If folding, the recommendation is to vary the folding points a little every time.

Control Lines and Mainsheet

When control lines do their job, tuning the sail and changing gears become much easier. All control lines should be non-stretch and, as purchase systems are made out of them, smooth and wear-resistant materials are necessary. To prolong their lifespan, reverse the lines or shift the loops before high-friction points get worn-out.

Mainsheet. The mainsheet should be lightweight, comfortable on the hands, and tangle-free. When sailing downwind or reaching in very light wind, a light mainsheet helps the boom to stay out. A 6-7 mm diameter sheet runs through the blocks smoothly and is comfortable to hold. A length of 13-14 m allows the boom to go out past 90° from the centreline. Tie figure-of-eights at both ends of the mainsheet. Some prefer to tie the tail end to the hiking strap to prevent true knots from forming in the mainsheet.

Before using a brand new mainsheet, soak it overnight in water to remove the soapy feeling. To minimise entanglements at the top mark, throw the mainsheet into the water and drag it along while sailing close-hauled before the race. This removes all the twists in the mainsheet.

Clove Hitch

Cunningham. The 6:1 purchase system in *fig. 2.10* can be rigged using a 5-6 mm diameter, 5.2 m line with two thimbles. A comfortable handle is helpful as a lot of tension is often required (*see boxed text*). The whole system can be rigged to lie on the starboard side of the boom, so that the cunningham grommet can be pulled down past the gooseneck when it is windy. However, this pulls the sail to one side, so the sail looks different on the other tack. To avoid this, some rig the system to straddle both sides of the boom when the wind is light, and rig it all to one side when the wind picks up.

Fig 2.10 Cunningham system.

Five Steps to a Comfy-Handle

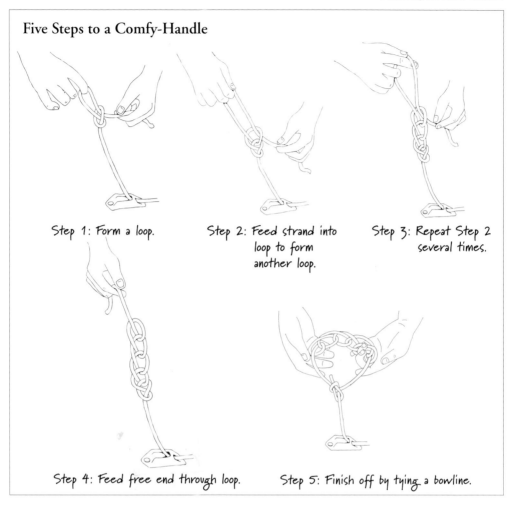

Step 1: Form a loop.

Step 2: Feed strand into loop to form another loop.

Step 3: Repeat Step 2 several times.

Step 4: Feed free end through loop.

Step 5: Finish off by tying a bowline.

Boom Vang. The 8:1 purchase system for the boom vang (*fig. 2.11*) can be rigged using a 5-6 mm diameter, 5.0 m long line. The portion of the line that is fixed to the lower block is around 1.8 m from the end where the bowline is. Adjust the position of this point such that the mast just manages to be absolutely straight when the vang is fully released. The tail should be long enough to allow the vang to be pulled while the buttocks are over the gunwale. With a good swivel, it is a lot easier to adjust the vang while the boom is out. Thimbles are not allowed for the vang.

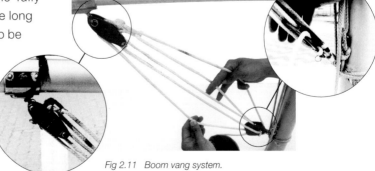

Fig 2.11 Boom vang system.

Check regularly for corrosion around the mast attachment tang, and for stress fractures on the tang itself as this area is subjected to high loads. As the vang key is subjected to high loads as well, attach a spare key as permitted by the Class rules. To prevent the vang from falling off before you get a chance to tighten it at the bottom mark rounding, hold the key in place using shockcord or electrical tape around the boom.

As it is difficult to adjust the vang once the boat is on a free leg of the course, the vang is best adjusted to the reaching or downwind setting just prior to rounding the top mark. Markings on the vang make it easier to get the setting right the first time, so that the vang does not have to be re-adjusted again after the top mark rounding. The recommended reference points used in *chapter three* are the 20 and 30 cm from block-to-block positions. To make these markings, sheet in till the boom end block and mainsheet block are 20 cm apart, take the slack off the vang, and mark the tail where it comes off the lower vang block. Do likewise to get the 30 cm mark, preferably with a different colour. Other marking systems are also used, but this is the simplest.

Outhaul. The 10:1 outhaul purchase system (*fig. 2.12*) can be rigged using a 5 mm diameter, 6.6 m line. The knots are positioned such that the tail end is forward but easily accessible. From the clew end of the line, mark the 1.92, 2.41, and 4.40 m points along the line. Tie loops at these points, inserting thimbles into the first and last loops. The middle loop serves to hold the strands together.

Fig 2.12 Outhaul system. Right: The markings on the boom are 5 cm apart (starting from the end of the boom). Notice that there is a triangular space between the clew tie-down and the sail for the outhaul line to pass through.

A 5 mm diameter, 75 cm long clew tie-down will go thrice around the boom to hold the outhaul grommet against the boom. Stopper knots at both ends are advisable. Spraying Teflon® or WD40® on the boom helps the tie-down to slide smoothly.

Markings to help make the outhaul settings more objective can be made at the end of the boom (*fig. 2.12 right*).

Traveller. The traveller system is rigged easily using a 5 mm diameter, 5.0 m long line to form one large bowline (*fig. 2.13*). Tape the two blocks rigidly together to prevent them from twisting when gybing.

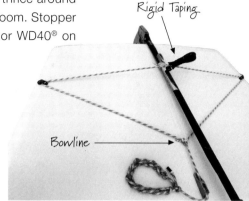

Fig 2.13   Traveller system.

OTHER ESSENTIALS

Wind Indicator

A wind indictor is useful in very light wind and when sailing downwind. It can be placed at the top of the mast (rarely done these days), the bow eye, or in front of the mast. Having it strapped to the mast (*fig. 2.14*), in front of the gooseneck is the most popular. In this position, it holds the outhaul up and is comfortably within the field of vision.

Fig 2.14   Wind indicator. With the indicator secured to the gooseneck using a string, it is less likely to be lost if another boat's mainsheet yanks the indicator off. Alternatively, attach the indicator upside down.

Compass

In the Laser, a compass is used to detect wind shifts. Of course, one can detect wind shifts without a compass on board, by noting changes in sailing angles with respect to other boats. But immediately after starting or rounding the bottom mark, it is not easy to tell if one is sailing on a header or a lift. In these situations, having a compass is an advantage. More will be said on the use of compasses in *chapter nine*.

Silva's racing compass, model 103R (*fig. 2.15*), designed for the Laser, is the most

Fig 2.15   Tactical Compass, bolted onto a base plate.

popular. The tactical scale is the easiest to read and use. Mount the compass on the base plate, and it is ready for use! Compass cards are balanced for the equator and the northern and southern hemispheres, so get the appropriate one for your area.

Water Bottle

Performance is adversely affected by dehydration. Get a good-sized bottle (> 750 ml) with a wide opening so that the inside can be cleaned and aired easily. Attach it to one of the hiking strap eyestraps using a shockcord. The "system" shown in *fig. 2.3 (pg 10)* is the simplest possible, but it takes time to detach and reattach the drink bottle. A method that saves the trouble of having to remove the bottle from the shockcord involves using a longer shockcord and passing it through the traveller fairleads.

Protest Flag

To protest on the water, a red protest flag must be displayed at the first reasonable opportunity and be removed only after finishing or retiring. The front end of the boom is a good place to have your protest flag (*fig. 2.16*) as it is easily accessible, easily seen when unfurled, and not in the way of anything.

Fig 2.16 Home-made protest flag slipped over the front of the boom. Simply pull the edge down to unfurl.

The foregoing preparations are simple, especially when compared against most other classes. Maintenance is even easier, so there is no excuse for leaving things like replacing worn ropes and loose rivets to the last minute. As a final note, do not forget to put the bung in before launching!

Chapter 3

Sailing Tuning

content by **Ben Tan** *and* **Jacqueline Ellis**
reviewed by **Rod Dawson**

C.E. CHEONG

*T*he Laser has only one sail, with three control lines. With no jib, spinnaker, slot, forestay, spreaders, or shrouds to worry about, the Laser sailor's life cannot be easier. Although there is no need to know as much as an aeronautical engineer, there are a few fundamentals about the sail and the airflow surrounding it that one must know in order to get the most out of the rig.

UNDERSTANDING THE SAIL

Sail Shape

Far from being a simple, flat triangular piece of cloth, the sail comprises several panels of resin-impregnated Dacron® sailcloth sewn together to form a 7.06 m² sail with a horizontal cross sectional shape shown in *figure 3.1*.

Fig 3.1. Section shape.

The section shape is defined by the:

Depth:	Distance between the deepest part of the sail and the cord.
Cord length:	Horizontal distance between the luff and the leech at any specified level.
Camber:	Ratio of depth to cord length.
Draft position:	Position of maximum depth.
Angle of attack:	Roundness of the luff (fig. 3.2).
Twist:	Variation in cord angle up the sail.

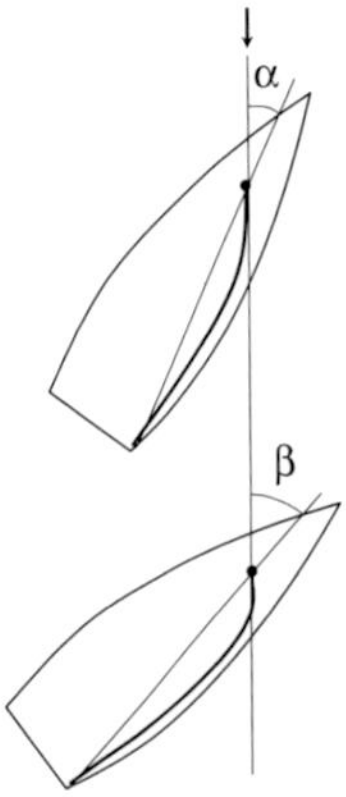

Fig 3.2 The roundness of the luff determines the angle of attack. Top: Small angle of attack (α). Bottom: Large angle of attack (β).

How the Sail Works

The curvature of the sail causes the air on the leeward side to travel a greater distance compared to the windward side, but within the same time *(fig. 3.3)*. This increases the speed of the leeward flow, resulting in a decrease in pressure (Bernoulli's principle), so the sail is "sucked" to leeward by a lift force. This may be an over-simplified explanation, but it will serve our purpose.

Fig 3.3 *Air flowing at a higher speed (closer streamlines) on the leeward side of the sail generates lift (arrow).*

The practical implication is that air has to flow across the sail for it to work effectively. That is why sailing by-the-lee or on the broad reach is faster than sailing on a direct run *(fig. 3.4)*. On a direct run, the wind "pushes" the sail with a force that is lower than the lift generated when air flows over the sail.

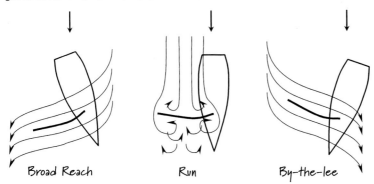

Fig 3.4 *Different airflow patterns. Left: On a broad reach air flows from luff to leech. Middle: On a direct run, there is no laminar flow, so this is slowest. Right: Sailing by-the-lee, with air flowing from leech to luff (reverse flow).*

The amount of lift generated depends on how much the airflow on the leeward side speeds up, and how well the flow adheres to the leeward side of the sail. In *fig. 3.5*, notice how the airflow tends to separate after the break point. Some separation is inevitable towards the leech of the sail, but the aim is to prevent the break point from moving forward towards the luff. To do this, the sail must not be too deep, especially in light air. More importantly, the sail must not be oversheeted.

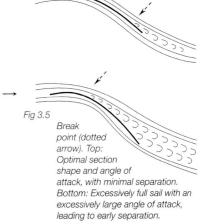

Fig 3.5

Break point (dotted arrow). Top: Optimal section shape and angle of attack, with minimal separation. Bottom: Excessively full sail with an excessively large angle of attack, leading to early separation.

Never Over-sheet

Over-sheeting not only causes early separation, but it also stalls the sail. A stall is when the flow becomes separated from *luff* to leech. When this happens, the leeward telltale droops. Stalling severely impairs lift. On the flip side, if the sail is eased out too far, then it will start luffing. Although both should be avoided, stalling is much more detrimental than luffing. If the sail is luffing, prompt recovery of speed can be achieved by trimming the sail in. If the sail is stalled, it takes a longer time for boat speed to recover after easing the sail.

Oversheeting is slow for another reason. The lift force, *L*, generated by the sail is approximately perpendicular to the boom. *L* can be resolved into a forward force, *f*, which drives the boat, and a sideways force, *s*, which heels the boat and causes sideslip (*fig. 3.6*). When oversheeted, *s* increases at the expense of *f*. For a sail that is luffing, the slight loss in *L* is partially compensated for by the increase in *f*, as *L* rotates forward with the boom. For this reason, there should be no hesitation in easing the sail when overpowered.

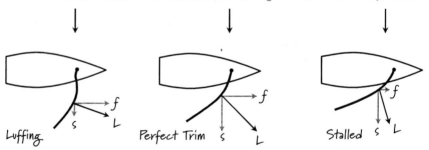

Fig 3.6 Resolving the lift force. L = lift. f = forward force or drive. s = sideways or heeling force.

Pay attention to the sail trim in the following situations:

- When sitting along the line before the start, luff the sail and never allow it to stall, especially in light wind, or the boat will be slow to accelerate off the line.
- When bearing away (e.g. top mark rounding or penalty turns), always ease the sail to avoid stalling.
- When the boat falls off the plane on the reach, the apparent wind shifts back. Thus, the sail should be eased, and trimmed back in only when the boat starts to surf again.
- When the boat decelerates on hitting waves upwind, ease the sail out and bear away a little to help the boat pick up speed.

CONTROLLING THE SAIL SHAPE

For simplicity's sake, we shall divide the sail into the upper, middle, and lower thirds. Each of the three control lines (and mainsheet) *predominantly* powers up or de-powers a third of the sail:

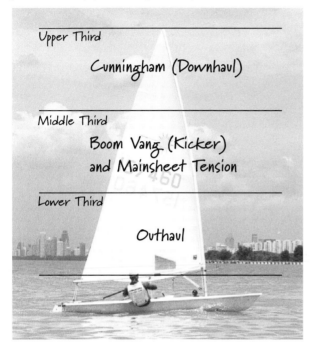

Upper Third

Cunningham (Downhaul)

Middle Third

Boom Vang (Kicker)
and Mainsheet Tension

Lower Third

Outhaul

Cunningham

Fold a handkerchief corner to corner, and hold the other two corners apart (*fig. 3.7*). Now, pull them apart and notice how a crease forms and how the middle of the handkerchief is drawn towards the fold. Similarly, when the cunningham is tightened, the sailcloth is drawn towards the luff, bringing the draft forward (*fig. 3.8 top row*). This increases the angle of attack (i.e. the entry is more rounded), resulting in a sail that is less prone to stalling, but with a lower pointing angle.

Fig 3.7 When tension is applied at 45° to the bias of the cloth, a fold appears along the tension line (right), and the cloth is drawn towards the fold (as shown by the mark on the handkerchief moving up).

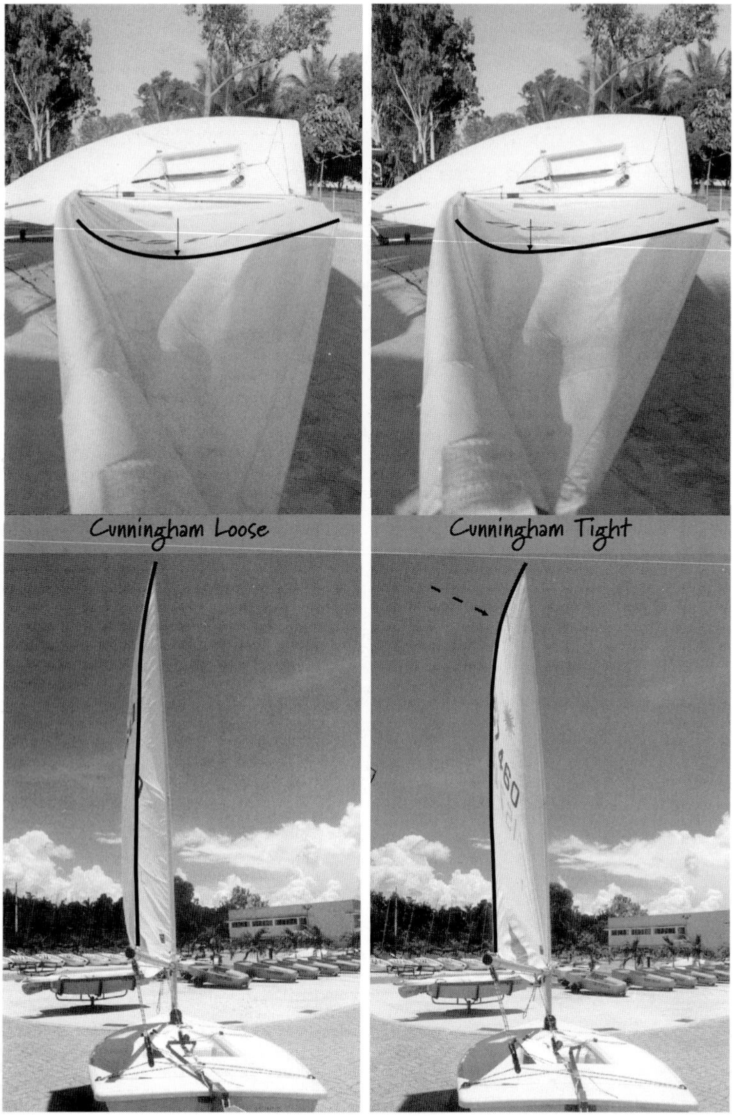

Fig 3.8
Top row: Effect of cunningham tension on draft position. The draft position (arrow) moves forward when the cunningham is tensioned (right).

Bottom row: Effect of cunningham tension on sail twist. Pulling on the cunningham opens the leech (right), thereby spilling air from the upper third of the sail (dotted arrow).

On the Laser, the effect of cunningham tension on sail twist is more significant. A tight cunningham increases the twist, opening the leech (*fig. 3.8 bottom row*). This "spills" air from the upper third of the sail, thus effectively de-powering the rig.

Upwind. When the wind is too light to hike, the sail should be powered up, so there should be little, if any, cunningham tension. A good guide is to tighten the cunningham just enough to remove the big creases, leaving behind the small ones that are called "speed creases."

If the boat cannot be flattened despite hiking fully, then it is time to de-power the sail. As the upper third of the sail has the highest heeling moment, power from that portion should be the first to be dumped. Pull *hard* on the cunningham until the grommet (i.e. the hole at the tack of the sail) reaches the gooseneck (or below the gooseneck if the sail is old and stretched).

Off-Wind. Other than when sailing close-hauled, the cunningham should always be completely loosened. The exception is when reaching in overpowering conditions.

Boom Vang and Mainsheet Tension

Mast bend and leech tension are determined by the vang and mainsheet tension. Upwind, both the vang and mainsheet control the leech tension and mast bend; when sailing off-wind, it is all left to the vang alone. As the vang or mainsheet is tensioned, the mast, especially the middle portion, flexes. This flattens (i.e. decreases the camber) the middle third of the sail. As wind strength increases, the upper third should generally be de-powered first, followed by the middle third.

Upwind. In medium wind, keep the mainsheet tension tight so that the leech is straight. There should be no vang tension, and only the slack in the vang is taken out to help tacking. The optimal amount of mainsheet tension depends on how much mast bend, and hence power from the middle third, is desired. As a rough guide, when sitting on the side deck, the

Jacqui's Tip for RADIAL SAILORS

"The very first difference I found with the Radial sail was when I sailed a Radial for the first time, just before the 1988 Women's Worlds in England. We didn't have Radials in Australia at the time. A full rig mainsheet is almost always sheeted block to block when going upwind so when I jumped into my Radial, I did exactly the same thing. The boat felt terrible – it seemed to be underpowered and stalling. I played around with the other controls to try and fix things but it wasn't until I eased the mainsheet by about 20 cm between the back blocks that the boat powered up and felt better. Easing the mainsheet like this proved to be a significant speed difference during the championship.

The distance between the blocks varies with wind strength, but you should never need to ease to more than 30 cm no matter how light the wind is. As the breeze increases you can gradually decrease the distance between blocks, right up until block-to-block when it is quite windy. After this, if you're overpowered, start to ease the sheet again (after you've trimmed with your vang and cunningham) to spill wind in order to keep the boat flat. The mainsheet trim is something that you need to play around with and find the setting that suits you, your weight and the conditions you are sailing in at the time. It is a great thing to practice with a friend when you are working on straight-line speed."

Jacqueline Ellis

distance between the boom end block and the mainsheet block should be somewhere between 30 cm and block-to-block, depending on wind strength (the stronger it is, the closer the blocks), chops (the bigger the chops, the further apart the blocks), and height (if you want to sail higher, the blocks should be closer). By the time the buttocks are over the side of the boat, the sail trim should have reached the block-to-block position.

Once the blocks are together, further mast bend is achieved by tightening the vang. In overpowering conditions, the vang should be so tight that when the mainsheet is eased, the boom moves outboard rather than upwards.

Fig 3.9 Reaching in medium wind.

Reaching. On the reach or run, the mainsheet is ineffective in controlling mast bend, so vang tension becomes the sole control. It is best to set the vang tension before the reach, while approaching the top mark on close-haul. For medium wind, ease the mainsheet until the blocks are 30 cm apart, and then release the vang and cleat again without allowing any slack. After rounding the top mark and sailing on the reach, the boom should be slightly above horizontal and the mast relatively straight (*fig. 3.9*).

In very light wind (drifting conditions), where a flatter sail is desired (to reduce separation), the vang tension should be higher. In this case, set the vang tension at approximately 20 cm rather than 30 cm from block-to-block.

On the other extreme, in very strong wind and rough water, a vang tension that is equivalent to further than 30 cm from block-to-block is a good idea, as it raises the boom above the waves and opens the leech to de-power the sail.

Downwind. The vang is loosest when sailing downwind. The mast should be straight, or almost straight, with the boom above horizontal to open up the leech (*fig. 3.10*).

Fig 3.10 Sailing downwind in light conditions.

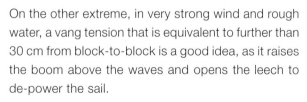

In strong winds, excessive sail twist results in the cord of the upper sail sections going past 90° from the centreline of the hull. The lift force thus acquires a vector that heels the boat to windward, increasing the likelihood of a death roll (i.e. a capsize to windward). To stabilize the boat in such conditions, put on more vang tension and trim the sail in such that the boom is about 75° from the centreline.

Outhaul

The action of the outhaul is the simplest to understand: it lengthens the cord, thereby flattening and reducing the camber of the lower third of the sail. The lower third of the sail provides a lot of drive with minimal heeling moment, so it should be the last to be de-powered as the wind strength increases.

At its loosest, the distance between the deepest part of the sail and the boom (i.e. the depth of the foot) should be 15 cm or one hand span, as measured from the tip of the little finger to the tip of the thumb with the fingers comfortably spread apart. This translates to distance of approximately 16 cm from the end of the boom to the corner of the clew. (The precise distance depends on how stretched the sail is.) Any fuller, the airflow separation will be excessive. To prevent the depth of the foot from accidentally exceeding 15 cm, the knots for the outhaul purchase system should be rigged such that this is the maximum depth attainable when the outhaul is fully released. A full foot is best for choppy water, and a wide range of wind strengths.

Upwind. In very light wind, where there is a tendency for the break point to move forward, a depth of 10 cm might be faster. The foot can also be flattened to a depth of about 10 cm in strong winds

Jacqui's Tip for RADIAL SAILORS

"*The Radial sail is cut more deeply in the foot, so measurements used for the full rig are a bit too much for the Radial. I too use the finger to thumb measurement, but having a smaller hand makes just the right difference (10-12 cm).*

A good thing to try on shore is to set up your outhaul to what you think looks right, then walk to the back of the boat to see how deep the sail really is – probably much deeper than you expected! Keep this mental picture with you when you are setting the outhaul on the water.

If you are on the heavier side of the Radial fleet, you can carry a deeper foot for longer as the wind increases, as this gives you more power and drive to keep the boat moving, especially in waves.

One thing that really annoyed me when sailing in heavy air with a very tight outhaul is the bottom scallop of the sail flapping against the boom. To fix this, gradually ease just a little outhaul until the noise stops."

Jacqueline Ellis

with minimal compromise on drive to cope with the waves. If it is even stronger and there is difficulty flattening the boat despite hiking fully and putting on lots of cunningham and vang tension, then it is time to flatten the foot of the sail further, until it is absolutely straight if necessary.

Off-Wind. The foot should be deep (10-15 cm) in almost all wind conditions when reaching or sailing downwind, as being over-powered is usually not a concern. The exception is on tight reaches in strong winds, where the heeling moment is still quite significant. In this situation, keep the same setting as on the upwind leg.

Traveller

The traveller should remain tight in all conditions. A loose traveller allows the boom to be trimmed in closer to the centreline, but without a jib to shift the break point towards the leech, this is not desirable in the Laser. In fact, if the boom comes inboard from the corner of the transom, you should use your foot to push it back to the corner.

The traveller is sometimes loosened slightly to allow the block to move across the tiller when tacking or gybing in very light winds. However, with a flat-profile carbon fibre tiller, this is usually not necessary.

SECTION SHAPE AND SAIL POWER

A full sail accelerates well, like a car on first gear, and it is desirable when:

- There is adequate weight and fitness to keep the boat flat.
- Sailing upwind in choppy waters. Short chops slow the boat down, and a full sail helps the boat to pick up speed after each wave.
- Reaching or sailing downwind.

Upwind, most sailors are already hiking maximally at around 12 knots, so the sail controls, trimming, and steering have to be relied upon to keep the boat flat in anything beyond that. *Do not be greedy for power* – de-power the sail if you have to. A flat boat is faster than one that is heeling to leeward, even if the heeling Laser has a more powerful rig.

In very light winds (*fig. 3.11*), a full sail tends to shift the break point forward, causing early separation. To encourage the leeward airflow to stick to the sail, a flatter sail is necessary. The smaller angle of attack associated with a flat sail also gives you a higher sailing angle when going upwind.

Upwind sailing in flat water and light to medium wind is another situation where a relatively flat sail is advantageous. As there are no waves to impede the boat, sacrificing power for pointing ability is an attractive option.

GUIDE FOR SAIL SETTINGS

The settings mentioned above are summarized in *tables 3.1-3.3*. These settings serve only as a guide. Experiment with and refine the settings to suit your sailing style, weight, and feel (some prefer more weather helm than others). Centreboard height has also been included.

Fig 3.11 Sailing close-hauled in very light wind. The vang is tightened to about 30 cm from block-to-block and the boom is let out to encourage the leeward airflow to stick to the sail.

For the purpose of the tables and the rest of this book, a relative wind strength scale that takes into account your bodyweight is used (body positions refer to the upwind leg):

Very light wind: Almost drifting conditions, where the bodyweight is over the centreline of the boat (*fig. 3.11*).

Light wind: Buttocks on the side deck.

Medium wind: Just managing to hike out (i.e. buttocks over the side, but with the torso upright).

Strong wind: Hiking almost flat out or flat out, and comfortably keeping the boat flat.

Overpowering wind: Difficulty keeping the boat flat, despite hiking flat out.

> *"The 'feel' of the boat is the most significant factor with sail tuning. Do you feel overpowered? Does it feel like the boat isn't flowing through the water easily? Do you feel that the boat is stalling or you just don't feel fast? If you do, then something needs adjusting! Acquiring a feel for the boat gives you an opportunity for trial and error, and with time you can learn to adjust your controls not by the 'numbers' or the 'general rules' you've been told, but by the 'feel' of the boat."*
>
> *Jacqueline Ellis*

Table 3.1 Upwind Settings.

	OBJECTIVE	CUNNINGHAM	BOOM VANG & MAINSHEET TENSION	OUTHAUL	CENTREBOARD
VERY LIGHT WIND	Flatten sail to bring break point aft	Speed creases only	Tension the vang to around 20-30 cm from block-to-block, then ease the boom out slightly past the transom corner	Depth of 10 cm at foot of sail	All the way down
LIGHT WIND	Full sail, especially in chops	Speed creases only	Mainsheet tension at 0-20 cm from block-to-block position	Depth of 10-15 cm at foot of sail	All the way down
MEDIUM WIND	Fully powered sail	Almost no creases	Block-to-block	Depth of 10-15 cm at foot of sail	All the way down
STRONG WIND	Start depowering the sail, beginning from upper third	Cunningham grommet at gooseneck level	Mainsheet at block-to-block with some additional vang tension	Depth of 5-10 cm at foot of sail	All the way down
OVER-POWERING WIND	Very flat sail, eased out to keep the boat flat	Maximum tension	Maximum vang tension, ease the boom outboard as far as is necessary to keep the boat flat	Straight foot	Fully down or 10 cm up

Table 3.2   Reaching Settings.

	OBJECTIVE	CUNNINGHAM	BOOM VANG	OUTHAUL	CENTREBOARD
VERY LIGHT WIND	Flatten sail slightly to help leeward airflow to stick to the sail	Release fully	Vang tension equivalent to 20 cm from block-to-block	Depth of 10-15 cm at foot of sail	About halfway up
LIGHT, MEDIUM, & STRONG WIND	Full sail, with leech slightly open	Release fully	Vang tension equivalent to 20-30 cm from block-to-block	Depth of 10-15 cm at foot of sail	About halfway (30-40 cm) up
OVER-POWERING WIND	Spill air from upper third of leech and keep boom high	Release fully (unless on tight reach)	Vang loose enough to keep boom above the waves and to spill wind	Depth of 10 cm at foot of sail, or use upwind setting	About halfway up or higher to reduce heeling moment

Table 3.3   Downwind Settings.

	OBJECTIVE	CUNNINGHAM	BOOM VANG	OUTHAUL	CENTREBOARD
VERY LIGHT TO STRONG WIND	Straight mast and open leech (especially when sailing by-the-lee)	Release fully	Vang tension equivalent to 30-40 cm from block-to-block	Depth of 15 cm at foot of sail	One fifth down
OVER-POWERING WIND	Stability	Release fully	Vang tension equivalent to 30 cm from block-to-block and trim sail in to de-power	Depth of 15 cm at foot of sail, or use upwind setting	One quarter to halfway down

outboard mainly 10cms

Chapter 4

Straight-line Speed on the Beat, Reach, and Run

content by **Rod Dawson**
reviewed by **Lock Hong Kit**

*B*oat speed is a pre-requisite in fleet racing. Without it, superior tactics and strategy will barely save the day. With it, one can look like a great strategist – sailors with superior speed have been known to follow the favourites around the course, mimicking their strategy and eventually taking them on speed to finish ahead.

In a simple boat like the Laser, the main determinants of boat speed are technique and fitness rather than equipment. Sail tuning and trimming also play a part, but they have been covered in the previous chapter. With the sail well tuned, we are ready to look at fast techniques for the upwind, reaching, and downwind legs.

UPWIND TECHNIQUE

At the 1996 Olympics 56% of the average race was spent sailing upwind, whereas reaching and running took up 13% and 31% of the race respectively. This being the case, a slight superiority in upwind speed will put quite a distance between you and the other boats. Boat speed off the starting line helps in pulling ahead of the first row, with the reward of clear air and freedom to tack. After the first top mark, positions do not usually change as much, so it is important to continue working hard for the rest of the first beat.

157460

Running 31%
8:50 min per leg

158022

Upwind 56%
15:57 min per leg

Reaching 13%
3:42 min per leg

157459

Breakdown of the time spent on the different legs of the course for the Laser class at the 1996 Olympics.

Superior straight-line speed when sailing close-hauled is dependent on:

- Getting to and staying in the optimal weight range of 78-83 kg for the standard rig, and 60-75 kg for the Radial rig (*chapters 11 and 12*). There are fast sailors who may not be within these weight ranges, but they are the exceptions. Also, the top sailors in the standard rig are in excess of 1.7 m in height.
- Fitness (*chapter 11*).
- A well-tuned and trimmed rig (*chapter 3*).
- Effective hiking technique and body movements.
- Skilful steering.

The first three are covered in the other chapters, so we shall discuss the latter two elements in detail here.

Hiking, Laser-Style

The flat deck that was designed for car-topping rather than ergonomic considerations has led to the evolution of a unique hiking technique for the Laser. This technique, characterized by straight knees and upper body, was made popular by the 1994 Laser World Champion from New Zealand, Nik Burfoot. Combined with the necessary body movements to exploit the lightweight boat, Laser-style hiking is a physically demanding (and painful) skill that presents the greatest hurdle for sailors new to the Class. Taking years to acquire, superior technique separates the men from the boys and the fast from the slow.

> *"Straight leg.*
> *Straight back.*
> *Boat flat.*
> *Upper body leaning out.*
> *Torque the boat.*
> *Don't cleat the mainsheet."*
>
> *Rod Dawson, on upwind hiking*

Why Hike? Hiking keeps the boat flat. With a flat boat, the mast is almost vertical and the lift is near the horizontal plane (*fig. 4.1 left*). This is desirable, as we want the boat to move in the horizontal plane after all. With a leeward heel, the lift acquires a downward vector that weighs the boat down, reducing its speed (*fig. 4.1 right*). Also, the horizontal vector is diminished.

Mainsheet and Tiller Extension. Good hiking technique is not possible without first mentioning a few points regarding the mainsheet and tiller extension. The mainsheet should not be wrapped around the hand – it will take too long to release it when a gust hits. If you are new to the Laser, you may cleat the mainsheet while sailing upwind, but eventually, it

Fig 4.1 *The lift, L, generated by the sail is perpendicular to the boom and the mast. Left: When the boat is flat, L is close to the horizontal plane. Right: When the boat heels, a downward vector, d, is created while the horizontal component, f, is reduced.*

Fig 4.2 Hiking position. The tiller extension is held in front of the body. The mainsheet is locked in the hand by using the thumb to bend the sheet over the index finger. Pressing the mainsheet against the thigh makes it easier to hang on.

is better to sail the boat with the mainsheet out of the cleats. This has the advantage of a quicker reaction to the wind and waves, and the tension in the mainsheet helps to support the bodyweight while hiking. "Locking" the mainsheet against the thigh (*fig. 4.2*) makes it easier on the hands. Sheet in using the hand-over-hand method, and never use your teeth – you may find them flying off when a gust hits.

In most conditions, the tiller extension is best held with the palm facing downwards, in front of the body (*fig. 4.2*) – not at the side as in some other classes. This position is the most efficient because only elbow movements are needed to steer the boat, whereas with the extension by the side, the whole upper limb would have to be mobilized to move the extension back and forth. In very light wind, some hold the extension by the side as it is thought to improve feel.

There are sailors who have extraordinarily long extensions (1.31 m) so that both the mainsheet and tiller hands are at chest level, providing additional righting moment. However, the long tiller extension makes tacking difficult, so try gradually increasing the length over time.

Hiking Strap. The hiking strap should be loose enough for the bodyweight to be far out, but tight enough for the lower limbs to be glued firmly to the deck, making the boat and body one unit so that body movements are transferred effectively to the hull. Whether hiking from the toes, top of the feet, or ankles, the gunwale should be at mid-thigh level or below. If the calves are not pressed as firmly against the deck as the thighs are, then tighten the straps or push your body further out. Also, if hiking from the toes, the strap should be tighter than when hiking from the ankles.

An adjustable hiking strap (*fig. 2.2, pg 10*) is useful (particularly if you are not of above-average height), as it can be tightened for the reaches and for marginal upwind hiking conditions.

Position. Hike from a position between immediately aft of the centreboard and approximately 30 cm aft of this position (measuring from the forward edge of the front thigh). The exact position within this is determined by the size of the waves – shuffle back if waves are coming over the bow, and forward in flatter patches.

Posture. Point the toes upwards or slightly outwards, avoiding the toe-in position as that disproportionately activates the outer quadriceps muscle relative to the inner quadriceps. It is more efficient to distribute the load evenly over the whole muscle. Furthermore, disproportionate development of the outer quadriceps pulls the kneecaps outwards, possibly leading to a condition called patellofemoral pain after some time.

Keep the knees as straight as possible (*fig. 4.3*). Ideally, they should be so straight that the gap between the back of the knees and the side deck is obliterated – neither light (when observed from astern) nor a hand should be able to pass through this gap. This is critical to good upwind speed because:

- The clearance between the buttocks and water is increased.
- Righting moment is increased.
- Knees locked in full extension help prevent the boat from "giving" (by heeling to leeward) every time a gust hits.
- When "locked-in," all your energy can then be transferred directly to the boat when you throw your body around to torque the hull through the waves.

Fig 4.3 Hiking flat out.

Chest Up

Straight Knees

Body Flat

Back Straight

Hiking from Toes

When you get that "locked-in" feel, you will know it and realize how effective it is. In light-medium wind, tighten the hiking strap to maintain that "locked-in" feeling.

Depending on the wind strength, the torso can range from being flat to vertical. But whatever position it is in, do not crouch – it reduces leverage, makes it harder to spot gusts, and may cause backache. Keep the lower back straight and the chest up. A straight back, especially when the torso is upright, is only possible with flexible hamstrings – long hamstrings allow flexion to take place at the hip joints, thus sparing the lower back.

Survival Tips. Hiking muscles undergo a static contraction for long periods, impeding blood flow through the muscles and making it difficult to sustain the contraction. To improve hiking endurance, transiently relax the muscles every so often (e.g. when going over a wave) to allow blood flow. If you are well "tuned-in" to your muscles, you can take these transient breaks at well-timed intervals so that your muscles do not become totally fatigued before you reach the top mark.

Battened hiking pants (*fig. 4.4*) distribute the pressure from the gunwale, allowing sailors to hike harder and longer. The battens help to lift the buttocks off the water and some even slide thicker battens into the pants to enhance this effect. These performance-enhancing garments are an essential part of the Laser sailor's sailing gear.

The flat-out hiking technique aims to keep the head almost level with the knees to achieve maximum righting moment. This is definitely fast but like all good things, it comes at a price. Besides limiting visibility, huge loads are placed on the joints (especially the ankles and knees) and hiking muscles (ankle dorsiflexors, knee extensors, hip flexors, and abdominals). However, with progressive and consistent training, the joints and muscles will eventually (it may take years, though) adapt to the stress placed on them by this fast technique.

Fig 4.4 Hiking pants improve hiking performance. They are made for all climates, from shorties for the hot to full steamers for the cold. Go for the ones with thick, wide, and stiff battens stitched into a neoprene wetsuit. For shorties, shoulder straps prevent the pants from slipping off. It is important to get the right length, as shorties that are too long will cut into the back of the knees, causing painful abrasions. They should not be too tight around the thighs, or blood flow will be impeded.

Steering

With a hull weight of only 60 kg, oncoming waves can adversely affect the Laser's upwind speed. Finding the path of least resistance through the waves with skilful steering is thus critical for good boat speed. Other than steering with the rudder, the lightweight Laser can also be steered upwind using the bodyweight.

Steering with the Rudder. As the bow ascends an oncoming wave, point slightly into the wind, and as the same wave passes under your body, bear away to the original course (*fig. 4.5*). While steering through the waves, try to avoid sailing over the higher portions of the crests. Instead, steer through a break in an oncoming wave front (i.e. a flatter patch), if it is not too far from your course.

The boat's weather helm aids in pointing, so there is no need to jab the tiller too hard when pointing up a wave, unless it is really choppy. Bearing away will require more rudder action. As a general rule, keep in mind that the rudder acts as a brake when used excessively. However, vigorous steering can be very effective in choppy conditions, giving you the height to climb off a boat to leeward. Sharp movements of the helm, aided by a slight leeward heel, in time with the waves can be used to push the bow to windward. The timing has to be spot-on so that the boat does not stall.

Much time needs to be spent on the water before you get a feel of what the optimal amount of steering is for different conditions. Waves that are close together will require more steering action, but there comes a point where they are so close that it is better to keep the tiller still.

Steering action and mainsail trimming go hand-in-hand: ease the mainsheet to help the boat bear away; sheet in again as you point up the next wave. This is done for the bigger waves, where course deviations are larger than usual. Put on more vang tension when doing this, otherwise the boom will rise and power up the sail as the sheet is eased, heeling the boat to leeward. Furthermore, the vang tension makes trimming a lot easier.

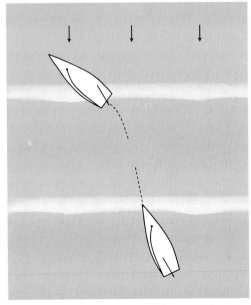

Fig 4.5 *Steering through the waves. Point up as the bow goes up the wave (bottom boat), and bear away as the same wave passes under your body (top boat).*

Steering with the Body. Earlier, it was mentioned that the boat should be kept flat at all times. The one exception is in choppy conditions and moderate to strong winds. Here, the boat is allowed to heel slightly to leeward, but it is subsequently flattened by throwing the upper body outwards and backwards as the crest of each wave passes under the boat (*fig. 4.6*), to power it through the chops. Throwing the bodyweight back not only helps the boat bear off, but it also keeps the bow from lifting off the water and slamming down as the wave passes.

Fig 4.6 Fore and aft movements to torque the Laser. From the usual hiking position (top), throw the torso out and back (bottom) as the waves passes under the body.

"Torqueing" the boat effectively requires a great deal of physical fitness and excellent technique. With the wrong technique, you will find yourself slower than those who hike flat-out to keep the boat flat without any body movements. To acquire the skill, learn to hike flat-out first. Once that becomes easy, torque the boat only for the bigger waves. As your fitness improves, do it more frequently. Remember – the very top sailors can maintain this for the whole race!

Light Wind Beating

When sitting on the side deck, hook the toes under the leeward handrail so that body movements will be transferred to the hull more effectively. Slide the buttocks in and out as the wind strength changes. Keep the bodyweight forward, next to the centreboard, to lift the transom above the water level, thereby reducing drag. In this position, sailing with the tiller extension by the side rather than in front of the body may increase sensitivity to the helm. In very light wind and flat water, keep as still as possible in order to maintain laminar airflow around the sail and water flow around the hull and foils.

In very light wind, a slight heel to leeward is fast, because it:

- Keeps the sail filled.
- Increases the weather helm and hence the feel for the boat.
- Reduces the hull's wetted surface area. As the Laser hull is relatively flat around the centreline and rounded on the sides, heeling the boat puts the rounder portion in contact with the water. The rounded portion has less surface area exposed to the water (compared to the flat area), and hence less drag. Sitting forward also reduces drag, since the hull is rounder at the front compared to the back.
- Cuts through chops better.

When the wind is light, the above benefits more than compensate for the deviation of the sail's lift from the horizontal plane.

When a larger set of waves is approaching, bear off to build speed to power through them. On the flip side, a flat patch can be used to gain a bit of height.

Beating in an Overpowering Wind

Despite its relatively small sail area, it does not take very much wind before the Laser is overpowered. When it is very windy, do not get disheartened – the others are also overpowered. If they do not seem so, it is because they have learnt how to handle the wind. You too can do it:

- Firstly flatten the sail. The cunningham grommet should be at the level of the gooseneck, if not lower. Throw your bodyweight back when tightening the vang. If you are not strong or big enough, use the foot to step on the part of the mainsheet between the mainsheet block and the boom as you pull on the vang. The vang tension is adequate when the boom moves horizontally outboard rather than upwards as the mainsheet is eased. Tighten the outhaul until the foot is straight.
- Ease the mainsheet out if you have to: it is faster to have the luff flapping and the boat flat, than to have the sail nicely trimmed and the hull heeling.
- Do not cleat the mainsheet: trim your sail continuously with the waves (sheet in as you point up the wave, and ease out as you bear down the wave) to keep the boat flat.
- Move slightly back (around 30 cm aft of centreboard) to prevent waves from coming over the bow.
- Hike flat-out and point or bear away to keep the boat flat.

REACHING TECHNIQUE

Planing – that is the key to being fast on the off-wind legs. He who catches more waves, stays longer on them, and finds the next one quicker is king of the reach and run. The ingredients for a fast reach are:

- Keeping the boat flat, or almost flat
- Riding the waves
- Weaving

Keeping the Boat Flat

A boat that is heeling will tend to broach when a gust hits. A flat boat, on the other hand, is much more lively and will surge forward with each gust. The rudder can really be a brake on the reach, so use the bodyweight to control the amount of heel and achieve neutral helm. If the same hiking strap length as the beat is used, the buttocks will tend to drag in the water. Tighten the strap if it is adjustable, or angle the body back to take up the slack.

The fore and aft position depends on the wind strength, size of the waves, and whether the boat is planing. Practice shuffling forward and aft: forward as the wind lightens and the boat starts to fall off the plane; aft when the gust hits and the boat starts planing.

Trim the sail continuously to keep the hull from heeling with the gusts and waves, holding the mainsheet either off the mainsheet block or forward boom block. The latter gives better feel for the sail pressure (especially when the wind is light) and more freedom for the upper body to respond to the gusts and waves. Trim according to the telltales, but do not hesitate to ease the mainsheet if the wind is strong.

Steer to keep the boat flat, bearing away quickly as soon as the gust hits, otherwise the boat heels, making it more difficult to bear away.

Aren't We Glad that the Laser Planes !

A floating boat displaces an amount of water equivalent to its weight. When it moves, it has to push aside this much water, thus creating bow, quarter, and stern waves. This is described as displacement sailing.

With increasing speed, the created waves become bigger, and the hull becomes trapped between its own bow and stern waves, unable to surmount the slope of its own bow wave. In this displacement mode, the 'terminal speed' is a function of the hull's waterline length (hull speed (knots) = 1.32 $\sqrt{L}$, where L is the waterline length in feet). With a waterline length of 3.81 m, the Laser's hull speed is less than 5 knots!

The good news is that when the wind picks up, the Laser is able to break out of the displacement mode and start planing. Its relatively flat hull-shape allows it to skim on the surface, displacing very little water, and freeing itself from the restrictions of displacement sailing. The faster it planes, the higher the hull is lifted off the water and the smaller the wetted area and corresponding skin friction drag.

Surfing

The aim is to be planing all the time. To catch a wave, position yourself to leeward of a sizeable wave and point the bow obliquely down the slope of the wave. In marginal planing conditions (i.e. smaller waves and lighter wind), point the bow further down the wave. As the wave picks the boat up, pump the sail once while throwing the bodyweight out and back to help the boat to overcome its inertia.

Once planing, hang on to the wave for as long as possible. This involves keeping the pressure in the sail by steering up and sheeting in as the boat slows down, and steering down to make ground to leeward when planing comfortably.

Before falling off the current wave, head higher to look for another good wave to hop onto.

Weaving

In weaving, the boat takes a winding course towards the next mark, steering down in a gust and up in a lull (*fig. 4.7*). When there are gusts, a weaving path to the next mark is faster than a straight one, the reasons being:

- Gusts are bodies of fast-moving air that migrate downwind. By bearing down in a gust, the boat moves downwind with it, thus spending more time in increased pressure.
- By bearing away, the boat can be kept flatter and thus faster if the wind is strong.
- In the lulls, sailing a higher course keeps the pressure in the sail and gives better speed. A higher course also brings the boat closer to the next gust.

In light and medium conditions, gusts are opportunities to steer down. In strong wind, lulls are opportunities to sail higher.

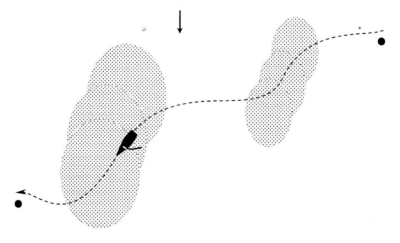

Fig 4.7 *Weaving. Bear away in the gusts; point up in the lulls. Note that the gusts migrate downwind.*

Light Wind Reaching

In light air, planing is impossible, so keep the bodyweight forward with a slight leeward heel to lift the stern clear of the water and reduce wetted area. This minimises drag. Move gently to avoid disturbing the flow over the sail, hull, and foils when trimming the heel of the boat to neutralise the helm and when steering with the bodyweight. Constantly trim the mainsheet for every little variation in the wind, using the telltales to increase sensitivity to wind changes.

Strong Wind Reaching

In strong air reaching, keeping the boat flat is of utmost importance in maintaining control. Work hard to catch the waves. It is actually safer to sail fast because the apparent wind is reduced, lowering the pressure on the rig.

When the boat heels to leeward, the small rudder and the bubbles from the bailer increase the likelihood of a "spin out," where laminar flow over the rudder is lost. The rudder feels lighter and becomes ineffective. Quickly re-establish laminar flow by throwing your bodyweight out to flatten the boat and jabbing the tiller to leeward to shake off the bubbles.

RUNNING TECHNIQUE

Downwind sailing has recently taken on a revolutionary fervour. Pointing the bow at the bottom mark and sailing on the rhumb line is a thing of the past. Instead, the top guys zigzag their way past other boats, deviating as much as 30° degrees from the rhumb line. With upwind differences in speed becoming smaller, the running legs take on greater importance. This is now one of the key opportunities to pass boats in a race.

Sailing By-the-Lee

This means sailing with the wind coming from the same side as the sail, the air flowing from leech to luff (*fig. 4.8*). Many find sailing by-the-lee awkward initially, but after some practice, they become converts.

Fig 4.8 Sailing by-the-lee.

The Pros of Sailing By-the-Lee. Reversing the flow across the sail is definitely fast in the Laser, and it has other advantages:

- It might not seem so at first, but sailing by-the-lee is more stable, even in windy and gusty conditions.
- It provides an additional option (apart from pointing) for manoeuvring through a gap in the wave ahead and for avoiding a nosedive.
- It provides additional tactical options like bearing away to avoid being blanketed by the boat astern, and getting an inside overlap at the bottom mark.

The speed superiority compared to a dead run or broad reach is greater in non-planing conditions. In bigger waves and medium to strong wind, getting the boat to surf becomes the priority – it does not really matter whether you are on a dead run, broad reach, or by-the-lee, so long as you are planing.

Fig 4.9 *An open and flicking leech are fast when sailing by-the-lee.*

Front is Back, Back is Front! As the flow is reversed, the rig is set up differently. Normally, some vang tension is put on to stop the leech from twisting excessively and spilling wind. However, when sailing by-the-lee, the luff becomes a very straight "leech," so there is no need to have too much vang on. In fact, the vang must be loose to open up the leech (which is now the "luff") to facilitate air entry, otherwise the boom will gybe over too readily (*fig. 4.9*).

Just as you would normally trim your sail using telltales along the luff to ensure laminar flow on both sides of the sail, by-the-lee sailing requires you to trim the sail such that air flows over both sides of the leech. When trimmed correctly, the leech will start flicking. Do not stop it – this is quick. This natural fanning of the leech is a legal way of pumping that can be encouraged by releasing a section of mainsheet and then stopping with your hand. Try to time this with a wave and it will improve your surfing.

On a broad reach, forcefully rolling the boat to windward causes it to surge forward; when sailing by-the-lee, a forceful roll to leeward has the same effect. Beware of the rules on propulsion!

To de-power, bear away and sheet in – not the other way round. Remember this when hit by a gust.

When sailing by-the-lee, you will tend to be picked up by waves from the leeward side, causing the boat to roll to windward. Anticipate these waves by moving your bodyweight to leeward early. Reacting too slowly results in the rudder coming out of the water and complete loss of rudder action.

Sail Trim

When sailing on a broad reach, trim according to the telltales. When sailing by-the-lee or on a dead run, the boom should be approximately perpendicular to the centreline. The

Averting a Death Roll

"The common running problem is the violent roll to windward that causes the boat to start to bear away radically. What do you do? Perhaps you pull the sheet in and move your weight in to correct the trim, but let us concentrate on the rudder. Do you push the rudder away from you (head up) or pull it toward you (bear away)? For most of you it is probably inconceivable to pull it towards you, but that is actually the right answer! You see the alternative is to push it away from you. Then the angle of the rudder will act as a lifting plane and lift the transom out of the water and accentuating the roll. If you pull it towards you, the rudder becomes a lowering plane and drives the boat both deeper 'by the lee' and forces the boat upright. At the same time, the rig once again becomes stable as the power on the leach is removed (more flow, less push) and the boat again becomes stable."

Steve Cockerill

lift generated by the sail is roughly perpendicular to the boom, so having the boom in that position will direct the lift straight ahead, in the direction you want to be heading. From here, trim in and out depending on how much power you want from the sail and where you are heading. A common mistake is to have the boom too far in or out without realizing it. If you are not good at judging where 90° is from where you are sitting, then marking the mainsheet will help. To do this, position the boom perpendicularly to the centreline (with some pressure on the sail) while on shore, and mark the mainsheet at the point where the forward boom block is. This will serve as your reference point.

When the wind is so light that there is not enough pressure on the sail to keep the boom out, ease the boom approximately 10° past the perpendicular, and heel the boat to windward. The weight of the boom will then keep it in position, allowing the sail to fill. The alternative is to move forward and hold the boom out yourself.

Hull Trim

When sailing downwind, a windward heel brings the sail's centre of effort directly over the centreline *(fig. 4.10)*, neutralizing the helm and thus reducing unnecessary rudder action. From this position, athwartships movements will steer the boat effectively (heel further to windward to bear away and heel to leeward to point).

Sit as far forward as is comfortable, without the bow digging into the wave in front. The windward heel (short of submerging the side deck) and forward position reduce wetted surface area and hence drag.

Fig 4.10 Heeling to windward when sailing downwind is fast. The centre of effort of the sail (indicated by the cross) sits directly over the centreline of the boat.

Posture

Three different postures are common, each for different conditions:

Knees in Front of Body *(fig. 4.11 top)*. As the body faces the leeward side of the boat rather than forward, it is easier to look behind for patches of increased pressure. Most adopt this posture in light and medium conditions, but some find this posture stable even when it is blowing.

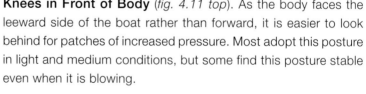

Front Knee Next to Centreboard *(fig. 4.1 middle)*. This is more stable, brings the bodyweight further forward, and makes it easier to move quickly to leeward to avert a capsize to windward.

Locked-In *(fig. 4.11 bottom)*. With stronger wind and bigger waves, the bodyweight is shifted back to prevent the bow from digging in. The front foot is jammed against the front of the cockpit while the back knee is lowered to the floor to lock the lower body into the hull while the upper body moves freely to promote surfing.

Fig 4.11 Common sitting postures for downwind sailing.

Surfing

As in reaching, planing is the most important consideration in downwind sailing – surf down waves and plane from one wave to another. Pick the right waves: some are too small to catch, and are better ignored; some are too steep, causing your bow to nosedive; some bring you too far away from the rhumb line. Sometimes, there are two sets of waves, each moving in different directions, giving you more options to keep the boat planing. In mixed waves, try to choose those that will bring you closer to the next mark or the favoured side of the leg.

To catch waves, the sheeting and body movements are similar to that described for reaching, except that you will not be hiking, and the bodyweight is thrown more backwards than outwards. By pointing the bow directly down the wave and aiming for the steepest part of the wave, you will achieve maximum speed. The trick from here is to not plough into the wave in front and to not lose the wave. Point the bow higher and give the mainsheet a big pump. If the boat starts to lose momentum, bring the bow around to sail by-the-lee and release about 50 cm of mainsheet and then stop it with your hand – this will cause the leech to fan, promoting you further along the wave. Remember, one pump per wave – make the most of it!

If the bow threatens to nosedive, point or bear away. Try to steer through gaps in the wave ahead, thereby "overtaking" it and getting onto its leeward slope to continue surfing. "Linking" waves this way keeps the boat planing endlessly.

Never mind if you have to deviate far off from your rhumb line, so long as you keep your boat planing. Some fast sailors make huge deviations, others smaller. As you zigzag downwind, stay away from other boats and also stay away from their blanket zones. If there are other boats nearby, affirm your rights (if you have right-of-way) to discourage others from getting in your way. Look back frequently to spot gusts that you can intercept, as sailing in gusts will make it easier to surf.

Running in Different Wind Strengths

Here are some fast downwind pointers for different conditions.

Light Wind:

- The top priority is to look for gusts and to intercept them. This will determine the path you take.
- The next priority is to keep your air clear and maintain good speed. Stay out of the other boats' wind shadows – particularly, try to stay in a gap between two groups of boats behind. The wind will be clear and possibly accelerated.
- Sail by-the-lee as far as possible as it is fast in such conditions.
- Heel to windward and shift your weight well forward to reduce wetted surface area.
- Steer with athwartships body movements to minimise rudder action.
- Avoid abrupt body movements in order not to disrupt the flow around the sail, hull, and foils.
- If it is really light, let your boom out past 90° from the centreline so the sail will fill and the boom will not keep coming over. Alternatively, move forward to hold the boom out.
- Handle the mainsheet from the forward boom block to get a better feel for the pressure on the sail.
- Keep all control lines loose (especially ensure the vang is loose so the leech of the sail will fan).
- Raise the centreboard high, leaving just enough in the water to facilitate steering. However, when you sail sharply by the lee you should drop it down a bit so the boat tracks properly and does not go sideways.

"Fundamentals play a critical part in effective downwind sailing in the Laser. Your ability to catch and maintain your position on waves is greatly enhanced by proper sail trim, weight placement, and efficient turning. By thinking about how all these factors interact and using each to enhance the other, you can maximize your downwind speed and resulting gains."

Nick Adamson

Medium wind:

- The top priority now shifts towards catching waves and staying on them. Being in the gusts will help with the waves as well.
- Sail higher or lower to avoid a direct run.
- Keep your weight forward, just aft of the centreboard. Steer using body movements.
- Adjust the heel so that the helm is neutral.
- Avoid digging the bow into the wave ahead.

- If you cannot quite get onto a plane, sail by-the-lee for maximum speed while looking for better waves. Shift your weight forward if you are not planing.
- Set up the sail so that the leech fans.
- Raise the centreboard almost fully up to allow the boat to roll a little.
- Try to be loose and mobile in the boat rather than planted in one position.

Strong wind:
- Here, it is easier to plane, so the challenge is to "link" waves and plane continuously.
- Lock-in the lower body for stability, keeping the upper body mobile.
- Put your weight back and steer up or down the waves to avoid digging the bow into a wave.
- Sail by-the-lee or go on a broad reach for stability (when you are in between waves).
- Keep the centreboard one quarter to halfway down for stability.
- Sail faster rather than slower! The apparent wind is reduced when you are planing, reducing the forces on your rig.

Watching the top guys in action best complements the above description on technique. This is now made possible with a CD ROM of top sailors in action, which you can watch over and over again (*see Recommended Reading*).

Next, you will have to spend lots of time on the water. No matter how detailed the above description, only experience gained on the water can help you fully appreciate all that you have read.

Robert Scheidt (left) and Ben Ainslie (right), two of the fastest downwind sailors in the world.

Chapter 5

Tacking, Gybing, and Penalty Turns

content by **Nick Adamson**
reviewed by **Alexandre Nikolaev** *and* **Lock Hong Kit**

*T*acks and gybes constitute only a small part of fleet racing, but they can adversely affect the final results if executed poorly. Apart from the obvious slide down the fleet resulting from a capsize, poor tacking and gybing skills severely limits one's tactical options. Imagine tacking to lee-bow an approaching boat and getting overtaken to windward instead, or gybing across to get an inside overlap on the boat ahead at the bottom mark, only to broach after the gybe (and possibly hitting other boats in the process)! These and other situations can be avoided by acquiring simple but good technique, together with lots of practice in different conditions. Penalty turns, another important skill, will also be described in the chapter.

TACKING

The Laser is a highly manoeuvrable boat where tacks and gybes should result in minimal loss in distance. When considering whether or not to tack during a race, the anticipated loss should be so small that it hardly constitutes part of the decision-making process. For example, when sailing in another boat's backwind, a Laser sailor should not quote lost distance from having to tack twice as an excuse not to clear his air.

The technique differs slightly when tacking in the different wind conditions. The roll tack is performed in light winds while the standard tack is used for all other wind strengths.

Standard Tack

1. Before tacking (*fig. 5.1a*):
    *   Ensure that there is a valid reason to tack. Needing a break from hiking is not a good reason!
    *   Look ahead to check that you are not tacking away from a good gust or shift and check your windward hip to ensure that you are not tacking into another boat's water.
    *   Ensure that the boat is moving at optimal speed. Hike out if you have to.

Fig 5.1. Standard tack

- If necessary, use your feet to push the mainsheet to the front of the cockpit to keep it out of the way during the tack.
- Take your aft foot out of the hiking strap and place it over the strap (i.e. you are now hiking off your forward foot only) so that it will smoothly rotate under the strap and become your new forward foot as you cross the boat facing forward. This will allow you to start hiking immediately on the new tack.

2. Try to initiate the tack in relatively flat water, as the Laser is a light boat that can be slowed down significantly by oncoming waves. As the bow goes up a wave, point slowly into the wind. There is no need to rush this stage as the boat is making headway in a favourable direction, into the wind. If the rig is not already at the block-to-block, sheet in as the boat points. To maintain boat speed going into the tack, stay out to keep the boat flat (*fig. 5.1b*) and shift your buttocks onto the side deck (from the hiking position) only after the heeling moment begins to diminish (*fig. 5.1c*).

3. As the bow goes past head-to-wind, move across the boat directly to a hiking position on the new tack (if the wind is strong enough to hike) (*fig. 5.1d and e*):
    - Resist the temptation to start moving across too early.
    - Face the front of the boat as you move to the other side, switching the tiller and mainsheet hands behind your back (*fig. 5.1e*). Note that throughout the tack, the mainsheet and tiller extension are in your hands, so you have full control of the boat heel and rate of turn at all times. If the tiller extension tends to get caught onto the mainsheet, try holding it at the tip when tacking.

d

e

f

- Time the rate of turn such that the next wave hits the new windward side of the bow, helping the boat to bear off onto the new course.
- Once the boat is past head-to-wind, ease the mainsheet as much as you have to in order to keep the boat flat, especially in strong wind. This is extremely important, as the boat will not accelerate smoothly while it is heeling. In lighter air, delay the move across a little to allow the boat to heel slightly to leeward on the new tack.
- Do not stop to sit on the side deck on your way to the hiking position on the new tack. If you have taken your foot out of the strap prior to initiating the tack, your new forward foot will be ideally positioned to support you as you go into an immediate hiking position.

4. Once you are on the new tack, the priority is to accelerate to full speed:
    - Hike to flatten the boat (*fig. 5.1f*).
    - Trim the sail in as the boat accelerates.
    - Tidy up the mainsheet last, *after* you have accelerated to full speed.

In the method described above, the mainsheet and tiller hands are switched while moving across, so that the changeover would have been completed before the end of the tack. This is very advantageous when doing double-tacks or a quick series of tacks. Some sailors switch hands only after getting onto the new hiking position. This is acceptable as long as speed and control are maintained throughout the tack. Other sailors sit on the tiller extension to hold it in place as they switch hands. If you do not already have this habit, it is best not to start since during the time that the tiller extension is under the buttocks, steering adjustments cannot be made, and the extension gets in the way of a good hiking posture.

Strong Wind Tack. When it is very windy, the boat tends to go into irons during the tack, not wanting to bear away onto the new close-hauled course. Below are some important tips to help the boat to bear away onto the new tack:

- Ensure good boat speed before going into the tack. It is the rudder that turns the boat round, and the boat needs to be moving for the rudder to work. Hike hard and bear away a little, if necessary, to pick up speed before tacking.
- Time the tack with the waves, such that the next oncoming wave hits the bow on the new windward side, helping the boat to bear away onto the new course.
- Prevent the boat from heeling after it has gone past head-to-wind. When it is blowing hard, a leeward-heeling boat will resist bearing away. On top of that, the boom-end will tend to catch the water, causing the boat to heel even more. To keep the boat flat, place your aft foot over the hiking strap just prior to moving across so that you can go straight into the new hiking position on the new tack. Also, ease the mainsheet out amply once the boat has gone past head-to-wind.

If you do get caught in irons during the tack, raise the centreboard a little and allow the boat to reverse. After the boat has gained some momentum in the reverse direction, push the tiller away from you to allow the boat to fall away to a close reach course. (You can help by pushing the boom out, away from you.) Once the bow is pointing at the correct angle to the wind, hike out aggressively and sheet in (taking care not to sheet in too fast, as you are trying to make the boat move forward without stalling the foils), keeping the boat flat as it gathers speed. You may need to give the tiller a couple of quick pulls to windward to keep the boat from rounding up, but centre your tiller as soon as you feel the boat responding with forward motion. If the conditions are really bad, easing the vang (in addition to raising the centreboard) will also help to prevent the boat from screwing up into the wind when the sail is sheeted in. When the boat is back on its close-hauled course, you might want to push the centreboard back down.

Roll Tack

The principles are the same as that for the standard tacks, except that here, the sail is used as a fan to "propel" the boat (*fig. 5.2*).

1. Before the tack, look ahead to ensure that you are not tacking away from a gust. Gusts are especially advantageous in light winds.

2. Initiate the tack by pointing the bow slowly into the wind. Heeling very slightly to leeward helps the boat point (especially in very light air), minimising rudder action (*fig. 5.2b*). With a bit more breeze, this is unnecessary as there should be sufficient weather helm. As the boat points, sheet in until the boom is block-to-block.

3. After the bow has gone past head-to-wind, aggressively heel the boat to windward to "fan" the sail (*fig. 5.2c*). Be careful not to do this prematurely as heeling to windward before you are head-to-wind creates counter forces (with the rudder turning the boat into the wind and windward heel turning the boat away from the wind) that will sap your momentum. You may need to move your weight in slightly as the sail unloads to keep the boat flat.

4. As the boat bears away to the new close-hauled course, ease the mainsheet liberally and pull yourself across to the new windward side by grabbing the windward gunwale with the tiller hand. Delay the move across to give the boat a substantial leeward heel on the new tack, with the gunwale dipping slightly below the water surface.

5. Before rolling the boat to windward:

    •   Ensure that the boom is eased just outside the leeward corner of the transom (approximately 30-50 cm from block-to-block) (*fig. 5.2e*). As the boat rolls to windward, the apparent wind shifts towards the beam, and therefore the sail should be trimmed accordingly.
    •   Ensure that the bow is pointing in the direction of the new close-hauled course with the tiller centred, so that the boat will accelerate in a favourable direction as you roll it to windward.

6. When the above two prerequisites are met, shift your weight out to flatten the boat (*fig. 5.2f*). Sheet the sail back in as soon as the boat is flat (i.e. when the apparent wind shifts forward) (*fig. 5.2g*). There is an optimal rate for the roll to windward. If done too slowly, the boat sideslips. If done too violently, there will not be enough time for the boat to accelerate. Experiment

Fig 5.2. Roll tack

with how much you ease out and how quickly you flatten the boat to find the ideal combination. In general, ease the sail out further as you flatten the boat faster.

In light wind, a good roll tack will actually result in a gain in distance (although the rules specify that the speed coming out of a tack or gybe must not be greater than it would have been in the absence of the tack or gybe). Bear in mind that "repeated tacks or gybes unrelated to changes in the wind or to tactical considerations" are disallowed.

GYBING

Standard Gybe

The standard gybe described below can be used for medium and strong wind (*fig. 5.3*).

1. Before gybing, get the boat to surf down a wave (if the waves are large enough). This reduces the strength of the apparent wind, making the gybe much less violent.

2. Bear away down the face of the wave. As you do so, sheet the sail in from the mainsheet block a few arm lengths (*fig. 5.3a*) and adjust the windward heel of the boat until you feel very little resistance from the helm. (The windward heel will help you eliminate rudder drag generated from turning.)

3. As your transom passes through the wind, help the boom gybe across by giving the mainsheet a tug (*fig. 5.3b*). Do not jerk too hard or the mainsheet will flick itself around the boom end.

4. As the boom comes across, move over to the other side, and bear away to trace an S-shaped course (*fig.5.4*). When crossing the centreline, you may use your forward hand to grab the mainsheet from the forward boom block (*fig. 5.3c*), reducing the slack in the mainsheet even further. This helps to prevent the sheet from getting caught around the transom corner and the boom from hitting the water.

    Before the boom slams onto the new gybe (*fig. 5.3d*), prepare to take advantage of the sudden push by ensuring that:

Fig 5.4 *S-shaped course taken during a gybe. When the boom slams onto the new side, the boat is close to a dead run.*

Fig 5.3. *Standard Gybe*

- Your weight is already on the new windward side to counter the heeling moment.
- The boat is close to a dead run course so that the slamming action pushes the boat in a downwind direction. The stronger the wind, the closer you will have to be to a dead run.

5. Switch the tiller and mainsheet hands, trim the sail, and continue planing down the wave (*fig. 5.3e*).

Strong Wind Gybe. Gybing in strong winds can be a scary experience. However, it can be done safely, without capsizing, if the following pointers are adhered to:

- The faster you go, the safer it is. Make sure that the boat is planing as you gybe – this reduces the apparent wind so that the forces acting on the rig are considerably less. If there is a need to gybe before you can get the boat planing, then at least try to gybe in a patch of relatively flat water.
- As soon as the boom crosses the centreline, start bearing away to align the boat in the direction of the wind to minimise the leeward heel when the boom slams onto the new side.
- Be very careful not to let the boom out past 90° to centreline prior to establishing control on the new gybe. This frequently results in the boat death-rolling.

Roll Gybe

Roll gybes (*fig. 5.5*) help to propel the boat in light wind, but they are also a useful way of preventing the mainsheet from getting caught around the transom corner. This happens when the mainsheet dips into the water as the boom comes in during the gybe, and it is then dragged back, around the corner of the transom. The windward roll prior to the gybe keeps the mainsheet out of the water to prevent this annoying problem.

1. Sheet in a few arm lengths from the mainsheet block, bearing away at the same time (*fig. 5.5a*).

2. Heel the boat a little to leeward (*fig. 5.5b*), grab hold of the hiking strap with the mainsheet hand (while still holding on to the mainsheet), and roll the boat to windward (*fig. 5.5c*).

3. As the boom comes across, move over to the other side, grabbing the mainsheet from the forward boom block as you go past the centreline to take more slack off the mainsheet (*fig. 5.5d*). On the new tack, allow the boat to heel to leeward such that the boom end just clears the water (*fig. 5.5e*).

4. With the tiller centred and the boat pointing in the direction you want it to go, roll the boat flat with your bodyweight and feel it surge forward (*fig. 5.5f*). Do not flatten the boat until the sail has filled on the new gybe to maximise the power generated by the manoeuvre.

Fig 5.5. Roll Gybe

5. Switch mainsheet and tiller hands, and trim your sail for the new course (*fig. 5.5g*).

Another method of gybing in light air, especially from a run to a run (rather than at a gybe mark), is to simply pull both strands of the mainsheet from the back to get the sail across. Instead of moving all the way back to grab the sheet, "pick" it up using the end of the tiller extension. This method requires minimal course alteration, and is therefore ideal when there are other boats nearby.

PENALTY TURNS

Penalty turns are similar to tacks and gybes in the sense that a 720° turn comprises two tacks and two gybes, while a 360° turn comprises one tack and one gybe. Tacking and gybing techniques are important, but there is more to it - you need to be able to bear away sharply and maintain speed through fast handwork.

Generally, when beating upwind, it is advantageous to start with a tack (after releasing the vang if it is blowing hard) since the boat is already sailing close-hauled. Likewise, start with a gybe on the downwind leg. On a beam reach, it is equivocal. The difference between starting with a tack or gybe is not great, so other factors must be considered, like keeping clear of other boats and clear air. For example, after touching the top mark, it is better to continue sailing on starboard tack and start with a tack to get out of other boats' way, and to remain in clear air after the penalty.

Here are some keys to good penalty turns:

- Use windward heel to help the boat bear away from the wind with minimal rudder action. Slight leeward heel is helpful while heading up, but is not as important.
- Monitor your boat speed and your rate of turn. Slow the turn down if you are losing speed.
- Match your rate of trim to your rate of turn to ensure that the sail is properly trimmed throughout the turns.

Penalty turns are not about finishing the turns as fast as possible – they are about losing as little ground as possible. In between the tacks and gybes of a 720° turn during the upwind leg, instead of going into the next gybe or tack immediately, stay on the close-hauled course a little longer to build up speed (*fig. 5.6*). It will take longer to complete the penalty, but you make better headway to windward in the process.

> *"If there is any class where it's sailor against sailor, it's the Laser class. You don't have to throw a lot of money at boats and equipment; you just have to work at sailing well."*
>
> *Nick Adamson*

Fig 5.6 *Minimising the distance lost during a 720° turn.*

Chapter 6

Around the Buoys

content by **Ben Tan**
reviewed by **Alexandre Nikolaev** and **Lock Hong Kit**

*W*ith the big-fleet racing that is typical of the Laser class, places are gained or lost at the marks within a matter of seconds, whereas between marks, boats are painstakingly overtaken one at a time. Being able to pass boats at the marks involves not only superior boat handling, but also a sound knowledge of the racing rules and a war chest of tactical tricks. This chapter looks at the boat handling elements, while the tactical aspects are dealt with in chapter nine.

Mark rounding involves more than turning the boat - there is much to do. Developing and practicing a routine for each mark will leave more time to think of other things like wind strategy.

The commonly used course configurations are shown in *fig 6.1*.

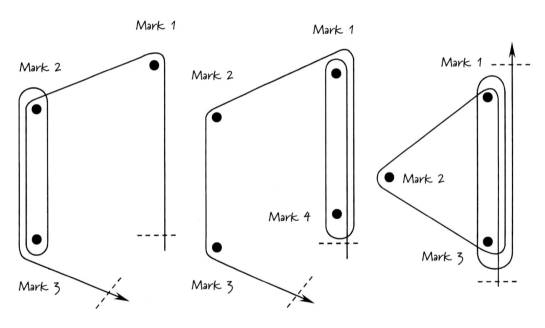

Fig 6.1 Commonly-used courses. Left: Outer loop trapezoid course. Middle: Inner loop trapezoid course. Right: Triangle course.

Fig 6.2 Rounding the top mark.

TOP MARK

The first top mark tends to be the most crowded, and also the most interesting. The routine described below is for a starboard tack approach (*fig. 6.2*).

1. **Where's the next mark?** Before getting into the crowd at the top mark, look for the next mark (i.e. the gybe or bottom mark) (*fig. 6.2a*). With an orientation of where the next mark is, you can sail straight towards it immediately after rounding the top mark and avoid sailing off course. Even if you are not in the lead, it is important to get your bearings, as the boat in front might not be heading the right way (e.g. he might be sailing high to free his mainsheet), and the normal tendency is to follow the boat in front.

2. **Disentangle the mainsheet.** Make sure the mainsheet is not knotted up, especially if you have the habit of kicking the mainsheet around when tacking and you have made lots of tacks during the beat.

3. **Ease the outhaul.** When the boat is about 10 m from the top mark, start easing the control lines. (This distance can be shortened, as you get more proficient.) If there is a need to ease the outhaul for the next leg, then point up slightly (to prevent the boat from heeling to leeward), transfer the mainsheet to the hand holding the tiller extension, and release the outhaul while staying as far out as it is possible (*fig. 6.2b*). Boom markings are useful here, as they will help you get the right setting the first time round (*fig. 2.12 right, pg 18*). Note that there are situations when there is no need to release the outhaul: when the foot of the sail is already set at its maximum fullness for the upwind leg, and when it is really blowing, in which case

e

f

the outhaul will be tight during the upwind leg, and it may be best to leave it there for the off-wind leg.

4. **Ease the vang.** Immediately after easing the outhaul, uncleat the vang tail, ease the mainsheet, and cleat the vang at the appropriate setting (using the markings on the vang tail) (*fig. 6.2c*).

5. **Ease the cunningham.** With smooth lines, all you need to do is to unleat the cunningham (*fig. 6.2d*). If it does not run freely, move forward and loosen the cunningham from the portion lying parallel to the mast. If you have not reached the top mark by now, hike out and go for speed till you get to the mark.

6. **Bear away and start planing.** At the mark, raise the centreboard, and bear away (*fig. 6.2e and f*). Focus on catching a wave as soon as possible. If you cannot raise your centreboard in time, then get planing first and raise it later.

Get the boat to plane as soon as you have rounded the top mark.

Having the ability to bear away sharply is useful, especially if the downwind leg is up next. If the intention is to sail to the left side of the downwind leg, spinning the boat around its axis will get you out of the blanket zone of the boats immediately behind, and it will also discourage the boat behind from following you to the left. To make a sharp turn, the boat must be almost flat, the mainsheet must be eased quickly (feed it through the mainsheet block if you have to), and the centreboard should be partially raised (especially if it is blowing hard). Be quick to move your weight towards the centreline to avoid capsizing to windward.

7. **Tighten the hiking strap and complete the vang and cunningham adjustments.** Only after the boat is planing (if the conditions permit) on the new course to the gybe mark, do you tighten your hiking strap (if you have to) for the reach.

If sailing downwind in light air, it is usually difficult to free the vang adequately while approaching the top mark, so there may be a need to release it further after rounding the top mark. At the same time, ensure that there is no tension on the cunningham.

The main objectives are to change the sail settings while losing as little speed as possible, and to get planing as soon as the top mark is rounded. The outhaul and the vang are difficult to release after rounding the top mark, so they should be freed before the rounding. If the cunningham cannot be freed or centreboard cannot be raised on time, it is not too difficult to do them after the rounding.

If you are just under the lay line, and tacking twice would put you too far above the lay line, then an option is to "shoot" the mark by pointing almost head-to-wind to take advantage of the boat's momentum to carry it past the mark. The Laser's lightness limits the momentum available, so it is important to be sailing at full speed prior to pointing. Also, think twice about trying to shoot the mark in an adverse current.

MARK 2 OF TRAPEZOID COURSE AND GYBE MARK

Mark 2 of the trapezoid course is passed to one side rather than rounded when sailing from a reach to a run. The priority is to maintain good boat speed throughout while picking the left or right side of the downwind leg. The vang needs to be freed for the run, preferably before passing the mark. If your weight is needed over the side of the boat, then free the vang after passing the mark, when sailing downwind.

For the gybe mark, there is no need to make any sail adjustments, unless one reach is tighter than the other. Again, the priority is to keep the speed up, so the vang is adjusted, if necessary, on the leg that does not require the body to be over the side of the boat.

BOTTOM MARK

There will either be a reaching exit or an upwind exit. For a reaching exit (e.g. passing mark 3 of the trapezoid course from a run to a reaching finish) the vang will need to be tightened for the reach, preferably before reaching the mark.

The upwind exit is much more difficult. Here, it is important to enter the mark wide, and exit close to the mark. This prevents others from squeezing between you and the mark, taking away your freedom to tack. Never allow your bow to be trapped to leeward of the boat ahead as you exit – slow down instead, and point directly at his transom. If the boat in front rounds wide, squeeze in between him and the mark.

The steps below are for an upwind exit (*fig. 6.3*).

1. **Plan ahead.** As you approach the bottom mark, take a quick look behind to see if there are any gusts (or any other factors) that might influence your decision on whether or not to tack immediately after rounding the bottom mark (*fig. 6.3a*).

2. **Hiking strap.** If you tightened the hiking strap earlier for the reach, loosen it for the beat.

3. **Mainsheet.** About 10 m from the mark, hold the mainsheet off the mainsheet block if you were trimming off the forward boom block earlier.

4. **Centreboard.** Lower the centreboard fully.

5. **Cunningham.** Tighten the cunningham, throwing your body weight back if you need to (*fig. 6.3b*).

a

b

c

Fig 6.3 Rounding the bottom mark.

6. **Establish rights.** Just before you enter the two-boat length circle, verbally declare your rights to the surrounding boats. To those who are inside but have no overlap on you, shout "Two lengths, no water!" (*fig. 6.3c*). To those who are overlapped on your outside, shout "Two lengths, water!" or simply "Water!" (If you are nice, you can add a "please" to the end of the sentences.) These succinct and universally understood statements are an important part of the mark rounding sequence as they minimise disputes.

7. **Wide entry, tight exit.** Approach the turn with the bottom mark at about 1.5 boat lengths abeam of you (*fig. 6.3d*). Sheet in quickly hand-over-hand as you point, aiming to exit as close to the mark as possible (*fig. 6.4*). Allow the boat to heel slightly to aid pointing, but flatten the boat once you are close-hauled (*fig. 6.3e*). Once on a close-hauled course, check your tactical compass to see if you are on a lift or header, and tack to get in sync with the shifts if you need to.

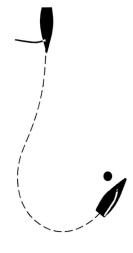

Fig 6.4 Bottom mark rounding: wide entry, tight exit.

8. **Tighten vang and outhaul.** Once settled on the beat and sailing at full speed, take the slack off the vang (*fig. 6.3f*) and tighten the outhaul if you need to. Tidy up the mainsheet if it is lying all over your legs.

In the photo sequence below, the boat rounds the mark to port. As leeward gates are increasingly used (due to congestion at the bottom mark), it is a good idea to practice rounding the mark to starboard as well.

d

e

f

Chapter 7

Wind Patterns and Strategy

content by **Ben Tan**
reviewed by **Meteorological Service Singapore** *and* **Jacob Palm**

*A*lthough they might seem haphazard, winds do abide by the laws of physics. Air and water temperature, the earth's rotation, the shoreline, the latitude, and a whole host of other factors determine the wind's behaviour. The wind assumes many different patterns, each with its own "personality." There are winds that arrive punctually each day and then progressively clock to one side predictably. There are winds that swing widely, as if unable to make up its mind. There are winds that do not even bother to turn up when they are supposed to. For each wind pattern, there is an optimal strategy to get you round the course in the shortest amount of time.

Once you learn how to recognise the numerous patterns, you can anticipate what the wind will do next, and that offers an obvious advantage. Sailing round the course over and over again will help familiarise you with the pattern, but you have only a limited amount of time before the start, and besides, the pattern may change as the day progresses. Hence, there is a need to be able to recognise patterns quickly. To do this, you must first be aware of the different wind patterns, and the reasons why the wind adopts those patterns.

"I have been sailing on many race courses around the world with a good deal of success because I have trained myself to take the trouble to learn the local wind and current conditions."

Paul Elvström

By wind patterns, we are referring to the behaviour of the surface wind. This is the wind near the earth's surface, and is therefore the wind we sail in. But to understand the surface wind, we will have to take a look at its big brother, the gradient wind, which is the wind that blows higher up in the atmosphere.

GRADIENT WIND

Being high up in the atmosphere (roughly more than 500 m above the earth's surface), the gradient wind is relatively free from the effect of friction or drag with the earth's surface. It is visible to us as moving clouds in the sky. Whatever the gradient wind does, it will have an effect on the surface wind.

The Driving Force Behind the Gradient Wind

The sun preferentially heats up the equator more than the other parts of the earth (*fig. 7.1*). The air above the heated land, in turn, gets hotter and rises, creating low pressure areas (lows). Cold air from the high pressure areas (highs) flows in to replace the rising air. This flowing air, on a global scale, is what we recognise as wind systems.

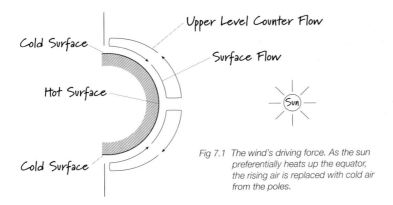

Fig 7.1 *The wind's driving force. As the sun preferentially heats up the equator, the rising air is replaced with cold air from the poles.*

Because of the earth's rotation, air does not flow directly from a high to a low. Instead, it blows across the pressure gradient (the Coriolis Acceleration). In the northern hemisphere, wind spirals around a low in an anticlockwise direction (as seen from the top), and around a high in a clockwise direction (*fig. 7.2*). The directions are reversed for the southern hemisphere.

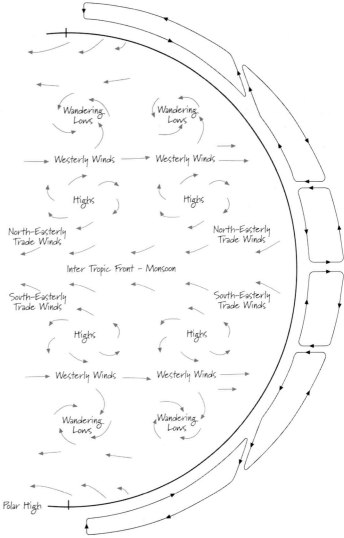

Fig 7.2 *Global circulation. The direction of the gradient wind is perpendicular to the pressure gradient.*

Fig 7.3 Weather maps. Top: Chart comprising isobars. Bottom: Streamline chart.

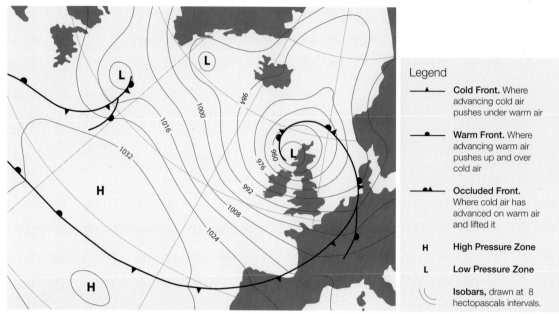

Legend

——▲—— **Cold Front.** Where advancing cold air pushes under warm air

——●—— **Warm Front.** Where advancing warm air pushes up and over cold air

——▲●—— **Occluded Front.** Where cold air has advanced on warm air and lifted it

H High Pressure Zone

L Low Pressure Zone

Isobars, drawn at 8 hectopascals intervals.

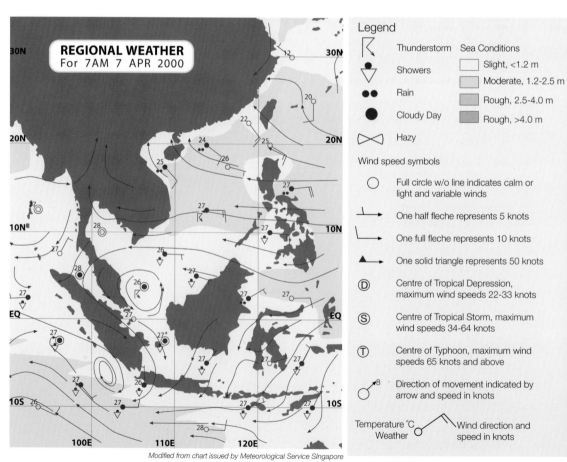

Legend

↙ Thunderstorm

▽ Showers

●● Rain

● Cloudy Day

⋈ Hazy

Sea Conditions

☐ Slight, <1.2 m

☐ Moderate, 1.2-2.5 m

☐ Rough, 2.5-4.0 m

☐ Rough, >4.0 m

Wind speed symbols

○ Full circle w/o line indicates calm or light and variable winds

One half fleche represents 5 knots

One full fleche represents 10 knots

▲ One solid triangle represents 50 knots

Ⓓ Centre of Tropical Depression, maximum wind speeds 22-33 knots

Ⓢ Centre of Tropical Storm, maximum wind speeds 34-64 knots

Ⓣ Centre of Typhoon, maximum wind speeds 65 knots and above

○↗8 Direction of movement indicated by arrow and speed in knots

Temperature °C
Weather ○ Wind direction and speed in knots

Modified from chart issued by Meteorological Service Singapore

Weather Map

Weather maps allow us to "see" the gradient wind. They consist of lines, called isobars, which join points on the earth having the same atmospheric pressure (*fig. 7.3 top*). The isobars form circles around the lows, which are called depressions or cyclones, and also around the highs, which are called anticyclones. Other frequently used terms in the isobar chart are the ridge, trough, and col (*fig. 7.4*).

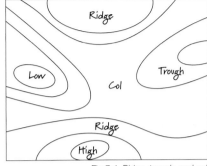

Fig 7.4 Ridge, trough, and col.

The strength and direction of the gradient wind can be inferred from the isobars. The closer the lines are, the greater the pressure gradient, and hence the stronger the wind in that area. The direction of the gradient wind is roughly parallel to the isobar. Parallel, but in which direction? As mentioned earlier, in the northern hemisphere wind circulates around a low in an anticlockwise direction (like a whirlpool), and a high in a clockwise direction. A way to remember this is to hold out your left hand. For the circulation around a high, do a "thumb's up" (*fig. 7.5*). The wind circulates in the direction indicated by your curled fingers (i.e. clockwise). For a low, point the thumb down. The fingers will curl in an anticlockwise direction, and that happens to be the direction of the wind around the low. To work out the wind direction from an isobar chart of the southern hemisphere, use your right hand instead.

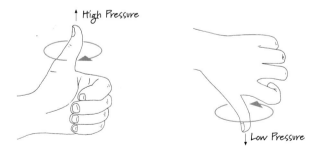

Fig 7.5 Using your left hand to remember the wind direction around the highs and lows in the northern hemisphere. The left hand shows the circulation (circular arrows) around a high (left) and low (right). Use the right hand for the southern hemisphere.

In the equatorial trough (doldrums), where the pressure gradients are minimal, the lines on isobar charts would be too far apart to be useful. Hence streamline charts, where the lines indicate the surface wind direction instead, are used in such areas (*fig. 7.3 bottom*).

Satellite Picture

Satellite images, like weather maps, give an instantaneous picture of the weather over an area. They are photographs taken from high above the earth's surface. Areas of high pressure are cloudless or sparsely littered with clouds, whereas the low pressure areas are cloudy. Clouds seen in the satellite picture map out wind patterns, as demonstrated by the swirls of a tropical storm in the centre of *fig. 7.6*.

Fig 7.6 Satellite picture showing a tropical storm over the South China Sea.

The Monsoons

Derived from the Arabic word for seasons, the Monsoons are persistent seasonal winds caused by difference in solar heating between the two hemispheres (as well as differences in temperature between oceans and continents).

They are most developed over Southern and Eastern Asia, where in the northern winter, the outflow from the Siberian anticyclone travel great distances as north-easterly or north-westerly winds across the Pacific coasts, southern China, Burma, India, and South China Sea. However, during the northern summer, the Siberian high disintegrates into low pressure systems while in the southern hemisphere, high pressure systems develop over Australia and the surrounding seas. These high pressure systems give rise to the south-easterly or south-westerly winds over Southern and Eastern Asia. Other continents like North Australia, Africa, and North America also develop Monsoon winds.

The winds may or may not bring rain, depending on whether there is a long sea track. For example, the Northeast Monsoon brings dry, cool weather from Siberia and China to most of the Southeast Asian Continent, but as the wind flows across the South China Sea, it picks up moisture, dumping it over countries to the south like Singapore and Malaysia.

SURFACE WIND

So far, we have been talking about the gradient wind, whose home is high up in the atmosphere. Let us now come down to earth and study the wind that we sail in – the surface wind.

Factors Influencing the Surface Wind

As the surface and gradient winds are adjacent to each other, they interact closely. Drag and stability are important determinants of this interaction.

Drag. Being near the earth's surface, the surface wind is strongly influenced by drag (i.e. friction against the earth's surface). If it were not for drag, the surface wind would be somewhat similar to the gradient wind. A forest exerts the greatest drag, while a smooth sea exerts the least. Tall buildings, however, should be treated as obstacles to the wind rather than as causing drag. Drag has two effects on the surface wind. Firstly, it reduces the wind speed. Secondly, it alters the wind direction. In the northern hemisphere, drag causes the surface wind to back (i.e. the direction of the surface wind rotates anticlockwise) from the direction of the gradient wind (*fig. 7.7*); in the southern hemisphere, the surface wind veers (i.e. wind direction rotates clockwise) from the gradient wind. The greater the drag, the greater the reduction in speed and change in direction of the surface wind compared to the gradient wind.

Fig 7.7 Effects of drag on the surface wind in the northern hemisphere. On land, where the drag is higher, the surface wind is backed further and the wind strength is reduced further compared to the smooth sea. For the southern hemisphere, the surface wind is veered from the gradient wind.

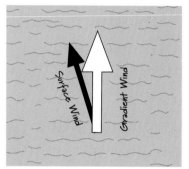 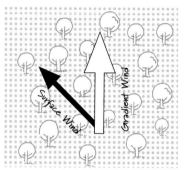

Stability. When the wind blows over a relatively warm surface, pockets of air are heated up and they rise, while pockets of colder air descend to replace them. In such a situation, the air is said to be unstable. The churning results in turbulent flow, and this allows faster-moving air from the higher altitudes to reach the surface, resulting in gusts and an overall wind speed that is closer to that of the gradient wind. Conversely, if the water or land temperature is cold, then there is less mixing (i.e. stable air) and airflow remains laminar and slower near the surface.

As the land gradually heats up during the day, the increasing turbulence causes the wind to strengthen progressively, peaking in the early or mid afternoon. The sea temperature, on the other hand, does not have as marked a diurnal variation due to the higher specific heat of water (i.e. it takes much longer to heat up a body of water), so this phenomenon is not evident over the sea.

Variations in Surface Wind Strength

The strength of the surface wind is never absolutely steady all the time – gusts and lulls are everywhere, even over a smooth surface like the open sea. The object of the game is to catch all the gusts, and avoid the lulls.

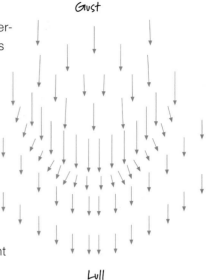

Gusts. With turbulence, descending pockets of faster-moving air (i.e. gusts) hits the water at an angle and fans out as shown in *fig. 7.8*. The fast-moving air whips up little ripples on the water surface, giving it a darker appearance (*fig. 7.9 left*). All competitive sailors must acquire a sharp eye for these gust patches. They are easiest to spot in flat water, and when the sun is at a certain angle. These patches usually have an elliptical shape (with the long axis along the wind direction) and tend to migrate downwind. If you can, go to a vantage point on the coast and observe these gusts, noting their behaviour in each set of conditions. How fast do they move? How long do they last? How frequent are they?

Fig 7.8 Wind direction in and around a gust. Longer arrows indicate greater wind strength.

Not all dark patches are gusts. Cloud shadows (*fig. 7.9 right*) tend to mimic gusts. Their appearance is different but if unsure, you can always look up to see if there is a cloud floating between the dark patch and the sun.

Fig 7.9 Left: Gusts can be seen on the surface of the water as dark patches of more intense ripples (arrows), while the area over the lull has a shinier appearance. Right: Not all dark patches are gusts. The dark areas on the water are cloud shadows, and not gusts!

The wind within a gust has its own speed and direction, so each gust is often accompanied by a wind shift. Sometimes, the wind backs every time a gust hits; sometimes, it veers with every gust; at other times, you get a combination of both (most common situation). It is said that in the northern hemisphere, gusts will veer since the surface wind is backed relative to the gradient wind, and these gusts descended from the upper levels; whereas in the southern hemisphere, gusts will back. In practice, the theory does not hold true all the time. This is probably because there are many other forces at play (each influencing the wind direction in its own way), with a particular one dominating over the others at any one point in time. The practical implication is that we have to place a greater reliance on observation, rather than theoretical predictions. Go out to the course early and make a mental note of the wind shift pattern as you beat up to the top mark. Do the gusts tend to come from the left, right, or both left and right? How big are the shifts, if any? How long do the shifts last? Is there periodicity, or is the timing of the shifts totally random? Build a mental picture of the shift pattern in your mind to help in your tactics and strategy.

Lulls. Due to drag, gusts eventually decay, becoming lulls. Soon, a fresher pocket of air will displace it. Beneath the lull, the water surface attains a relatively smooth and shiny appearance compared to a gust patch. Avoid these "holes." However, not all smooth and shiny patches are lulls. A thin layer of oil on the water can have a similar appearance, so do not get fooled, especially when racing in an area with a heavy traffic of powered vessels. Oil on the water can be seen when in close proximity but at a distance, the shape of the shiny patch and odour are useful clues that help in differentiating the two.

Wind Bands. In the open sea, the surface wind does not distribute itself in a perfectly uniform manner. It has a tendency to organize itself into bands of strong and light wind (*fig. 7.10*). These bands may be approximately 1-8 km apart. Sometimes, rows of clouds, called cloud streets, line the top of the light-wind bands.

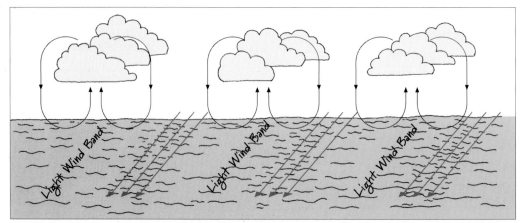

Fig 7.10 Alternating strong wind (straight arrows) and light wind bands over the sea. "Cloud streets" demarcate the light bands.

Shore Effects on the Surface Wind

The shore influences the surface wind in a variety of ways, depending on the direction of the wind in relation to the shoreline and the hemisphere involved. As dinghy races are held close to shore, it is important for Laser sailors to understand these shore effects.

Wind Blowing Off the Shore. In the northern hemisphere, as the surface wind blows over the land, it is backed relative to the gradient wind. Over the water, it is backed to a lesser degree, so an offshore wind veers over the water (*fig. 7.11*). In the southern hemisphere, the off shore wind backs over the water. The veer may not be

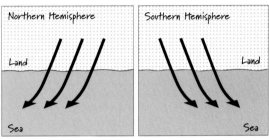

Fig 7.11 An offshore wind veers over the water in the northern hemisphere and backs in the southern hemisphere.

immediate, so the location of the wind bend in relation to the shoreline varies. To locate the bend, sail close-hauled towards the shore on one tack and look for a progressive change in the boat's heading.

Wind Blowing Onto the Shore. With an onshore wind, the bend occurs over the land, so it is of no relevance to sailors.

Wind Blowing Along the Shore. When the wind blows along the shore, the difference in drag between land and sea causes the wind to converge or diverge along the shoreline depending on the hemisphere and wind direction (*fig. 7.12*). When they converge, a band of stronger wind, the convergence zone, results. As the converging air is forced upwards, a row of clouds along the shore

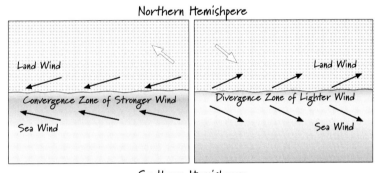
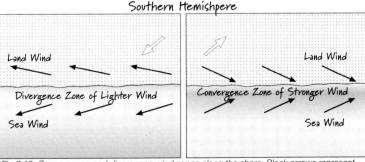

Fig 7.12 Convergence and divergence wind zones along the shore. Block arrows represent the gradient wind.

may form to mark its location. When the winds diverge, a light-wind divergence zone arises. The zones vary in width, so their presence and location will need to be ascertained before the start of the race by sailing across the zones.

Wind Blowing Off a Coastal Cliff. With the wind blowing off a coastal cliff, the veer (in the northern hemisphere) or back (in the southern hemisphere) will still occur, but the bigger concern now is the eddies (*fig. 7.13*). If the top mark is in the region of the eddies, then be prepared for random shifts and gusts as the zone is entered. It will be difficult to cover another boat in such situations as two boats in close proximity can be sailing in different winds. A better strategy would probably be to take advantage of the frequent shifts and gusts to sail your own race once your boat crosses into that zone.

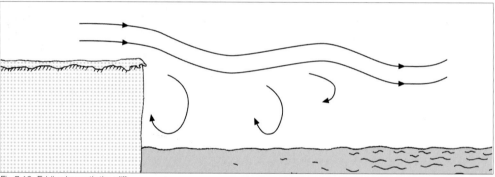

Fig 7.13 Eddies beneath the cliff.

Barrier Effects on the Surface Wind

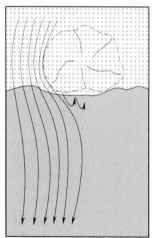

Fig 7.14 Wind bend around a hill.

Obstacles Along a Shoreline. Buildings and trees that line the shore are examples of obstacles that will influence an offshore wind. Directly downwind of an obstacle is its wind shadow, where airflow is disturbed. How far downwind does this disturbed area extend? That depends on the density of the obstruction and, more importantly, its height. It has been said that the disturbed area extends downwind to a distance roughly equivalent to 30 times the height of the obstruction (i.e. 300 m for a 10 m tall tree). In practice, it is advisable to sail upwind towards the shore to get a more precise picture.

A Hill on the Shore. Unlike a tall building, a hill near the water can be big enough to not only cast a wind shadow, but also cause a the wind to bend around it (*fig. 7.14*).

Gaps Along the Shoreline. Besides casting a wind shadow, obstacles that are not uniformly distributed along the shore will funnel an offshore wind through the gaps in the line of obstacles. When racing, this is obviously the place to be (in the absence of other factors like current). River mouths and similar openings in the shoreline will also have a funnel of stronger wind passing through them (*fig. 7.15*).

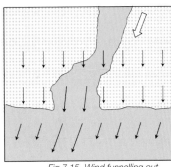

Fig 7.15 *Wind funnelling out through a river mouth in the northern hemisphere. The block arrow represents the gradient wind.*

Islands. Quite a few regattas are hosted at seaside resorts that are dotted with little islands. Again due to the greater drag as wind blows over the island, there will be a band of stronger wind on one side of the island, a wind shadow to leeward, and a wind bend below the island (*fig. 7.16*).

Barrier Effects at the Start. When sailboats are bunched together, as in the starting line or at the top mark, they present a barrier to the surface wind. At the start, a long line of boats will affect the wind in several ways (*fig. 7.17*):

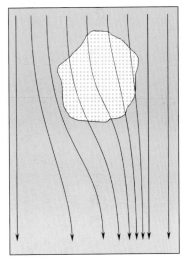

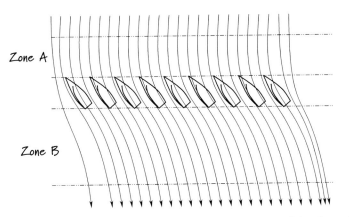

Fig 7.17 *Barrier effects at the start. In zone A, the wind is slightly lighter; in zone B, the wind is even lighter, and it is also deflected.*

Fig 7.16 *Wind direction and strength in the vicinity of an island in the northern hemisphere. Note the wind bend in the lee of the island and the stronger wind (represented by closer streamlines) on the right hand side of the island. In the southern hemisphere, the strong wind band will be on the other side of the island, and the wind bend will correspondingly be reversed.*

- The air decelerates slightly in front of the fleet, resulting in a zone of lighter air.
- The wind speed directly behind the first row of boat is understandably reduced.
- The starboard tackers' sails deflect the wind, creating a lift for boats crossing behind on port tack.

Sea Breeze

Rising air (updraught) over the land and sinking air (subsidence) over the sea, driven by a temperature difference between land and sea as the sun rises, give rise to the sea breeze (*fig. 7.18*). Clouds developing just inland of the shoreline are a manifestation of the updraught, and are therefore indicators of a sea breeze circulation. The shoreline is the birthplace of the circulation, since the temperature gradient is greatest there. As it matures, the circulation extends further out to sea and further inland at the same time. Hence, on a sunny and calm day, sail close to the shoreline if you want to be the first to take advantage of an anticipated sea breeze.

How will an incumbent gradient wind affect the sea breeze circulation? If the gradient wind is in excess of approximately 20-25 knots, the sea breeze will not develop regardless of the direction of the gradient wind. A lighter gradient wind will either reinforce or hinder the sea breeze from developing, depending on its direction relative to the shoreline (quadrant effect). Generally, an offshore gradient wind increases the onshore sea breeze. But how can this be? Going back to *fig. 7.18*, note that the sea breeze is onshore, but the higher altitude return flow is offshore. An offshore gradient wind pushes the return flow along, while the sea breeze tucks itself under the gradient wind. An onshore gradient wind opposes the return flow and prevents the sea breeze from ever developing (*see boxed text*).

Fig 7.18 Sea breeze developing around the shoreline.

As the sea breeze gets stronger, it may either back or veer. After its peak, towards the end of the day, be prepared for a progressive reversal in direction.

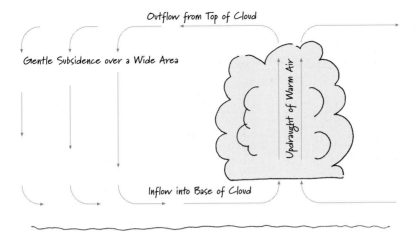

Fig 7.20 *Circulation around a non-raining cumulus cloud.*

to the sailor: it merely tells us if we are on the same side of the cloud as the sun (white cloud) or on the side opposite to that of the sun (black cloud).

Over land, areas that get especially hot, like a large open car park, can have clouds sitting over them on a calm day. Towards the late morning, clouds may form just inland of the shoreline, hinting that a sea breeze is developing (*fig. 7.21*). At sea, the surface temperature is more uniform, but clouds can still appear:

Fig 7.21 *Cumulus clouds forming just inland of the shoreline.*

- Cloud streets form over bands of light wind in open water.
- Clouds form over a convergence band along the shoreline.
- In temperate latitudes, frontal clouds form when advancing cold air (cold front) displaces warm air upward (*fig. 7.22*). These appear as a single line of cumulus clouds. Under the clouds, expect the wind to veer (northern hemisphere) or back (southern hemisphere).

Fig 7.22 *Frontal clouds form when a cold front displaces warmer air upwards.*

Since cumulus clouds indicate an area of rising air, the wind under the cloud tends to be light (except for a convergence band). Avoid sailing under a large, low-level cloud if possible.

Raining Clouds

So far, we have been discussing non-raining cumulus clouds. What happens if it rains? Below raining clouds, the rain chills the air as it falls and, at the same time, the water droplets "drag" the air down with it. The result is an outflow of cold air away from the cloud. The outflow varies in strength, and radiates outwards (*fig. 7.23*).

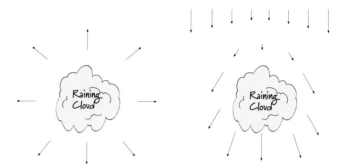

Fig 7.23 *Wind pattern around a raining cloud in calm weather (left) and in a surface wind (right).*

THE WEATHERMAN SAYS ...

Many sailors criticise weather forecasts as being inaccurate, blaming the forecast for losses. Before we make the weatherman our scapegoat, we ought to bear in mind that:

- Not many meteorologists forecast coastal weather, and even a shipping forecast is not put together with sailboat racing in mind.
- A meteorologist looks at weather at a larger scale, whereas we sailors are interested in the weather on a relatively tiny racing course.
- Meteorologists do not have the advantage of the additional information that we can gather before the race, like nearby clouds (the clouds they see are from satellite photos), and local wind trends (knowing which way the wind is clocking an hour before the start can help us make predictions).

In fact, if we add the absolutely up-to-date information from our own observations to the information provided by the meteorological service, our "forecast" for the racing area should logically be more accurate than that of the meteorologist. Do not rely only on the weatherman's forecast.

How can the meteorological service help us? To complement our own observations, we need the latest:

- Weather map
- Satellite picture
- Weather forecast

A little of the meteorologist's opinion goes into writing the forecast, and if you have a distrust for his opinion, then at least make use of the objective information – the weather map and satellite picture. As each map or satellite image gives an instantaneous record of the weather, information on trends will have to be extracted from the forecast or serial maps and images. Useful trends to note are the movements of the highs and lows (which direction and how fast), pressure changes, and movements of fronts.

Where can we get weather information? At major regattas, weather maps and forecasts (with or without satellite pictures) are posted on the notice board. These will be the latest postings. Another good source is through the Internet, where many meteorological services provide updated information, including the latest satellite images. Other sources include the newspapers and radio (forecast only).

WIND STRATEGY

In the preceding paragraphs, we discussed the different wind patterns for many different situations. Once familiar with the different patterns, you can start developing strategies for different wind patterns to get the most out of each.

Detecting Wind Shifts

There are two common ways to detect wind shifts: using relative boat angles or relying on a tactical compass.

Boat Angles. When beating upwind with another close-hauled boat in sight (*fig. 7.24*), changes in wind direction will

Fig 7.24 Detecting wind shifts using boat angles. Initially, you (Black) and your rival (White) are even. If you are lifted (Light Grey), White will appear to have "moved" ahead relatively; if you are headed (Dark Grey), White will appear to have "moved" astern relatively.

change the other boat's position relative to you. Headers and lifts can be detected this way, provided that there are other boats around on the same tack and that the reference boat sails at the same speed and height.

Although this method eliminates the need for a costly compass, it has its disadvantages. At the start, it is quite hard to tell if starting on a lift or a header until the first shift arrives. Also, if you are the first to round the bottom mark, there will be no boats to use as a reference. Using the boat's angle to the waves and using landmarks are not precise enough.

Tactical Compass. When sailing close-hauled with a compass, a change in the compass bearing indicates a wind shift. Telling if you are on a lift or a header at the start (based on readings collected before the race), and immediately after rounding the bottom mark (based on readings taken during the previous beat) becomes easy. Compasses can quantify the shifts and are very sensitive, sometimes too sensitive in the sense that it detects headers that are so small that they may not be worth tacking on.

Fig 7.25 Silva's tactical scale. Left: Reading of 18 on the tactical scale when on starboard tack. Right: Reading of 8 on the port tack.

The Silva tactical compass has a scale that saves us from having to remember one bearing for the starboard tack, and another totally different number for the port tack. The scale is marked such that if the compass reads "18" on one tack, then it reads "8" on the other if the wind direction remains steady (*fig. 7.25*). The corresponding reading after each tack is either plus or minus 10, so only one number needs to be committed to memory. For the compass to be an asset to the sailor, he must be aware of the following:

- The tactical scale is based on a 40° sailing angle. This is true in most conditions, but not in light winds, where the Laser cannot point that high. In these situations, a pair of numbers will have to be remembered.
- As pointing angles change with a change in wind strength, a lull might be misinterpreted as a header. If you go strictly by the compass, you will be tacking on every lull! Give an allowance of a few degrees when you hit a hole before interpreting it as a true header.
- Do not stare at the compass during the beat! Keep your head out of the boat (e.g. looking out for gusts).

Rather than staring at the compass, a much better way to sail is to detect the shifts using changes in boat angles, and then use the compass to confirm and quantify the shifts. The compass will show exactly how much you have been headed (or lifted), and whether you have been headed (or lifted) past the median wind direction. (If you have been headed, but not past the median, then you are actually still on a lift, although you are now not lifted as much.) By using the compass to supplement shift reading via boat angles, rather than relying solely on the compass, the sailor is forced to keep his head out of the boat to check boat angles. Also, by looking at the compass only after a shift is suspected due to changes in boat angles, sailors will not be confused or disturbed by the very small shifts (which are not worth acting on) picked up by the overly sensitive compass.

Sailing in the Three Basic Shifts

There are three basic wind patterns: oscillating shifts, persistent shifts, and progressive shifts. Oscillating shifts can be superimposed on the other two.

Oscillating Shifts. This is when the wind swings back and forth about a median direction. It is very hard for the wind not to oscillate at all. A phenomenon called wind-waves will induce regular oscillations in the wind direction. (An explanation of this phenomenon is beyond the scope of this book: *see Recommended Reading* for text by Frank Bethwaite). On top of this, in unstable air, there are different pockets of air, each with a slightly different speed and direction reaching the surface.

"When behind, never give up because until the finish, there are always opportunities to win. Don't sail on the obviously wrong tack just to split with the opposition. This only reduces future opportunities to pass. Chip away at their lead by taking the shifts – this will frustrate them."

Rod Dawson

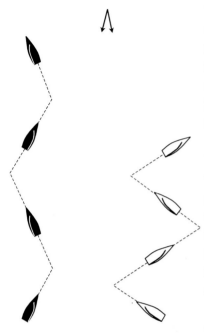

Fig 7.26 Black and White have equal speed (i.e. length of both wakes are the same) and each had three oscillating wind shifts at the same time interval. Black stays on the lifts and tacks when headed; White does the direct opposite. The result: Black ends up way ahead.

The timing of the oscillations can be regular (e.g. one shift every 3 min) or irregular (e.g. a shift occurring at 30 s, and the next one 3 min later); frequent (e.g. every 30 s) or infrequent (e.g. every 15 min). The magnitude of the change in direction can also be regular (e.g. 5° left ➤ 5° right ➤ 5° left, etc.) or irregular (e.g. 5° left ➤ 4° left ➤ 12° right ➤ 3° left ➤10° right, etc.).

The basic rule is to tack in a header and stay in a lift. This is the fastest way to the top mark (*fig. 7.26*). Getting a header is good when you have been on a tack for some time, as it means that you have been sailing on a lift all this while. On the other hand, if you are lifted, then you were on the wrong tack prior to the shift. Here are a few pointers on making the best use of oscillating shifts (with no progressive or persistent shifts):

- Unless trying to work your way to one side of the course, tack only on headers that have shifted past the median. Take, for example, a wind from a bearing of 100°N - 114°N, and a median of 107°N, and you are presently lifted on starboard with the wind from 114°N. If headed by 5°, you should not tack as you are still in a lift. Wait till you have been headed more than 7° before tacking. The reading for the median wind direction is obtained by sailing on a long upwind beat before the race.

- With each wind shift, you are sailing into a different body of air. Between two bodies, there will be a small transition zone where the wind direction is midway between the two. In this zone, the wind direction is not settled and, if you tack immediately when headed, the wind might shift back to its original direction. This can be frustrating, as you would have to tack back, only to tack again when the header finally decides to stay. Therefore, there are times when it pays to sail deeper into the shift. In different conditions the size of the transition zone varies, but on average, wait about three seconds after you have been headed before tacking. Again, you will need to do a beat before the race to see whether the shifts occur sharply and decidedly (in which case you can tack immediately), or whether the wind eases itself slowly into a new direction.

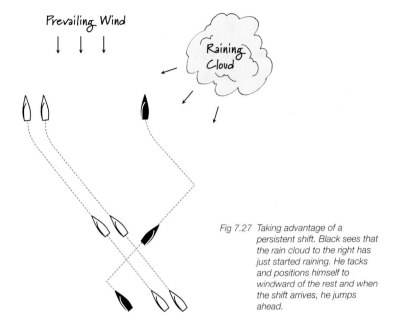

Fig 7.27 *Taking advantage of a persistent shift. Black sees that the rain cloud to the right has just started raining. He tacks and positions himself to windward of the rest and when the shift arrives, he jumps ahead.*

Persistent Shifts. Shifts are said to be persistent when the wind swings to one side and stays there till the end of the beat or race. Situations when this might arise include the onset of a sea breeze, a large raining cloud bringing a new wind that might stay for the rest of the race, and the arrival of a cold front. The last oscillating shift on the upwind leg is treated as a persistent shift.

When two boats are lifted, the windward boat gains; when they are headed, the leeward boat gains. Hence, the idea is to be on the favourable side of the fleet when the persistent shift arrives. To do this, the persistent shift (*fig. 7.27*) needs to be anticipated.

The new wind does not usually come instantaneously. It takes a little time to develop, as in a sea breeze. Wind from a nearby rain cloud will enter the course much faster, but still not instantaneously. There is therefore a progression towards the new direction. Hence, if a progressive shift (i.e. the wind direction starts deviating out of its oscillating range) is sensed, look around to see what is happening. Is a new wind coming? You might be caught out if you assumed the wind would oscillate back to its original direction.

Progressive Shifts. As the name implies, the wind will clock either left or right gradually. Progressive shifts occur when:

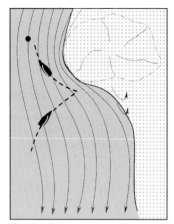

Fig 7.28 Taking advantage of a wind bend around a hill.

- A new wind is taking over an existing one. Whenever a wind shift is accompanied by a general change in wind strength, suspect a progressive shift.
- There is a wind bend, e.g. an offshore wind, a hill obstructing the wind (*fig. 7.28*), and an island.

If two boats are sailing close-hauled on the same tack, and the wind shifts to one side progressively, the boat on the side that the wind shifts to (i.e. the inner boat) will gain. This is likened to two runners running around a track, one on the innermost lane and the other on the outermost. The former, of course, has an advantage over the latter as he has to cover less distance. The way to sail a progressive shift is to sail on the headed tack first, and later tack to enjoy the lift towards the top mark (*fig. 7.29*). On each of the tacks, you would be on the inner circle. Tack before reaching the conventional lay line, or you will overstand the mark.

It is critical that progressive shifts are differentiated from oscillating and persistent shifts, as the response is entirely the opposite: you sail on the headed tack at the beginning of a progressive shift, whereas you tack on a header if it is an oscillating or persistent shift.

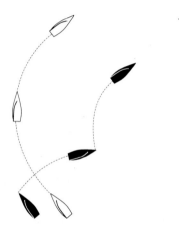

Fig 7.29 Taking advantage of a progressive shift. Black and White are initially even on starboard tack. Black tacks and gets progressively headed on port tack; when he tacks back onto starboard, he is progressively lifted ahead of White. On both tacks, he is on the inner circle. Black arrows represent a progressive veer as both boats beat upwind.

Wind Shifts on the Downwind Leg

So far, we have been discussing shifts when sailing upwind. Do we need to be concerned about wind shifts when sailing downwind? Generally, no. This is because the overriding priority in downwind sailing is surfing and intercepting gusts. Furthermore, the Laser can sail almost just as fast whether it is on a broad reach, run, or by-the-lee, as long as it is planing (unlike most boats). If a big shift brings you too far away from the bottom mark, simply gybe across.

Sailing in Gusts

Gusts are always present on the sailing course, so it is important to make full use of them on every leg of the course.

Upwind Leg. When sailing upwind:

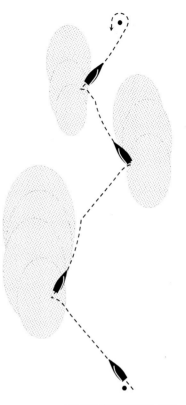

- Remember that the gust patch on the water moves downwind, so aim to intercept it, rather than sailing directly for it (unless it is so big that you cannot miss it). If a gust is ahead to leeward of your course, do not try chasing it as it would have migrated further downwind by the time you get there.
- If there is a gust patch ahead and slightly to windward (*fig. 7.30*), sail towards it. As the gust is approached, the boat will tend to be headed progressively over several seconds. Do not tack immediately or you will be tacking away from the gust. Sail deeper into the header until you reach the shoulder of the gust, then tack.
- Likewise, if you are headed while merrily sailing along, do not tack instinctively - look several boat lengths in front before tacking (a gust in that location will tend to give you a header before you even reach it) to ensure that you are not tacking away from a gust.
- Look up the course for gusts. Aim to string together a series of gusts so that you are practically sailing in one gust or another almost all the time. Gust hopping (*fig. 7.30*) in this way requires a keen eye and forward planning of your course.

Fig 7.30 Gust hopping. Note that black tends to get headed as he approaches the gusts. The gust patch migrates downwind, but black manages to intercept them, stringing them together so that he spends more time sailing in gusts than in lulls.

Reaching Leg. Sail high in a lull, and low in a gust (*fig. 7.31*). This is termed weaving. Sailing closer to the wind in a lull increases boat speed, getting you out of the hole faster. As the next gust will come from upwind, a higher angle increases the chance of intercepting a new gust. Sailing low in a gust allows the boat to stay with the gust longer, since the gust migrates downwind.

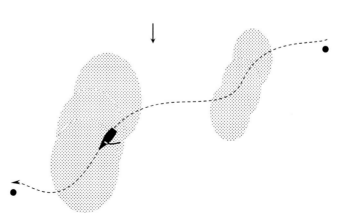

Fig 7.31 Weaving. Sail high in a lull and low in a gust.

Also, a lower angle makes the boat more manageable (if it is blowing hard) and makes it easier to catch waves.

Downwind Leg. Again, the idea is to sail in as many gusts as you can. To spot the gusts, look behind. Once you find one, intercept the gust as it crawls downwind. Do not worry about making large course deviations to get to the gust, as you will be partially compensated with a higher speed from sailing at a closer angle to the wind, and more than compensated once you are planing in the gust. While within a gust, sail in a more downwind direction, and try not to sail out of the gust while riding the waves.

It takes a lifetime to understand the wind we sail in. There will be many instances where we make wrong predictions and suffer losses. But if we analyse each mistake and if we steadily build up our mental library of wind patterns, then one day the wind will become our faithful friend.

Chapter 8

Currents

content by **Ben Tan**
reviewed by **Jacob Palm**

*L*ike air, water is also a fluid. It too is influenced by drag and flow gradients, and its flow can also be turbulent or laminar. The similarities do not end there. Fortunately we race only on the surface of the water so there is no need to discuss currents to the level we did for the wind. Here, we shall discuss a few flow characteristics and their implications to the racing sailor.

FLOW CHARACTERISTICS

Driving Force

The gravitational pull of the moon and sun creates the tides that drive the ocean currents, while in rivers, slopes cause water to flow from higher to lower ground. Strong and sustained winds blowing over the water's surface in many parts of the world can also drive currents.

Usually, the current flows in one direction when the tide rises, and the opposite direction when it ebbs. Tide tables (*fig. 8.1*) tell us the times of the high and low tides (there are two high and two low tides per day) in advance, but you will have to ask a local which way the tide flows between those times. As flow reverses at the high and low tides, pay special attention to the tide times when it falls during or around the duration of the race. The change in direction may not occur at precisely the indicated times because of the momentum effects of the water, and because the tide table used may be for a location kilometres away from the racing area.

Fig 8.1 Tide table from a club newsletter.

Do not take the water you sail on for granted – sailing on The Wash in Norfolk, UK, is possible only during the two hours before and after high water. Outside of these four hours, the water disappears! If this photo were taken hours later, only mud flats would be seen. During the four hours of racing, judging the lay lines in the tidal area can be challenging, and capsizing is strongly discouraged!

Other than the times, the tide table also states the high and low water levels. The difference between the two gives an indication of the strength of the current. In some parts of the world, the difference may be several metres. During the month, there will be spring and neap tides (*see boxed text*), when the current will be stronger or weaker respectively than usual. If racing in an area with strong tidal flows, make it a point to have a quick look at the tide table before getting onto the water.

Ocean Tides

Did You Know …

- *Tides are due to the gravitational pull of both the moon and sun over the surface of the earth. The pull of the sun (solar tide) is only about half that of the moon (lunar tide).*

- *The ocean surface bulges at two points: the first is the point nearest the moon (A) due to a maximum gravitational pull from the moon; the other is on the opposite end of the globe (C) due to a minimum in lunar pull. Therefore, as the earth rotates, each location on earth encounters two high tides (points A and C) and two low tides (point B and its opposite side), representing a semidiurnal change in water level. A full cycle takes 24 hr 56 min as the moon only passes overhead an hour later each day.*

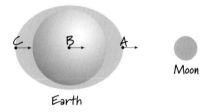

- *The moon oscillates by 23° on either side of the equator (declination), causing the tidal bulges to be asymmetric. This diurnal rhythm is superimposed upon the semidiurnal rhythm above, and therefore the high and low tides vary in level each day.*

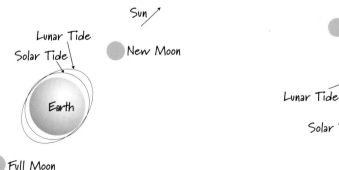

- *Every 14 days, the moon will either be on the same (new moon) or opposite side (full moon) of the earth as the sun. In either situation, the gravitational forces of the moon and sun are aligned, and they "join forces" to create spring tides.*

- *When the sun and moon are at right angles, they counter each other, leading to neap tides.*

Water Depth

Just as drag slows the wind at the earth's surface, friction against the bottom slows the current adjacent to it. The implication is that the current over shallow areas is weaker than that in deeper waters (*fig. 8.2*).

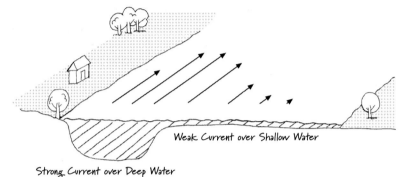

Weak Current over Shallow Water

Strong Current over Deep Water

Fig 8.2 *Effect of water depth on the surface current.*

When racing, remember these simple rules:

- In an adverse current (i.e. the current brings you away from the next mark), sail over shallow areas (e.g. shoals, shoreline), and cross any channels quickly.
- In a favourable current (i.e. the current brings you towards the next mark), sail over deeper waters and avoid the shoals.

How deep is the water over the racing area? This is where a map of the area will help. Read the contour lines on the map to get an indication. If, under the course, the bottom is flat then the current will probably be uniform.

Bottlenecks

Water flow is accelerated through a bottleneck or narrowing in the channel or river. This is because the same volume of water has to get through the bottleneck.

When a continuous bar lies across the current, it presents a "hidden" bottleneck (*fig. 8.3*). The water flows through a smaller cross-sectional area and is accelerated through the shallow area. This is

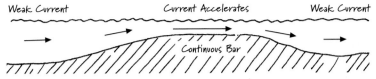

Fig 8.3 *Stronger current over a continuous bar, which acts as a bottleneck.*

the exception to the above rule that states that the current over a shallow area is weaker. However, note that the bar has to be continuous, otherwise the water will simply flow through the break in the bar. Such continuous bars that lie across a current are relatively rare.

Bends and Eddies

In a curved waterway, centrifugal force increases the current along the concave shore, compared to the convex shore (*fig. 8.4*). The stronger current cuts a deeper channel on the concave side, while on the convex side, the weaker current allows the deposition of sediments and may be accompanied by eddies. These are the forces that carve out a meandering river.

Eddy currents can also form along an irregular shoreline (*fig. 8.5*). These areas tend to be shallow.

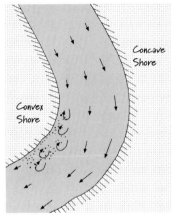

Fig 8.4 *Current differences in a curved waterway. The current is stronger along the concave shore.*

Current-Wind Interactions

Imagine floating on the water, with absolutely no surface wind. In a one-knot current, you would be experiencing a one-knot wind from direction opposite to that of the current. This 'current wind' is significant only in strong tides.

When water and wind flow in opposite directions (i.e. the current wind and the true wind are in the same direction), the current wind adds on to the true wind, leading to an increase in apparent wind over the water surface. This increases the size of the waves, making the sea choppy. When the current and wind are in the same direction, then the apparent wind is reduced, leading to a smoother sea.

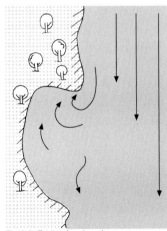

Fig 8.5 *Eddies forming along an irregular shoreline.*

Other than the waves, the changes in apparent wind also affect boats. For example, a boat that is lee-bowed by the current (i.e. sailing with the current hitting the leeward side of the boat) will experience a stronger apparent wind than one that is not. However, since races are seldom held in drifting conditions, the current wind is usually insignificant compared to the true wind, so changes in apparent wind are negligible.

Current Indicators

Tide tables give us a large-scale impression of the strength and direction of the currents. Contour maps show the underwater topography, but do not indicate current directions. These sources of information will complement – but not replace – indispensable onsite observations of the current to help us plan our race strategy. Such observations include:

Current Around the Marks. The wake of a buoy will give an indication of the direction and strength of the current. To quantify the flow, throw a sponge (or a plastic bottle two thirds filled with water) into the water just next to the buoy. After one minute, note the distance and direction that the sponge has drifted away from the buoy. This can be repeated at each mark of the course to obtain a picture of the currents in the racing area.

As this is tedious, it is worthwhile only in areas with tricky currents, and even then only the coach boat is fast enough to collect data from all parts of the racing course before the race. If you do not have a coach, visual assessments at the top and bottom mark of the course prior to the start should suffice. In places with a uniform current, a glance at the flow around the pin or anchor line of the start boat is adequate.

In tidal areas, it is a good idea to check the current as each mark is rounded during the race. This allows us to track changes in the current, and can provide an earlier indication of when the current will reverse. If there was some current at the last mark, and it has now disappeared, be prepared for a reversal in the direction of the current. The practice of checking the current at every mark also reduces the risk of drifting into the marks, since the sailor would be aware of the current throughout the race. Even if your coach has measured the currents at every part of the course and fed the information to you before the race, it is still necessary to check the current during the race as conditions can change with time.

Direction of Anchored Boats. In the absence of wind, a boat anchored at the bow will point in the direction the current is coming from. This tells us the current's direction in an area without us having to sail there to make observations. However, be mindful of two situations. Firstly, in a slack current, the anchored boat will be aligned along the wind's direction instead. Secondly, some boats or ships may be anchored at both ends, so do not use them as current indicators.

Appearance of the Water. Eddy currents and up swells can be seen on the water surface. A line of floating debris, small chops, and colour differences (*fig. 8.6*) can delineate two adjacent currents. *Fig. 8.7* shows how staying on one side of such a line can make a huge difference during a race.

Fig 8.6 Two different bodies of water, each with a different colour. The brown, sediment-filled water on the left belongs to a heavy outflow at the mouth of a river during an inland thunderstorm, while the darker water on the right is part of a relatively still body of sea water. The Lasers in the distance are wisely avoiding the brown water (adverse current) while making their way towards the camera.

Fig 8.7 Currents around a major regatta venue in Singapore. The lighter coloured water is the outflow from the river above, presenting an adverse current to the two boats. Black sails to the left of the line demarcating the two bodies of water, out of the adverse current, and makes significant gains.

TACKLING THE CURRENT

With an understanding of the currents, let us now discuss strategies for sailing in them.

Starts

It is important to know the direction of the current before the start, as the information will influence the race strategy for the start and the rest of the race. A convenient time to check the current is when fixing your transit for the start. While at the mark or committee boat, look at the water flow around the mark or the boat's anchor line, either before or after fixing the transit.

If there is an adverse current (i.e. current flowing from the on-course to the pre-start side of the line), stay close to the line before the gun, especially if the wind is light. In situations where it is a struggle just to get to the starting line (i.e. light wind and strong adverse current), you might even want to stay above the line and dip down just before the start, provided that neither the I Flag nor the Black Flag is displayed. There is typically a sag in the middle of the starting line when the adverse current is strong, providing you with an opportunity to do an impressive start, clear ahead of the other boats if you anticipate the situation and fix an accurate transit.

In the case of a favourable current, stay well below the starting line before the start to reduce the risk of a premature start. Beware of boats coming from behind to push you across.

Upwind Leg

Take advantage of current differences between the left and right sides of the course, if any. On approaching the top mark, currents make it difficult to call the lay lines. If you are not sure, it is better to tack early than to risk overstanding the mark.

Reaching and Downwind Legs

Figure 8.8 shows a common occurrence when the wind is light and there is a strong cross current on the off-wind legs. To avoid taking a longer route to the next mark, fix a transit soon after rounding the top mark and use it to stay near the rhumb line.

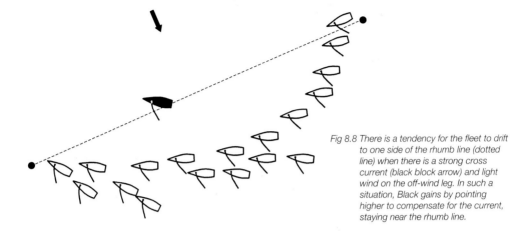

Fig 8.8 There is a tendency for the fleet to drift to one side of the rhumb line (dotted line) when there is a strong cross current (black block arrow) and light wind on the off-wind leg. In such a situation, Black gains by pointing higher to compensate for the current, staying near the rhumb line.

For a light wind reach, you can then weave above and below your rhumb line: sail above the rhumb line during a lull, and bear away below the rhumb line when a gust hits. However, if the cross current is slack and there is enough wind, then it is not necessary to steer a course near the rhumb line. Clear air and surfing become the overriding priority.

On the downwind leg, in non-planing conditions and a strong cross current, do not deviate too far from the rhumb line unless you have spotted a good gust to one side of the line. In planing conditions, you can make wide deviations away from the rhumb line, as long as you keep planing.

Currents in some areas like the Solent in South England are notoriously tricky to understand compared to other areas. But if we bear the above principles in mind and make use of up-to-date observations on the course, effective strategies can be developed to help us get to the finishing line faster.

Chapter 9

Tactics, the Art of Positioning

content by **Ben Tan**
Reviewed by **Jacob Palm** *and* **Lock Hong Kit**

*T*actics is the art of positioning with respect to other boats. It is analogous to a game of chess. Like world chess champion Garry Kasparov, you need to have a picture of where you are in relation to the others, to assess the vulnerability and strength of your current position, to rationalize your next move, and to think two or three moves ahead. The difference is that in sailing, making a move requires a much greater physical effort.

Strategy refers to the race plan in which one tries, in the absence of other boats, to trace the fastest course around the marks, taking the wind pattern, current, waves, and geographical features into consideration. In fleet racing, tactics and strategy are closely interlinked. For example, when approaching a starboard tack boat on the upwind beat, your decision whether to cross his bow and continue on port tack or to tack before crossing paths (i.e. tactical decision) depends on how favoured you think the right side of the course is (i.e. race strategy). For this reason, we shall discuss racing tactics in conjunction with strategy.

PRE-LAUNCH PREPARATIONS

Racing strategy is based on prior information gathered, complemented by our own observations. The gathering of relevant information begins way before the race. The night before, read the sailing instructions. What is the course configuration? How big is the course? How close is the course to the shoreline? These, and other contents in the sailing instructions will influence our strategy.

On the way to the club the next day, look up to the sky and note the speed and direction of the low clouds to get an idea of the prevailing wind. If the observed wind is in the direction of the seasonal wind, then the wind direction is likely to be steady. If the direction is as forecasted, then the rest of the weather forecast is more likely to be reliable. If it is in excess of 20 knots, then a sea breeze is unlikely to develop, regardless of the wind direction.

On arriving at the club, drop by the notice board and have a look at the:

- Weather map, satellite picture, and weather forecast.
- Tide table.
- Changes to the sailing instructions, if any.

If the weather and tide information is not provided, then look to other sources like the Internet and newspapers. Tide tables are published in advance, and may be found in the club newsletter.

There is much to do like rigging the boat, checking equipment, pre-race nutrition (food and water), and stretches, so a routine needs to be developed. Aim to launch early enough to arrive at the racing site half to one hour prior to the start.

PRE-START

While sailing to the racing area, have a look around. What are the clouds telling you? Which way is the current flowing? Information from weather forecasts, weather maps, and satellite pictures need to be assessed in conjunction with on-site information.

At the race area:

1. Spend up to three minutes doing some hiking and warm-up tacks to "wake" yourself up and loosen any sore muscles.

2. Check the current at the bottom mark.

3. Next, beat up to the windward mark, taking note of the wind pattern. Make a note of the compass readings for the lifts and headers on each tack, as well as the median reading. Also, time the shifts to see how frequent and regular they are. Try out how deep into the wind shifts and gusts you have to sail before the wind settles. Play the shifts to practice getting in sync with the lifts and headers. If you suspect say, a wind bend in an offshore wind, or a progressive shift in a building sea breeze, sail on to see if the wind indeed clocks progressively to the left or right. In other words, now is the time to confirm your suspicions and "theories."

4. If you have a partner whose speed is similar to yours, spend a little time speed testing. Set up your sail as best you can, and pace with your partner to see if you are up to speed. If you are, remember the settings; if not, tune your sails again. Do not get carried away or overly worried if you are not moving well – the race has not started yet.

5. Another thing you can do with your partner at this stage is to do a split pair, i.e. cross tacks and sail on opposite tacks for a specified duration, say 3-5 min, and then tack and sail towards each other. If there is time and the course is small, sail to the lay lines before tacking. If one boat is distinctly ahead of the other, then the side that boat went to may be favoured. Note that conditions can change. Go back to the starting point, switch sides, and split tacks again if time permits.

6. When you reach the top mark, assess the current at the mark. Take a break, and while doing so, do a round of stretches, focusing on the hiking muscles.

7. While testing the upwind leg, do not lose track of the time, especially in light wind. Make your way back to the starting line, riding the waves to "tune-in" to them.

8. Get back to the starboard end of the starting line in time for the warning signal, preferably with a few minutes to spare. While waiting for the warning signal:

   • Have a drink, and take a leak if necessary.
   • Get an orientation of where all the other marks are, and go through the order of the marks in your head. Even at top-level racing, rounding the wrong marks is not unheard of!
   • Check the current again to see if it is still the same as before. Note especially the direction of the current in relation to the starting line, as it has implications on your strategy for the start.

THE START

Just after the starting signal, a boat that is just one boat length ahead of another might be 20 positions apart, whereas at the finish, the distance between two successive finishers might probably be a few boat lengths. Hence, at the start, every inch translates to more positions gained or lost than any other time during the race. Whatever the size of the fleet, consistent starts are possible with a consistent routine:

1. **Start Timer.** Get close enough to the committee boat to start your timer against the warning signal. In big fleets, flapping sails can drown the signal, so keep the committee boat in sight and use the warning flag rather than the gun to mark your time. While waiting for the timing, keep the boat standing on starboard tack, so you have right-of-way over port tackers, and are less likely to be interrupted.

2. **Fix the Transit.** Next, it is time to take an accurate transit from the starboard end (*fig. 9.1*). By this time, the starting line has been laid and the race committee will not make further adjustments to the line. Transits are essential to a good start, as they accurately indicate your position relative to the starting line. As other boats will want to fix their transits at this time, move away from the line as soon as you are done to give others their turn.

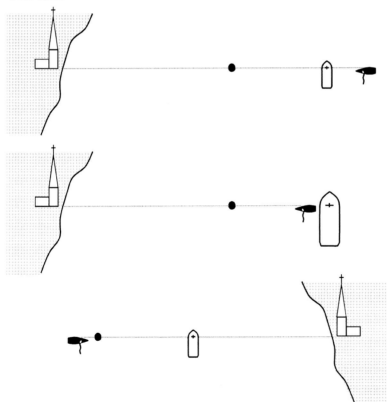

Fig 9.1 Three possible ways of fixing a transit at the start. Top: This is the most accurate, but is possible only with a small committee boat. Stand up, if necessary, to fix your transit. Middle: With a big committee boat, fix the transit from the pin side of the committee boat. Get as close as is reasonably possible to the staff of the committee boat. Bottom: If there are no landmarks on the port side of the starting line, then fix the transit from the pin end. This is accurate, but you will need to look over your shoulder to check your position at the start.

3. **Determine Line Bias.** Unless the starting line is square, one end will be further upwind than the other (*fig. 9.2*). Starting at this biased end gives you a head start over those at the other end. After fixing your transit, sail along the starting line, until you reach the middle. Here, point directly into the wind to check the starting line bias (*fig. 9.3*).

In shifty conditions, the starting line might be port biased one minute, and starboard biased the next minute. In such conditions, it pays to determine the line bias again nearer the starting signal and hang around the middle so that you can rush to either end in time.

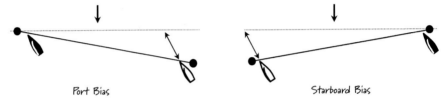

Port Bias   Starboard Bias

Fig 9.2   An uneven starting line gives those at the biased end a head start. In each case, Black gains over White by a distance indicated by the double-headed arrows. The bold arrow represents the wind direction.

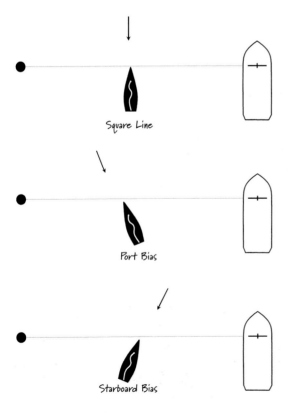

Square Line

Port Bias

Starboard Bias

4. **Plan Strategy for Start and Beat.** Bear away towards the pin end to allow others to check the line bias. On your way there, stand up to look for large gust patches that might be coming down the course. If a fleet started before yours, look at the boats to see how each side is doing and where the wind pressure is. Have another look at the clouds, and try to incorporate the information you have gathered thus far (weather information, tide information, messages from the clouds, observed wind pattern, observed current, split pair result, line bias, etc.) into your starting and upwind strategy:

Fig 9.3 Line bias. At the middle of the starting line, point straight into the wind. Sighting from below the boom, the end of the line that the bow is pointing closer to is the windward or biased end.

- If the line bias and the favoured side of the course are both on the left, then start on the port end and continue sailing on starboard tack.
- Likewise, if the line is starboard biased and the right side of the course is favoured, then start at the starboard end and tack soon after to get to the right side. In this case, freedom to tack after the start is valuable.
- If the line bias and the favoured side of the course are opposite, then you will have to decide which is more important.
- If the line is square, start at the end nearest the favoured side of the course.
- If unsure of the favoured side, start at the biased end of the line (or the middle if the line is square) and play the shifts up the beat.

5. **Approach the Starting Line.** With about three minutes or more to go, clear your foils (especially if the water is filled with plastic bags, leaves, and other debris) and empty the cockpit of any water by "kicking" it out the back. Start looking for a parking space in the front row of boats. The best way to do this is to sail below the starting line on port tack, starting from beyond the pin end and adjusting your speed along the way (*fig. 9.4*). This approach provides excellent control over your position relative to the starting line: as you approach starboard tackers that are too early (i.e. too close to the line), sail behind them; if they are late, cross in front of them. If necessary, do a few runs along the line to survey the front row for parking lots. While sailing back and forth, take note of how long it takes to reach your desired starting spot, especially in light wind. If you are early, there will be lots of gaps to pick from. But if you leave your approach too late, it will not be easy to find a space, especially at the biased end of the line, and you might be forced to start in the second or third row.

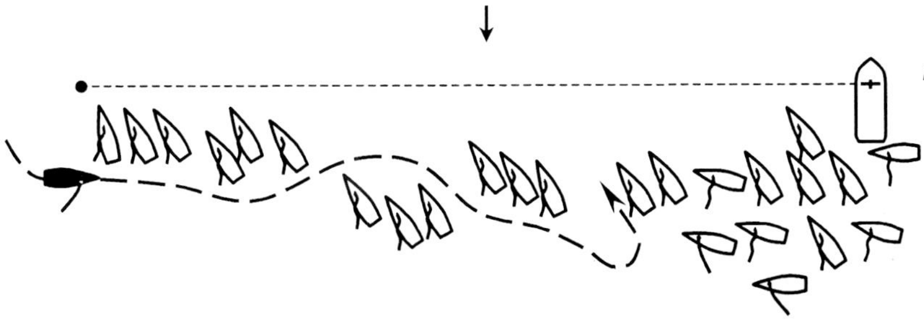

Fig 9.4 Port tack approach to the starting line. Black sails on port tack along the line and takes his pick of the gaps available.

Being in the front row should be a top priority, especially in a big fleet. There, you are automatically ahead of those in the rows behind (unless they manage to clear their air soon after the start, or the line is heavily biased).

Going for the Ends. Earlier, you had decided on the end to start at. You can now choose to take the aggressive and risky option of starting right next to the pin or the committee boat (or inner distance mark), or the conservative option of starting near the end, on the edge of the crowd (*fig. 9.5*). The choice depends on:

* The size and standard of the fleet, as well as the length of the starting line. The bigger and better the fleet and the shorter the line, the harder it is to win the ends.
* How biased the line is.
* How favoured one side of the upwind leg is expected to be.
* Whether there are any starting penalties, e.g. black flag. Starting at the committee boat end increases the risk of getting caught for being on the course side of the line, whereas those further down the line can avoid being caught – even if they are over – by hiding their sail numbers behind the adjacent boat. (This is harder with bow numbers.)
* Your upwind boat speed. If you obviously lack the speed to keep up with the rest, starting at the starboard end and tacking immediately to clear your air is an option to consider.

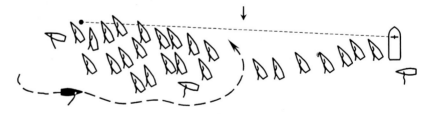

Fig 9.5 Starting on the edge of the pack. Top: Black starts to windward of a port-end pack. Bottom: Black starts to leeward of a starboard-end pack.

If you decide to gun for either end, it is important to be there early and have good boat control to hold your position. Sometimes, we have to take risks, but most of the time, the conservative approach pays since the champion is decided over a number of races, not just one. The idea is to sharpen your starting line skills (especially boat control) to such a high level that to you, starting at the ends is no longer considered risky!

Once you have made up your mind on where you want to start and there is adequate time, do a practice start near your desired starting point to get a feel of the angle, acceleration, and timing for that particular set of conditions.

Look Upwind for Gusts. As you make your final approach on port, stand up (preferably) and take a quick look to windward for gust patches (especially in light wind). This will influence your decision on the gap you select along the line. For example, if you had decided to start at the port end and work towards the left after the start, and you spot a big gust patch migrating down on the right side, you may want to start more on the right, intercept the gust after the start, and then resume your original strategy by working back towards the left. The later you stand up to look for the gust the more useful the information is. However, as the starting signal draws nearer, your attention will be needed elsewhere.

> *"Look up the course and try to work out what is going to happen at the start. Position yourself to capitalize on the first shift rather than necessarily trying to 'win' the start."*
>
> *Rod Dawson*

6. **Create and Protect the Space to Leeward.** You should have found your space on the first row about a minute before the start (depending on how crowded the line is). Your job now is to create a space to leeward (*fig. 9.6 left*). This space gives you

Fig 9.6 Creating and protecting a space to leeward. Left: Black points up to create a leeward space. Right: Black angles his boat almost parallel to the line, with sails flapping, to discourage other boats from stealing the space. If white does tack to leeward of Black, he has to give Black time to keep clear.

room to accelerate into just before or after the start, and it also reduces the likelihood of receiving backwind from the leeward boat. To create this space, make sure your centreboard is fully down, and point up. In light wind, you may wish to scallop (*fig. 10.7, pg 163*) if you are confident of your boat control.

Once a space is created, others will be tempted to slip into it. Keep a watch out for this. You can tell that someone is thinking of stealing your space by looking at his eyes: as he sails past, he will be looking at either your leeward space or you. Quickly bear away to occupy the gap with the length of your hull, pushing the boom out so that the boat will not move forward. After he sails past, point up again to continue working on creating that space to leeward.

Keep your bow even with the adjacent boats. If they inch forward, you usually do not have a choice but to follow. However, avoid sticking your bow out, at least not yet. If you are very sure that they are already over the line at this stage, you might want to bail out (before your number gets recorded) by falling out of the first row and finding another gap to start in. Push your boom out to reverse if there is very little time left, but bear in mind that under the current rules, "a boat moving astern by backing a sail shall keep clear of one that is not." If you cannot bail out, make sure that your sail numbers are hidden! The decision to bail out must be made as early as possible (preferably with at least 20 s to go) as you will need time to gybe or tack and sail through dirty wind to find another gap to start in.

7. **Sheet in and Go!** Novices often get caught off-guard at the start when the boats around them, from sitting perfectly still, suddenly sheet in and zoom off, leaving them blanketed. Generally, it is rare for a good fleet to start sheeting in with less than five seconds to go, so be on your guard before then. Lateness is usually attributable to adopting a passive approach. Instead of sheeting in only after others have begun to do so, make your own call as to when the best time to sheet in is, using your transit to assess how close you are to the line. The idea is to be the first to accelerate, but not to do it so early that you start prematurely. When using your line transit, do make an allowance for the part of the boat in front of you – if you are

exactly on the line according to your line of sight, then the part of the boat in front of you is already across.

Boat control, line judgement, and quick acceleration are vital to a good start.

Other Approaches to the Start

The port tack approach described above is the most versatile, as it accommodates many possible situations (e.g. port or starboard biased line, currents in different directions, different wind strengths). For example, if there is strong current pushing the fleet to the pre-start side of the line, you can compensate for the current by crossing in front of starboard tackers and staying close to or even above the line (if the black or I flag rule is not applicable). In light wind too, it is advisable to cross in front of starboard tackers. This keeps you close to the starting line in case of a further drop in wind strength. Furthermore, it is difficult to break through a blanket zone in light wind to join the first row from behind.

Other approaches like the dip start and the port tack start are alternative starting strategies:

Dip Start. When the wind is light and there is a strong adverse current for the upwind leg, the fleet might have difficulty sailing up to the starting line. Some do not even make it to the line at all. Dip starts can be used for such situations. This is where the boat stays above the starting line before the start and dips down to the pre-start side of the line before beating to the top mark (*fig. 9.7*). Such starts are possible only if the black, I, or Z flag rule is not enforced.

Fig 9.7 Dip start. Black stays above the starting line, and dips down just before the starting signal to start. The block arrows represent a strong adverse current.

Port Tack Start. Occasionally, the starting line can be so biased towards the port end that it becomes almost impossible to cross on starboard tack. If you see this while approaching the line on port tack as described above, consider starting on port tack instead of tacking onto starboard (*fig. 9.8*). To be successful, timing is essential, and the leading starboard tack boat has to be late. If you are unable to cross in front of him, then look for a gap in the line of starboard tackers to sail through. If the leading boat executes a perfect pin end start, and there are no gaps visible further up the line, then you are in trouble! Hence the risk of port tack starts.

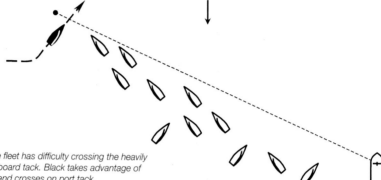

Fig 9.8 Port tack start. The fleet has difficulty crossing the heavily biased line on starboard tack. Black takes advantage of their predicament and crosses on port tack.

THE UPWIND LEG

This challenging leg takes up the greater part of a race, so it pays to be a strong upwind sailor, in terms of speed, tactics, and strategy. Brawn and brains must work together.

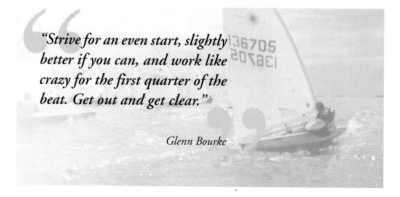

"Strive for an even start, slightly better if you can, and work like crazy for the first quarter of the beat. Get out and get clear."

Glenn Bourke

First Hundred Metres

For the first hundred metres after the start, the priorities are:

- *To stay in the first row.* This means hiking hard and sailing fast. Besides speed, pointing ability also helps, as it prevents you from getting backwind from the leeward boat.
- *To get in sync with the shifts as soon as possible.* There is no point in having good boat speed if you are going to use it to sail in the wrong direction! If at the start, starboard is the lifted tack, then stay and focus on boat speed. If starboard is the headed tack, then tack as soon as you can. Break out in front of the first row and tack across the fleet if you have Robert Scheidt's speed. If not, pinch up to backwind the windward boat, encouraging him to tack, and you can follow soon after as he will clear the way for you. Alternatively, turn to the windward boat and ask, "Can I tack?" If you were both on an obvious header, it is to his benefit to tack as well, and he would do so if he were free to tack. If not, he would ask the guy to his windward for permission to tack, and so on.
- *To sail in clear air.* If you get buried at the start, clear your air as soon as you can. Tacking onto port puts you on a lift arising from the deflection of the wind by the first row of boats. If starboard tack is the lifted tack, then tack back into the next gap that comes along in the first row. When tacking to clear your air, think a step ahead by looking upwind to ensure that you are not tacking out of a starboard tacker's disturbed air into a port tacker's wind shadow.

Sailing in Clear Air

Sails have an area of turbulent flow surrounding them. When sailing close-hauled, there will be a blanket zone, where the wind shadow is cast, and a backwind zone of dirty air (*fig. 9.9*). The blanket zone extends approximately five boat lengths (some authors estimate it at six times the height of the mast) down the line of the apparent wind rather than the true wind. The backwind zone extends about a boat length to windward and 3-5 boat lengths aft. If the leeward boat's wind indicator (which shows the apparent wind direction) is pointing directly at the windward boat, then he is being blanketed.

The blanket and backwind zones can be used to control other boats, as in covering and herding, to be discussed later. When sailing in disturbed wind, both boat speed and pointing ability are lost.

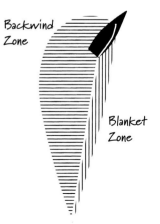

Fig 9.9 Disturbed air surrounding a boat. The size of the blanket and backwind zones vary with the wind strength.

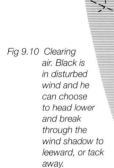

Foot

Tack

Fig 9.10 Clearing air. Black is in disturbed wind and he can choose to head lower and break through the wind shadow to leeward, or tack away.

Therefore, an attempt should be made to get into clear air by tacking away or footing through the wind shadow (*fig. 9.10*). When forced to tack away from the desired tack (i.e. sailing on a lift or towards the favoured side of the course) to clear your air, remember to tack back soon to resume your race plan.

If the boat to leeward is not quite close enough to give you backwind, you will need to maintain your height or even point higher (pinch) to stay out of it. Many find this difficult to achieve, and the tendency is to fall to leeward. To avoid this, resist looking at the leeward boat and instead, focus on your own boat speed. Staring at the waves in front of your bow helps to keep your eyes away from leeward boat while improving your steering at the same time. Try it during practice. If you fail and fall into the backwind, it is practically impossible to pinch your way out of it, so it would be better to tack or foot through to leeward immediately.

The Thinking Sailor – Upwind Tactics and Strategy
Sail Your Own Race. Once the post-start drag race of the first 100 m winds down a little, tactics and strategy come further into the foreground. The boat that devises the perfect strategy for the particular set of wind pattern, current, wave, and geography will sail an ideal course around the marks, crossing the finishing line in the shortest time possible. It is important to sail your own race and resist straying from your strategy, unless new and updated information (e.g. the sea breeze dying earlier than expected) arises.

Other boats in the fleet and self-imposed desperation are the two main culprits that cause a sailor to deviate from his strategy. In fleet racing, the idea is to position yourself in relation to the fleet in such a way that you have clear air while sailing according to your strategy. If you need to tack to clear your air, do so but do remember to tack back (unless you were on the wrong tack earlier).

Positioning. Tactics is all about positioning. Your opponent's position relative to yours can be described as one of the four possibilities illustrated in *fig. 9.11*. In the figure, both boats are on the same tack, and one of these four positions arises when either you (Black) or your opponent (White) tacks into it.

There should be well thought-out reasons for every tack – tacking simply to give the sore thighs a break will not do. The relative position we tack into depends on:

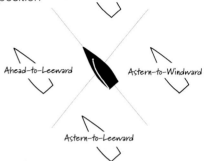

- *Whether the next shift is a lift or header.* As the windward boat gains in a lift and the leeward boat in a header (*fig. 9.12*), tactically it is desirable to be windward of the fleet when the wind lifts and leeward when it heads.

Lift   **Header**

Fig 9.11 Positioning. The terms describe White's position relative to Black's.

Fig 9.12 Left: The windward boat (Black) gains in a lift. Right: The leeward boat (White) gains in a header.

- *Where the favoured side of the course is.* If the left side is favoured (e.g. progressive wind shift, persistent shift, more wind, favourable current, smaller waves, etc.), you would want to keep to the left of the fleet.

Let us consider our options as we approach a boat (or fleet of boats) on the opposite tack:

Tacking Ahead-to-Leeward of Approaching Boat. When you are ahead of the approaching boat, you (Black) can choose to tack before or after crossing his bow. Tack before crossing when:

- You are sailing in an oscillating wind pattern, and your opponent is on a lift and you are on a header. By tacking to his leeward, you gain when both of you are headed by the next shift.
- Your opponent is sailing towards the favoured side of the course (e.g. progressive shift towards that side). By tacking early and below him, you will be closer to the favoured side than your opponent.

Tacking Ahead-to-Windward of Approaching Boat. When you are ahead of the approaching boat, tack after crossing his bow when:

- You are sailing in an oscillating wind pattern, and your opponent is on a header and you are on a lift. In this case, you are tacking on a lift so that you can stay with him, sacrificing further gains to protect your lead.
- Your opponent is sailing towards the disadvantaged side of the course. By tacking after crossing his bow instead of carrying on, you are sacrificing further gains to protect your lead.

In both circumstances, you are deviating from the desired strategy of staying on a lift and sailing towards the favoured side so that you can stay with your opponent. A way to get the best of both worlds, i.e. to stick to your strategy while staying with your opponent, is to tack in his wind, forcing him to tack. When he does so you can tack back (but delay your tack so that he has clear air) and continue with your race plan.

Tacking Astern-to-Windward of Approaching Boat. If you are behind your opponent, cross his transom and tack astern-to-windward (*outside* his backwind zone) when:

- You are sailing in an oscillating wind pattern, and your opponent is on a lift and you are on a header. By tacking, you get yourself back in sync with the oscillations. If you had tacked earlier, before crossing his transom, you would have tacked in his disturbed air.
- You were on a lift, and you tacked because you have reached the lay line.
- Your opponent is sailing towards the disadvantaged side of the course but you wish to stay with him. By tacking only after crossing his transom, you will be closer to the favoured side than he is.

Tacking Astern-to-Leeward of Approaching Boat. If you are behind the approaching boat, do not tack in his wind shadow unless you do not have a choice (e.g. you have already overstood the top mark). If you wish to tack before crossing his transom, do it early so that you are in front of his wind shadow. The possible reasons for tacking before crossing are:

- You are sailing in an oscillating wind pattern, and your opponent is on a lift and you are on a header. By tacking to his leeward, you stand to gain more than your opponent when both of you are headed by the next shift. (You should tack as soon as you realize that you are on a header.)
- Your opponent is sailing towards the favoured side of the course. By tacking early and below him, you will be closer to the favoured side than your opponent.

Leverage. This describes the separation between two boats on the beat. The further apart, the greater the leverage. In the scenarios above, we did not mention how far apart the two boats should be. The separation depends on how sure you are that there is an advantage to being on one side of your opponent and how big that advantage is. For example, if you were extremely sure that the wind would shift left, then you would position yourself as far left of your opponent as possible. When the shift arrives, your gains would be greatly magnified (fig. 9.13). However in sailing one can rarely be a hundred percent sure, so it is not advisable to stray too far from the fleet. The greater your leverage, the greater your potential gain but the greater your risk.

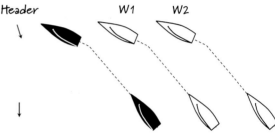

Fig 9.13 *Leverage. Black has a greater leverage over W 2 compared to W1. In a header, Black gains over W1 by one boat length, and over W2 by two boat lengths.*

Punters will sail almost all the way to the lay line to get maximum leverage. *Banging corners* is a high-risk strategy. If your predictions are accurate, you stand to gain heaps, but if wrong, then finishing dead last becomes a very real possibility. The only time when risk taking is possibly justified is when there is nothing to lose, as when you are already in the back of the fleet. Winning a series requires consistency, and to achieve consistent results, conservative tactics are the way to go.

"To succeed, you need the statistical adroitness of a mathematician, the analytical dexterity of a scientist, the clinical mentality of a hit man, and perhaps most importantly the conservatism of an accountant. My approach is based on a simple numbers game; there's seven races, nine legs per race, a certain number of boats to defeat. During the race I always chip away at the boats in front; making small gains, then getting back to the fleet.

There are gamblers in most fleets, whose hallmark is to take a punt and hit a layline. When it comes off they are temporary heroes, but the odds are generally against them."

Glenn Bourke

A lead is not "confirmed" until one boat crosses the bow of another. Once ahead, it is justifiable to tack back towards an opponent to consolidate the lead (i.e. to realize the gains) and reduce the leverage. However, avoid being too conservative and carrying this to the extreme by staying so close to a rival that you lose out on the shifts. Remember – you are racing in a fleet and sailing your own race (i.e. sticking to your strategy) will get you to the finishing line faster. If you have a decent strategy, sailing the fastest possible course, without covering, is an effective offensive tactic, and offence is one of the best defences.

Very often, we are unable to decide whether the left or right side of the course is favoured. In such a situation, it is best to "take the middle path" and play the shifts near the middle of the course. If you suspect the left is favoured but cannot be sure, then play the middle left of the course, and so on. This reduces your leverage on the fleet and also your risk, while allowing you to take advantage of the shifts.

Crossing Tacks, and the Unwritten Rules. When approaching a boat on the opposite tack, the decision whether to cross or to tack needs to be made quickly, based on strategy and tactics. Once the decision is made, the next step is to carry it through – your opponent can prevent you from carrying out your strategy by taking your wind or lee-bowing you. Let us see how we can encourage the approaching boat to give us what we want. We will presume that you are on what you perceive to be the desired tack (usually the lifted tack), and that you want to remain on your tack; if you were not on the desired tack, you should have tacked long before meeting the approaching boat.

> "*Don't fall into the speed-testing trap*"
>
> *Rod Dawson, on the importance of sticking to a strategy rather than getting caught up with boat speed.*

Approaching on Port Tack. If you are not sure whether you can cross the bow of the starboard tacker, then ask, "Can I pass?" Most of the time, he would wave you on. The reason is that he is presumably on what he perceives as the desired tack, and he would want to stay on that tack. Saying no is almost equivalent to asking to be lee-bowed by you. Of course, if you are obviously unable to cross his bow, the right thing to do is to bear away and cross his transom instead of asking for permission to cross in front!

If you asked if you could pass ahead and he responds immediately with a no, then duck behind his transom to stay on your desired tack. You will not lose much distance compared to tacking and being held on the disadvantaged tack. However, if he responds too late for you to bear away, then you would have no choice but to tack in his lee-bow, forcing him to tack away. This benefits no one, as both would end up on what each considers the wrong tack.

Approaching on Starboard Tack. On starboard tack, you have the right-of-way. To stay on your desired tack, wave on (or shout, "Hold your course!" to) port tackers that ask if they can cross. Duck behind their transoms if you need to – it is less costly than being lee-bowed or slam-dunked. Furthermore, you should only be happy that they wish to continue sailing on what you perceive as the wrong tack. Do not starboard another boat just for the sake of it.

If a port tacker on a collision course looks like he has not noticed your presence, then shout, "Starboard!" as soon as you can, so that if he decides to tack instead of ducking behind you, he will do so far to your leeward, sparing you from his backwind. Also, shouting at the last minute might startle him and cause him to panic right in front of you.

If you are on a header or sailing towards the disadvantaged side of the course, you may want to "bounce" the port tacker onto starboard tack before you tack onto port. (Do this only if other boats are out of contention and it is a two-boat race between the two of you.) To encourage him to tack, shout "Starboard!" repeatedly (and hysterically) to make him think that he will not be able to make it across your bow and that you are going to hold your course and hit him if he does not do anything. This will encourage him to tack on your lee-bow. You then tack immediately onto port, towards the favoured side and onto a lift. Of course, a smart port tacker will realize what you are up to and ask you to hold your course (and you have to if the boats are close) while he ducks below you to continue towards the favoured side or to stay on a lift.

Freedom to Tack. It is important to be able to tack when you need to, say when you are headed. If there is a boat on your windward hip (i.e. astern-to-windward of you), and you cannot tack and clear his bow or transom, then there are a few options you can take:

- Pinch to windward, until the windward boat is in your backwind. He will then have to tack to clear his air. When he goes, you are free to tack.
- If both of you are on starboard tack, foot to leeward (or slow down a little), and tack when there is enough space for you to bear away below the windward boat's transom. Crossing another boat's transom might not be appealing, but if you are sure that you are on a header, or that you are heading towards the disadvantaged side of the course, then you will gain in the end. (If you are the one to windward and a leeward boat makes a huge effort to duck under your transom, then you should double-check to see if you are going the right way.)
- If both of you are on port tack, foot to leeward and tack when there is enough space to do so. Before tacking, you may want to warn the windward boat by shouting, "Tacking!" Bear in mind that you have right of way as a starboard tack boat only after you have borne away onto a close-hauled course.
- Ask the windward boat, "Can I tack?" If the both of you are indeed sailing on a header, then it is to his advantage to tack as well (assuming an oscillating shift). If he realizes this, he will tack and you can then follow suit after sailing on for about a boat length to ensure that you do not tack into his backwind. If he wants to stay on his course (i.e. he disagrees that the both of you are headed, or he is working his way to one side of the course for some reason), then it pays for him to say yes to your request and duck below you (if necessary). By doing this, he is allowing you to get on what he perceives as the wrong tack. By saying no, he is inviting you to pinch up to backwind him.

> *"When leading, minimise the risks but continue to play the shifts."*
>
> Rod Dawson

Covering an Opponent. To protect a lead over another boat, covering tactics are used. The leading boat covers the trailing boat by staying between the trailing boat and the top mark (generally) and keeping the trailing boat on the same tack, so that whatever advantage the trailing boat gets (e.g. a favourable wind shift), the leading boat is likely to get also. The opposite of covering is splitting tacks, where the leading and trailing boats go on opposite tacks to different sides of the course. With the boats apart, there is nothing the leading boat can do if the trailing boat gets a nice gust or favourable shift for example, and overtakes him. When covering, the ideal path (i.e. the fastest course round the marks) is traded for tactical advantage over the trailing boat, unless the trailing boat can be manipulated to tack whenever the leading boat wants him to.

The covering boat should not disturb the trailing boat's air unless he wants the trailing boat to tack. With clear air, the trailing boat is more likely to stay on the same tack as the covering boat, making the latter's job much easier. The leading boat can cover from either windward or leeward of the trailing boat. In either position, the covering boat can choose to give the trailing boat clear air (i.e. loose or open cover) or disturbed air. Let us look at the significance of each of these positions:

Covering from Windward, Trailing Boat in Clear Air. After crossing well ahead, the covering boat (Black) sails on and tacks only when the trailing boat is out of his wind shadow (i.e. loose cover). This position is used when:

- The trailing boat is close to and sailing towards one of the lay lines.
- The trailing boat is sailing in the wrong direction, e.g. he is on a header or sailing towards the disadvantaged side of the course. The surer you are that he is on the wrong tack, the further you can sail on before tacking to be on the same tack.

Covering from Leeward, Trailing Boat in Clear Air. The covering boat tacks before crossing the trailing boat's bow. This position is used when:

- The wind direction is oscillating and the leading boat is in a header, tacking onto a lift. When the next shift arrives (a header for both boats), the leading boat pulls further ahead.
- The covering boat has reached the top mark lay line (i.e. the trailing boat overstood the mark).
- The side of the course that the trailing boat is sailing towards is the favoured side.

Covering from Windward or Leeward, Trailing Boat in Disturbed Air. The covering boat tacks dead to windward or lee-bows and backwinds the trailing boat when:

- The covering boat wants the trailing boat to tack towards the rest of the fleet (herding) or a nearby lay line.
- The covering boat wants to initiate a tacking duel, knowing that his tacks are superior.
- The covering boat has inferior speed but superior tacks and is trying to slow the trailing boat down with his dirty wind by covering from dead to windward.

Whether the covering boat tacks dead to windward or lee-bows the trailing boat depends mostly on whether he can clear the trailing boat's bow comfortably.

Note that the dead to windward position will result in a loss to the leading boat, whether the shift is a lift or a header.

Covering from Astern-to-Windward. If the covering boat is unable to cross the other boat's bow, he can still control the other boat by crossing close behind the transom and tacking into the astern-to-windward position. This takes away the covered boat's freedom to tack and is used to prevent him from tacking towards the mark. After holding the covered boat past the mark, the covering boat tacks and rounds the mark first (*fig. 9.14*).

It is impossible to hold this position for long as the covering boat tends to fall into the other boat's backwind (if he is not already in it), so do not try this too far from the lay line.

While protecting your lead by covering another boat, do not lose track of your race strategy. Keep in sync with the shifts and lead your opponent to the favoured side of the course while covering him, so that your position in the fleet is not compromised while you protect your lead.

In fleet racing, do not lee-bow or tack dead to windward of another boat unless you have a tactical reason to do so, e.g. when only the two of you are in contention for the series win and only your placings relative to each other,

Fig 9.14
Holding a boat past the top mark. Black tacks onto White's weather hip and prevents White from tacking until they have gone past the lay line. As Black is in White's backwind, he will not be able to hold this position for long. Before trying this, ensure that there is no crowd at the mark.

rather than your fleet position, matters. Backwinding or taking another boat's wind for no specific reason will encourage him to do it back to you when he gets the opportunity in the future. Before tacking, make it a point to check that you are not tacking in someone else's wind , especially if your decision to tack was not in response to a wind shift or other strategy. If you do tack on top of someone for a reason not obvious to him, an apology is a good idea.

Breaking Cover. If you are the one being covered, and you are under loose cover (i.e. your wind is not disturbed), there are a few ways to break the cover:

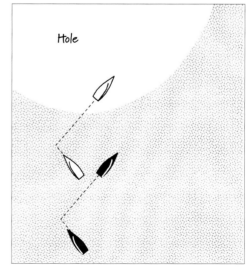

- *Playing the Shifts.* If you have a good strategy and are confident that you are better at reading the shifts, the best and preferred way to break the cover is to sail your own race. By doing so, you are sailing at your fastest, and that gives you the best chance of closing the gap between you and the covering boat, while improving your position in the fleet.

- *Disadvantaging the Covering Boat.* Attempt to disadvantage the covering boat by using obstructions, wind shadows, adverse currents, adverse waves, etc., knowing that he will tack whenever you do so (*fig. 9.15*). The covering boat might choose not to tack into a disadvantaged position (if he is aware of it), in which case the cover is broken. Alternatively, the covering boat may choose to stay with you, sacrificing fleet position for tactical advantage over you.

- *Superior Tacks.* If you are confident of your tacks, you can initiate a tacking duel, doing a series of tacks in succession. By getting caught up in a tacking duel with you, his fleet position will suffer (unless roll tacking in light wind) – and so will yours – so he will think twice about staying with you.

Fig 9.15 *Attempting to disadvantage the covering boat. Black "leads" White into a hole (e.g. from an island, large anchored ship, etc.), ensuring that he stays out of it himself.*

Covering a Few Boats. Once the art of covering a single boat is mastered, progress on to covering a few boats at a time. This is not easy. The objective is to:

- "Herd" those boats you are covering onto the same tack – when someone tacks and strays off from the pack, take his wind to encourage him to tack back and stay with the rest (*fig. 9.16*). This keeps them together, so it will be easier for you to keep an eye on them. Likewise, do not blanket someone who is on the same tack as the pack, or he will tack away and make it difficult for you to cover.
- Position yourself such that you are in the triangle formed by the boat on the extreme right, the boat on the extreme left, and the windward mark (*fig. 9.17*).

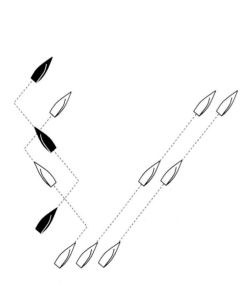

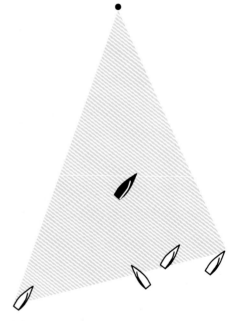

Fig 9.16 *Herding. Black is covering the three Whites. When one of them tacks, Black tacks dead to windward of him, encouraging him to tack back.*

Fig 9.17 *Protecting a lead against the fleet. Black stays in the triangle formed by the top mark and the Whites furthest to the sides.*

THE TOP MARK

The first top mark tends to be crowded, so planning the approach is a necessity. A mistake at this time would translate into a drastic drop in hard-earned placings.

Approaching the Top Mark

The mark can be approached from the right side of the course, the left, or the middle. The decision on which approach to take is dependent on:

- *Your upwind race strategy.* For example, if the left side of the course is favoured, you will tend to approach from that side, on port tack.
- *Wind shift.* When sailing in oscillating shifts, the side you approach from depends on where the shifts brings you.
- *The expected crowd.* In large, competitive fleets and short upwind legs, expect the top mark to be jam-packed, unless you are at the front or tail end of the fleet. In crowded situations, being on starboard tack has its advantages, so a starboard tack parade forms as boats "queue" to round the mark (*fig. 9.18*).

Fig 9.18 Starboard tack parade.

Lay Lines

Avoid the Lay Lines. To get to the top mark in the shortest possible time, the shifts should be played till the last moment if possible. Avoid committing to the lay lines early when racing in a fleet as any wind shifts thereafter cannot be taken advantage of. If lifted while on the lay line, the boat would overstand the mark; if headed, it would lose out to all the boats to leeward.

The Lay Line as a Tactical Weapon. An upwind contest between two boats is practically over when the boats reach either one of the lay lines. Hence, the leading boat can use the lay lines to protect a lead. When the trailing boat is sailing away from a lay line, use your backwind and blanket zones to force him to tack towards it. While he is sailing towards the lay line, give him clear air to encourage him to continue on. Once the trailing boat reaches the lay line, it is game over for him, at least until the top mark. Not only will he be unable to take advantage of wind shifts to catch up with you, there is also nothing he can do if you sit on his wind all the way to the mark.

If you are the one being covered, do avoid the lay lines. For example, while sailing towards a lay line, use the slightest header as an excuse to tack away from it. At the same time try and shake off the covering boat.

Judging the Lay Lines. It is not easy to judge if you are on the lay line, especially from afar, and in a current. If unsure, tack. Tacking too early necessitates two extra tacks to make the mark but in the Laser, the distance lost during each tack is minimal. Overstanding the mark usually results in a much greater loss in distance.

The Starboard Tack Parade
At the end of the first windward leg, the fleet would usually not have spread out yet, so a starboard tack parade tends to form at the mark. There are two ways to approach the queue:

Joining the End of the Queue. The conservative approach is to go to the starboard lay line early and join the end of the queue (*fig. 9.19 Black*). This approach is the safest, but not the fastest. Besides not being able to take advantage of headers, boats along the line will disturb one another's air and slip to leeward. Each new entrant to the line will tack a little further to windward of the others, resulting in a whole line of boats that are actually above the lay line. Those who tack right on the lay line will be in dirty air, and end up not making the mark (*fig. 9.19 W1*). Boats who cannot make the mark will have to gybe around and sail down the queue in the hope of finding a gap to slip into not too far down the line (*fig. 9.19 W2*). In big fleets, there are occasionally some boats that make it round only after the second or third attempt, when the queue thins out.

The Port Tack Approach. Here, the mark is approached on port tack, with the aim of "cutting the queue" and tacking right at the mark to round it, hoping that there is a break in the line of starboard tackers at the mark (*fig. 9.19 Grey*). Anticipation, timing, and a keen eye for gaps in the queue are keys to a successful port tack approach. If unsuccessful, not only will places be lost, but also the chances of having to do turns or attending a protest hearing in the evening are high.

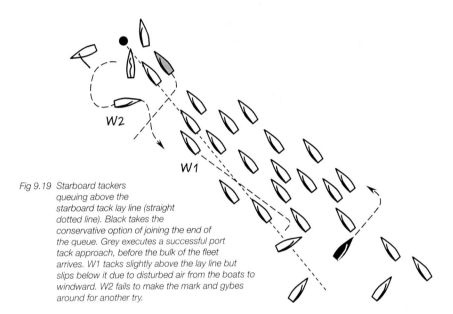

Fig 9.19 *Starboard tackers queuing above the starboard tack lay line (straight dotted line). Black takes the conservative option of joining the end of the queue. Grey executes a successful port tack approach, before the bulk of the fleet arrives. W1 tacks slightly above the lay line but slips below it due to disturbed air from the boats to windward. W2 fails to make the mark and gybes around for another try.*

The rules do not work in the port tack boat's favour. Firstly, room to round the mark does not apply "between boats on opposite tacks when they are on a beat to windward or when the proper course for one of them to pass the mark is to tack." Secondly, when inside the two-length zone, even if the port tack boat manages to complete the tack in time, he is in the wrong if the starboard tack boat has to sail above a close-hauled course to avoid contact. If the starboard tack boat bears away instead to avoid a collision, establishing a leeward overlap in the process, the port tack boat has to keep clear. Thirdly, a boat that intentionally hits a mark knowing that a 360° penalty turn is much less costly than gybing round to make another pass may have to pay dearly for that decision, since the rule states, "If a boat has gained a significant advantage in the race series by touching the mark, she shall retire."

Crossing Tacks Near the Mark

As boats from both sides of the course converge at the top mark, there will be many port-starboard encounters. Quick thinking and thinking a few moves ahead can help gain additional places at the mark. The objective is to protect the right and maintain freedom to tack for the mark. A few scenarios are possible when two boats meet near the mark or starboard tack lay line:

You are on Port, on a Collision Course with a Starboard Tacker. Whether you tack below him or cross his transom to tack on his windward hip will depend on whether he can make the mark. If the starboard tacker is comfortably above the lay line, tack below him to avoid overstanding the mark. If he cannot make the mark, cross his transom and tack when you reach the lay line.

A possible though imprecise way to judge if the starboard tacker can make the mark is to see where his boom end is in relation to the corner of the transom. If it is block-to-block, he is either on or below the lay line. If the boom is outboard, then he is above the lay line.

You are on Starboard, on a Collision Course with a Port Tacker. If you can make the mark, shout across to the port tacker and warn him not to tack in your water. In response, he may duck behind your transom or tack earlier to avoid tacking in your water. Either way, you will have clear air on your way to the mark. Alternatively, he might ignore your warning and lee-bow you. To avoid this, sail free (provided you can still make the mark) but hold your course (the right-of-way boat has to hold his course) as you approach him. When he tacks to lee-bow you, point up to avoid his backwind (*fig. 9.20 left*).

If you cannot lay the mark, then tack before meeting the port tack boat. Alternatively you may want to deceive the port tacker into thinking that you can lay the mark easily so that he will tack below you and subsequently tack two more times to get to the mark. To do this, ease your boom out when he is looking at you. If the port tacker falls for it and lee-bows you, tack onto port, and later tack back onto starboard. When you next meet, you still have the starboard tack advantage (*fig. 9.20 middle*).

If, on the other hand, the port tacker knows that you cannot make the mark, he will duck behind you. To avoid giving him the starboard tack advantage when you next meet, tack immediately after he crosses your transom, and hold him on port tack until you reach the lay line *(fig. 9.20 right).*

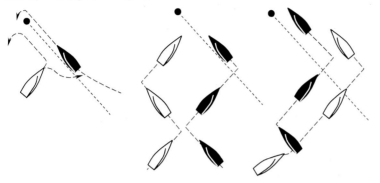

Fig 9.20
Crossing tacks at the top mark.
Left: Black overstood the top mark but rightly bears down to get onto the lay line so that White is not given the opportunity to tack on his lee-bow and make the mark. In response, White should duck Black's transom.
Middle: Black tricks White into lee-bowing him, tacks away, and tacks back onto a starboard advantage when they next meet.
Right: White takes the smarter option of ducking Black's transom to get to the right, but Black slams a tack close to White to take away his freedom to tack to the mark. To tack for the mark, White has to either slow down or sail free to create some room between the two boats.

You are on Starboard, Comfortably Ahead of a Port Tacker.

When a port tacker crosses your transom, he will naturally sight down the centreline of your boat to see if you can make the mark *(fig. 9.21).* If you are in close contention with the port tacker for the series, you may want to deceive him into thinking that you are below the lay line when you are not. He may then sail on, and overstand the mark. To deceive the port tacker, bear away slightly (without easing the sail) to point your bow below the mark as he glances at you. If you cannot make the mark, you can deceive the port tacker into thinking that you can (causing him to tack too early) by pointing your bow above the mark as he looks at you. These tricks do not work on the more experienced sailors, so you would be better of sailing your own race in a good fleet.

THE REACH

The number one priority for the reach is to get the boat planing, as there is a great disparity in speed between a Laser that is surfing and one that is not. The course taken does not matter so much, as long as the boat is planing.

Before starting the reaching leg, get an orientation of where the next mark is (i.e. the gybe mark or the bottom mark), so that immediately after the rounding, you can get the boat planing in the general direction of the mark. Once the boat is planing, fix a transit

Fig 9.21
As White crosses Black's transom, he sights down Black's centreline to see if he is on the lay line.

to keep track of your deviations away from the rhumb line, especially in light, non-planing conditions.

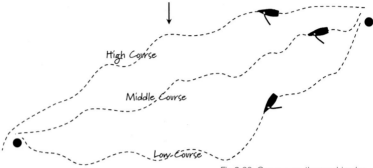

Fig 9.22 Courses on the reaching leg.

High or Low ?

Weaving, or sailing high in the lull and low in a gust, is an effective wind strategy for the reach. The median course can be high, low, or in the middle (*fig. 9.22*). Your decision on the course to take at the start of the leg depends on:

- *Changes in the prevailing wind strength.* In a quickly strengthening breeze (e.g. arrival of a storm), sail high so that as the breeze gets stronger, you can use it to sail low. In light conditions, a new wind will generally come from above the course (unless the wind reverses), so sail high to look for gusts or a new wind. If the wind is dying quickly, say at the tail end of a convection storm, sail low so that you can get a higher angle and better speed as the wind dies.

- *Gusts.* If there is a gust at the start of the reaching leg, go down with the gust. If starting the leg in a lull, then sail high. Hence the gust and lull at the beginning of the leg tends to commit you to a high or low median course for rest of the reach.

- *Current.* The current plays a bigger role in light wind. It is not uncommon to see the fleet being pushed far above or below the rhumb line by the current. These boats sail a big arc to get to the next mark. With a strong cross current and light wind, the transit saves you from sailing the extra distance. Stay near the rhumb line unless you spot a new wind coming, in which case you should head towards it.

- *Clear air.* Boats that sail high are more likely to have clear air. For the low course, clear air is only possible some distance below the rhumb line.

- *Inside overlap.* In a short reaching leg and a competitive fleet, a crowd may converge at the next mark. Sailing low would give you the advantage of an inside overlap at the mark.
- *Room to manoeuvre.* To surf and weave, you need to deviate quite a bit depending on the waves, gusts, and lulls. With other boats around, it is difficult to do this, so if possible, stay away from the fleet. Usually, the fleet tends to sail high as they luff each other up, so there is more room to manoeuvre below the rhumb line. However, Laser sailors realize the importance of riding waves so even below the rhumb line, you will often find a crowd there. To keep your immediate vicinity free of boats, consider sailing low immediately after rounding the top mark if the boat in front goes above the rhumb line, and vice versa.

Unlike the beat, the middle of an off-wind leg is generally slow (depending on the crowd) due to blanketing by a long line of sails above the rhumb line. The exception is when you are at the leading or tail end of the fleet. In a mid-fleet position, your options are narrowed to either a high or low course. If you decide to go low, stay committed to your decision (unless you spot a new wind coming from the top) as a half-hearted effort puts you in lots of dirty wind.

Covering on the Reach

To protect your position on the reach, stay between your opponent and the next mark. He would then have to pass close to you when overtaking. If he comes surfing up to you, you would benefit from whatever gust or wave that he is riding on. Likewise, if protecting your lead against the fleet, stay in the triangle formed by the next mark, the most windward boat, and the most leeward boat (*fig. 9.23*).

A common mistake when covering is to respond excessively to the boat behind. The trailing boat will go high and low depending on the gust and waves he is getting. If the covering boat were to mimic his every move, then he would not be sailing optimally

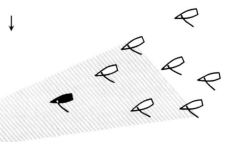

Fig 9.23 Covering on the reach. Stay within the triangle.

in his own set of gusts and waves. The idea is to stay roughly – and not exactly - between the opponent and the next mark, while riding your own waves and gusts. Hence if the boat behind points while you are in a gust, go ahead and ride the gust downwind, and point up only when you are out of the gust. Sailing fast is the best defence.

Overtaking on the Reach

The boat ahead can be overtaken to windward or leeward. The choice depends on the overtaking boat's abilities (e.g. if you are light and the wind is overpowering, leeward is the better option) and strategy (to go high or low).

Overtaking to Windward. Before getting too close to the boat in front, decide if you wish to pass him to windward or leeward. Do not wait till the last minute before deciding as passing close to windward will only encourage the defending boat to luff up, to the detriment of both boats. By pointing early and giving him a wide berth, not only will you reduce the likelihood of a luffing match, but you will also have more space to ride the waves down. Wait for the right opportunity - take advantage of a lull to sail high and avoid wasting a good wave or gust by pointing in them.

Overtaking to Leeward. As before, make your move before you get too close and sail far to leeward of the boat ahead. If you get too close, the blanketing effect, although not as significant as most other classes of boats, can kill your speed. Wait patiently for a big gust or wave, and then make a bold and definite move to break through his wind shadow. If you succeed in coming out on the other side of the wind shadow, point up a little to protect your position and pick up some speed before falling off the plane, otherwise you would just be overtaken back.

Look out for Opportunities to Overtake. For example, if you see the boats ahead getting involved in a luffing match, seize the opportunity to take the whole bunch to leeward. You will not succeed all the time, so it is a good idea to time your leeward assault just before reaching the next mark. If you do not break through to leeward, you will at least have an inside overlap advantage at the mark.

Luffing Matches

Luffing matches, where two or more boats get caught up pointing higher and higher away from the rhumb line, are detrimental to those involved. If in the middle or back of the fleet, a luffing match within your bunch would only allow the leaders to pull away. To keep the leaders within striking distance, it may be better to cooperate and follow one another in Indian file (for non-planing conditions). The leaders will have a harder time trying to pull away (especially on the run), so everyone in the group has a chance to catch the leaders.

Another form of group cooperation (to keep the leaders within striking distance) is to avoid blanketing the leeward boat purposefully and unnecessarily. After overtaking to windward, bear away as soon as the overlap is broken so that the leeward boat does not have to endure your dirty air any longer than is necessary. The leeward boat could have luffed up on you, but chose not to, so you should at least return the favour by not sitting in his wind.

THE DOWNWIND LEG

On rounding the top mark at the start of the downwind leg, hop onto a wave and get the boat planing as soon as you can. More and more, the downwind leg seems to be the one separating the winners from the losers. The overwhelming priority is downwind speed.

As the Laser can be sailed by-the-lee just as well (if not better) as on the broad reach, wind shifts do not feature highly on the mental checklist of the Laser sailor. Gusts, on the other hand, make a huge difference - make it a habit to look upwind for gust patches at regular intervals, just as you would look upwind on the beat. You should be able to sail just as comfortably looking behind.

Another critical skill is wave-catching. With big waves, anyone can get the boat planing, but the expert sailor is able to string together a series of waves such that he seems to be planing all the time. He is also able to plane in conditions that less able sailors consider as non-planing conditions.

Other than speed, downwind strategy and tactics also have a part to play in winning races.

Lasers, Lasers on the run, your capsized friend is not having fun.

Left or Right ?

One of the first decisions you will need to make at the start of the downwind leg is to go left or right. Those at the tail end of the fleet have an additional option of sailing down the middle. Use information gathered during the beat to the top mark to help in deciding the favoured side. The factors that will favour one side over the other include:

- *Starboard tack parade.* Boats that have yet to round the top mark will amass at the left side of the downwind leg, so most would tend to go towards the right to avoid the blanketing effect. This affects the leading and mid-fleet sailors.

- *Gusts.* After sailing towards the first gust of the leg to intercept it, you will tend to be committed to that side. Also, the wind might not be even on both sides of the course (e.g. a band of strong wind to one side of the course due to the funnelling of an offshore wind by geographical features).

- *Current.* In light winds, it is common to see the fleet pushed to one side of the rhumb line by a cross current. Distance is unnecessarily lost as the boats sail around an arc. In a strong cross current and light wind, fix a transit at the start of the leg to save yourself from travelling the extra distance. Stay near the rhumb line unless you spot a new wind or an approaching gust. In a favourable or adverse current, the strength of the current may be different on each side, especially if the water depth is different.

- *Inside overlap.* If the downwind leg is short and the racing is close, and you foresee a crowd at the next mark, consider going left to get an inside overlap advantage at the mark.
- *Blanketing by boats astern.* Boats rounding later blanket the boats ahead. To avoid the wind shadows, the boats ahead will have to commit themselves to either side of the pack, where the wind is clearer. Once a commitment has been made, it is difficult to change your mind and switch sides, as that would mean having to sail across a large area of disturbed air.
- *Room to manoeuvre.* To surf the waves and intercept the gusts, course deviations are inevitable and quite significant at times. With other boats in the vicinity, there is limited room to make these course alterations, so it pays to stay away from the fleet by going to the sides.

Blanketing as a Means of Overtaking

On the upwind leg, the leading boat has an advantage over the trailing boat as he can use his blanket and backwind zones as tactical weapons. For the downwind leg, it is the trailing boat that yields these weapons. However, in fleet racing, it is pointless to blanket one another unless the boats are in the leading pack. As on the reach, the boats behind should avoid slowing one another down in order to keep the leaders within striking distance.

While it is unreasonable to blanket the boat in front all the way down the run, it is somewhat justifiable to do so on approaching the bottom mark (since all the boats will converge anyway) to get an inside overlap. To blanket the boat in front, keep the leeward boat in line with your wind indicator. The Laser's solitary sail is relatively small, so do not expect the boat ahead to come to a halt. In planing conditions, a more effective way to overtake the boat in front is to be better at riding the waves.

Protecting a Lead

The boat ahead avoids being blanketed by moving away whenever his wind indicator is pointing directly at the boat astern. By riding the waves, the usual course deviations make it hard for the boat behind to maintain his dead-to-windward position.

To defend his position, the leading boat has to rely on his downwind speed, and this is dependent on clear air. He should sail his own gusts and waves to find the fastest course to the bottom mark. At the same time, an attempt should be made to stay on the same side of the course as the trailing boat so that he is unlikely to be the sole beneficiary of a good gust or set of waves.

THE GYBE AND BOTTOM MARKS

When rounding the gybe or bottom marks together with a pack of boats, having an inside overlap confers a significant advantage. The tactics at the rounding of these marks therefore revolve around the rules governing the passing of marks.

It can get messy at the bottom mark.

Giving Room and Keeping Clear

The area around a mark within a distance of two hull lengths is the two-length zone. At the point when a boat enters this two-length zone, the presence or absence of an overlap determines who gets to round the mark first. In the presence of an overlap, the inside boat gets room to round the mark. In the absence of an overlap, the boat that is clear ahead has the right to round first. It is noteworthy that the rights are established at the point when one of the boats enters the two-length zone. Thereafter, even if the overlap is broken, the rights are upheld. On the same note, it does not matter if an overlap is established after that point in time.

The line used to differentiate boats clear ahead, clear astern, and overlapped is a line abeam from the aftermost point on the boat (i.e. the back of the rudder). Since the line is abeam of the rudder, angling the boat can shift it (*fig. 9.24*).

Disputes arising from incidents at the mark are often related to whether or not there is an overlap. These can be avoided if sailors verbally acknowledge who has room to round and who does not (especially when there are more than two boats converging at the mark). Just before one of you enter the two-length zone, let those around know whether or not they have room. For those on the inside who do not have room over you, shout loud and clear, "Two-length, no overlap!" For those on your outside who have to give you room, yell, "Two-length, water!" For those who do have room over you, wave them forward.

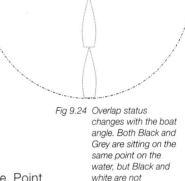

Fig 9.24 *Overlap status changes with the boat angle. Both Black and Grey are sitting on the same point on the water, but Black and white are not overlapped, while Grey and White are.*

Rounding in the Presence of Other Boats

It is critical to get an overlap just before the two-length zone. Point or bear away to blanket the boat in front or surf down a wave into that crucial overlap. If you have an inside overlap, then you are entitled enough room to pass the mark and to gybe if that is part of passing the mark. Ask for room to come in reasonably wide and aim to exit close to the mark to prevent the next boat from squeezing in between you and the mark. If gybing, warn the outside boat that you are about to do so if he is too close.

If you have to give another boat room, sail out wide so that you can point your bow at the other boat's transom as he exits the mark. Slow down (by pointing up and allowing the sail to luff) to avoid overlapping your bow to his windward or leeward. From clear astern, you are ready to squeeze in between him and the mark if he does a bad rounding (*fig. 9.25*). Even if you do not manage to squeeze to windward, you gain the freedom to tack after rounding.

Fig 9.25 *Bottom mark rounding. Left: Black sails out wide and keeps astern of White, which subsequently does a bad rounding. Black points up from directly astern to take advantage of White's error. Right: Black failed to swing out wide and ends up trapped to leeward of White.*

This applies when you are caught on the outside of a bunch of boats as well – stop the boat to let them pass and round close to the mark yourself rather than rounding to leeward of the bunch. But before you slow down, make it clear to the boats behind and outside of you that you have water over them and they have to round after you (unless they want to go to your leeward). Boats within a pack are very likely to get trapped under one another, so there are often good opportunities for you to squeeze through to their windward.

At the gybe mark, being able to squeeze in to windward of the boat in front gives you the option to sail high on the next reach and with that comes clear air and an inside overlap at the next mark. For the bottom mark, squeezing in to windward confers even greater advantages – freedom to tack into clear air immediately after the rounding and control over the boat that is now ahead-to-leeward. Conversely, it is very costly to get your bow trapped under the leeward quarter of the boat or boats ahead. You lose your freedom to tack, and will be sitting in dirty air for a long time!

The Leeward Gate
The gate is used more frequently in races to ease the congestion at the bottom mark (*fig. 9.26*). With it, sailors are forced to consider their upwind strategy as they approach the bottom, as a choice has to be made between the two marks. The factors to consider are:

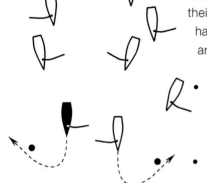

Fig 9.26 The leeward gate. Black rounds the more upwind end.

- *Which is the more upwind mark?* The gate is much shorter than a starting line, so the difference is not great. On the other hand, in a competitive fleet, every inch counts. The favoured end is gauged by eyeballing.
- *Which is the closer mark?* Obviously, with all else equal, it would be most convenient to round the mark closest to you.
- *Which side of the upwind leg is favoured?* It is not easy to round one mark and cross over to the other side of the course when there is a fleet coming down on the run.
- *Which is the less crowded mark?*
- *Is the wind backed or veered at the moment?* Coming down from a Laser's zigzag run, this is not easy to gauge, and

even a compass may not help you with this one (until after you have rounded the mark).

THE FINISH

Upwind Finish

It is important to continue hiking hard to keep your boat speed up towards the finish. The others are tired as well, so this is your chance to take them! This is the time to focus on your own speed and not allow yourself to get distracted by other boats.

The finishing line, like the starting line, can have a biased end. However, unlike the starting line, it is not possible to test the line bias. The favoured end of the finishing line to cross is the leeward end. There are two ways of determining the bias from a distance (*fig. 9.27*). The first is to use the flags on the staff of the finishing boat. Compare the angle it forms with the finishing line. If perpendicular, the line is square; if obtuse, the committee boat end is the favoured end to finish; if acute, then the other end is favoured for the finish. The other method is to compare the orientation of the finishing line with the angle of the waves. Assuming that the wave crests are perpendicular to the wind, the favoured end to finish is the end that meets the wave last as it moves downwind. Frequently the waves are not perpendicular to the wind (e.g. new wind or progressive shift), so ensure that they are at a right angle first before using this method. If unable to decide from a distance, then keep your options open and sail towards the nearer end (tacking if necessary) as you approach the line.

Fig 9.27 Identifying the favoured end of the line to finish. Here the starboard end is favoured to finish. Note the obtuse angle between the flag on the staff of the committee boat and the line, and the angle of the line in relation to the waves. Black luffs up just before the finish to cross ahead of White.

In a close finish, pointing into the wind just before crossing the line may help gain one or two positions. The Laser loses its momentum very quickly, so it is costly to make the mistake of pointing too early. It takes practice to get it right, especially if attempting this in the middle of the line.

Once the line is crossed, sail away from the finish line and other boats to avoid rule infringements, especially in light winds where drifting into the mark is a real possibility.

Reaching Finish

If the last leg is a reach to the finish, the decision to go high or low often determines the outcome at the finish. Most will tend to sail high as the leg tends to be short, with little time and opportunity to break through to leeward of the boat ahead. This will also make it easier to protect the boat's wind.

Go low if the leeward end of the line is definitely nearer and it is windy (in which case lighter sailors might not have a choice). If you are lucky, the boats ahead might luff one another up, clearing a passing lane to leeward for you.

AFTER THE FINISH

The race might be over, but not the series (unless we are at the last race of the series). It is now time to get ready for the next race:

> *"There is no magical recipe for winning. Just as a game of chess is always different from previous games, so are races - there are countless permutations. The more situations you have been in, the better your ability to analyse and anticipate the situation you encounter next. Just keep racing and racing and racing."*
>
> *Jacob Palm*

1. Start rehydrating and replenishing your energy stores as soon as possible whether the next race is in half an hour or the next day. If the last race for the day has just been completed, then try to get some calories and water into your system on the way back to shore, or very soon after returning to shore.

2. Analyse the course so that mistakes are not repeated in the next race. Discuss with your coach and friends to get a different angle if possible.

3. Finally, give your mind a break. Even if the next race is coming up soon, take a few moments to "re-set" your mind and start the next race on a clean slate rather than harping over a past mistake. If that was it for the day, then do spend a few hours relaxing after you have packed up, finished all repairs (if any), and analysed the day's racing. As sailing races are stretched over days, mental breaks need to be incorporated to prevent staleness. During these short breaks, it is best to avoid anything that has to do with sailing, if possible.

Chapter 10

Drills for All Skills

content by **Ben Tan**
reviewed by **James O'Callaghan**

*A*n effective training session starts with having a clear overall training plan that sets out the objectives and exercises or drills for the day. During the session, you need to stay focused on this plan, working hard to rectify weaknesses and meet the set objectives. Effective and creative drills are a sure-fire way to improve your sailing skills. This chapter will show you how to optimise the use of on-water drills and set out some basic but highly effective drills that are practised by top sailors throughout the world. But ultimately, do not be afraid to experiment – mix and match elements from different drills to suit your own training needs.

GETTING THE MOST OUT OF YOUR TRAINING SESSION

Being successful requires not only long hours on the water, but also a high training efficiency – aim to get maximum results out of every training session:

- *Set specific goals for each drill.* Break the skill down to different elements and rate your own performance for each element. For example, if you wish to improve your tacks, ask yourself which element of tacking do you need to improve. Is it speed across the boat, flattening the boat after the tack, hand changeover, etc.? Rate these different elements on a scale of 1-10 so that you can assess whether you have improved. This is particularly useful as a means of helping you concentrate when training alone.

- *When learning a new skill, do it when you are fresh so that you will acquire the skill quickly.* Later, when you are better at it, increase the level of difficulty by doing the drills under pressure. For example, you can progressively reduce the size of the course on which you are practicing your mark rounding.

- *To analyse your technique, boat handling, and sail settings, video cameras are very useful.* Get your coach or some other helpful person to capture you in action. This will offer you a different perspective, and you will notice mistakes that you would never have realized otherwise.

- *An intense training session will give you a good physical workout at the same time.* For fitness development, sailing has the advantage of specificity over dry-land training. Similarly, practice races are more specific to racing than training drills, so it is a good idea to end every session with a race round a course.

- *Use a training logbook to record your analyses of races, mistakes made during races and training, and most importantly, how you intend to rectify those mistakes or weaknesses.* Also, note down areas that you performed well in to reinforce your strengths. Even if you do not ever refer back to your logbook, the act of writing in it forces you to think about what you are doing rather than training blindly. Other entries into the logbook can include serial measurements of your weight and fitness level (to keep track of your progress); wind pattern, weather, and current observations; and notable pointers from your coach, literature that you have read, or discussions with other sailors and coaches. Your yearly planning instrument (*chapter 15*), which describes your overall training plan, should be kept in the back of your training logbook to remind you of the big picture.

- *Although Laser racing is an individual event, training in the Laser should be a team effort.* You will always learn more if you have one or more training partners around and this is applicable to your gym work as well. By sharing go-fast tips and helping one another, your training group will improve as a whole, and individual players will be less of a threat during races.

BASIC DRILLS

As sailing involves a multitude of skill, training drills are needed to specifically develop each skill (*table 10.1*). Learn a large variety of drills so that you can have a fruitful training session regardless of the weather or available resources. You should have drills for the occasions when your training partners are not around, for times when your coach cannot be on the water with you, for days when there is hardly a whiff of wind, and also for days when it is blowing hard.

Table 10.1 Summary of basic drills, categorized by type of skill targeted.

SKILL	DRILL
Feel	■ Look, No Rudder! ■ "Broken" Tiller Extension ■ Eyes Covered ■ Night Sailing

Boat handling	■ Tacking Drills
	   o One-Boat Tacking
	   o One-Boat Continuous Tacking
	   o Tacking Duels
	   o Tacking on the Whistle
	■ Gybing Drills
	   o One-Boat Gybing
	   o One-Boat Continuous Gybing
	   o Gybing on the Whistle
	■ 720° and 360° Drills
	   o 720° and 360° Race
	   o Short Course Turns
	■ Short Course Mark Rounding
	■ Starting Line Boat Handling Drills
	   o Parking
	   o Sailing Backwards
	   o Scalloping
	   o Start-Stop Drills
	■ Balancing Drills
	   o Standing Up
	   o The Windsurfing Tack
	   o The Windsurfing Gybe
	   o Rock & Roll Your Way Home
	■ Group Games
	   o Follow the Leader
	   o Ball Tag

Speed	■ One-Boat Speed Testing ■ Two-Boat Speed Testing
Judgement	■ Time-Distance Judgement Calls ■ Judging the Lay Lines
Awareness	■ Where's the Top Mark?
Tactics	■ Starts ■ Short Course Racing ■ Match Racing and Team Racing
Reading wind shifts	■ Long Beats

DRILLS FOR DEVELOPING YOUR FEEL

It is your feel that makes you fast in light wind, that hints to you that the wind has shifted, that reduces unnecessary rudder action, that tells you your sail is luffing even without having to look at it.

Look, No Rudder!

Try this in light winds. Raise your centreboard halfway up and sail slightly below a beam reach. Keeping the boat on a windward heel, move back to raise your rudder, and quickly move forward, next to your centreboard before the boat screws up into the wind (*fig. 10.1*). Keep the boat on the reach by adjusting the boat's heel. Heel to leeward to point, and heel to windward to bear away.

Fig 10.1 *Sailing with the rudder lifted up.*

TO DEVELOP
• Feel
• Steering with your bodyweight

NO. OF BOATS
1

SET-UP REQUIRED
Nil

"Broken" Tiller Extension

Remove your tiller extension and tie the tail end of your mainsheet to the tiller using a clove hitch. Once this is done, sail on a close-hauled or reaching course (*fig. 10.2*). While controlling your rudder with the mainsheet, you are forced to cut down on unnecessary rudder action. However, when using a proper tiller extension, do not hesitate to jab the tiller to leeward if the conditions are choppy.

TO DEVELOP
• Feel
• Steering with minimal rudder action

NO. OF BOATS
1

SET-UP REQUIRED
Nil

Fig 10.2 *Using the mainsheet as the tiller extension.*

TO DEVELOP
- Feel
- Use of non-visual cues

NO. OF BOATS
1

SET-UP REQUIRED
Nil

Eyes Covered

Blindfold yourself and sail close-hauled (*fig. 10.3*). Rely on the other senses: the boat's heeling angle, the pressure on the sail, the weather helm, the wind blowing across your ears, and the sun's position as felt by your body surface will all help you stay on course.

Fig 10.3 Sailing upwind blindfolded. Besides pulling your shirt collar over your head, the eyes can also be covered by pulling your cap over them, or by using a handkerchief.

TO DEVELOP
- Feel
- Use of non-visual cues

NO. OF BOATS
1 or more

SET-UP REQUIRED
Coach, torch lights, light sticks

Night Sailing

Get a coach to conduct a race at night. The coach positions himself at the windward mark, with a light so that the sailors know where to aim. With restricted vision, your remaining senses become remarkably better and you learn to steer the boat in reaction to these heightened senses.

For obvious safety reasons, this would need to take place in familiar areas that are away from commercial traffic. In addition, each participating boat should have a light stick attached to it.

BOAT HANDLING DRILLS

These drills are aimed at helping you master sailing manoeuvres like tacking, gybing, penalty turns, and mark rounding. They also include starting line and balancing skills. They help you to know the boat better, and some of them may even double up as fitness training.

TO DEVELOP
- Good tacks
- Fitness

NO. OF BOATS
1 or more

SET-UP REQUIRED
Whistle and coach if the group is large

Tacking Drills

One-Boat Tacking. If you are training alone, set a target of say, 20-50 tacks. Start tacking repeatedly. As soon as you have accelerated to full speed on the new tack, commence the next tack. Alternatively, you can set your countdown timer to repeat every 30-

60 s. Focus on coming out of the tacks with good speed. Do standard or roll tacks, depending on the wind strength. Throw in a few double-tacks now and then.

One-Boat Continuous Tacking. This really raises your heart rate, even in light winds. As an extension of the double-tack, keep tacking without stopping, until you have completed a predetermined number of tacks, say 20. If you have a partner, challenge him to be the first to complete 20 tacks.

Tacking Duels. Pair up, and start on opposite tacks with your partner. After crossing, the boat behind strives to overtake the one in front by doing dummy tacks and double tacks, or by pure tacking perfection (*fig. 10.4*). The leading boat tries to cover.

Fig 10.4 Boats crossing during a tacking duel.

The boat behind must do a tack within 20 s, in order to avoid turning this into a drag race or a test of playing the wind shifts. The duel ends when the leading boat is overtaken or after a predetermined time. For the next round, the winner of the previous duel now crosses behind (or you can take turns crossing behind) to start another duel.

One important skill to develop during tacking duels is to make judgement calls relating to crossing boats. Can you clear your opponent's bow? If your opponent is close on your windward hip, can you clear his transom when you tack?

Tacking on the Whistle. This is for bigger groups. Line up on one tack, equally across the wind. On the whistle (blown by one of you or the coach, if present), sheet in and sail close-hauled. One whistle signals a single tack, while two whistles signal a double-tack.

Gybing Drills

One-Boat Gybing. When training alone, set a target of say, 20-50 gybes. Start gybing, one after another. Do standard or roll gybes, depending on the wind strength, and throw in a few double-gybes now and then.

TO DEVELOP
• Good gybes
• Fitness

NO. OF BOATS
1 or more

SET-UP REQUIRED
Whistle, and coach if the group is large

Gybing Drills

One-Boat Continuous Gybing. This is another physically demanding drill for very light winds. Do a gybe, and immediately follow it up with another one, and another, until you have completed, say, 20 gybes. In very light wind or totally calm conditions, you can sail an almost straight course. That is, you are actually rocking your boat by jumping from one side deck to the other repeatedly. This is a good way to practice changing tiller and mainsheet hands under pressure.

Gybing on the Whistle. This is for bigger groups. Form a single line on the beam reach. On the whistle (blown by one of you or the coach, if present) bear away onto the run. One whistle signals a single gybe, while two whistles signal a double gybe.

720° and 360° Drills

720° and 360° Race. No marks are required for this. Starting from any point of sail, do a 720° or 360° turn. Practice your turns in both clockwise and anticlockwise directions, and in all conditions (especially in strong wind).

TO DEVELOP
• Quick penalty turns
• Fitness

NO. OF BOATS
1 or more

SET-UP REQUIRED
Nil or short course

To make things more interesting, challenge other boats to see who finishes the turns faster. Sail on an agreed point of sail with the boats more than two boat lengths apart and, on the whistle (or a verbal cue), start the turns together. Shout out loud once you have completed the turn, so that the group can tell who has won. The focus during this training drill is to finish the turns as fast as possible in order to improve boat handling skills. However, bear in mind that during a race, the challenge is not to finish the penalty as fast as possible; rather, it is to minimise lost ground (*chapter 5*).

Short Course Turns. When doing short courses, perform a 720° or 360° turn after rounding every mark. This will improve your fitness. Here, the focus is not to complete the turns in as short a time as possible, but to complete the turns while losing as little ground as possible.

Another way of incorporating penalty turns in a short course is to have the leading boat at every mark do a 720° or 360° turn soon after the rounding, so that the lead changes hands and the fleet stays together.

Short Course Mark Rounding

Depending on the number of marks you have, there are a variety of courses you can set, as shown in *fig. 10.5*. These short courses are great for training with more than one boat. The slowest boat starts first, and the fastest boat, last. Alternatively, the coach can set up a starting line. Chase one another around the course, overtaking as many boats as possible, until the coach terminates the drill. Everyone must re-set their sails at the top and bottom marks. Imposing a 5-tack minimum on the upwind beat and 720°

TO DEVELOP
• Smooth, controlled rounding
• Fitness

NO. OF BOATS
1 or more

SET-UP REQUIRED
1-3 marks

Short Course Mark Rounding

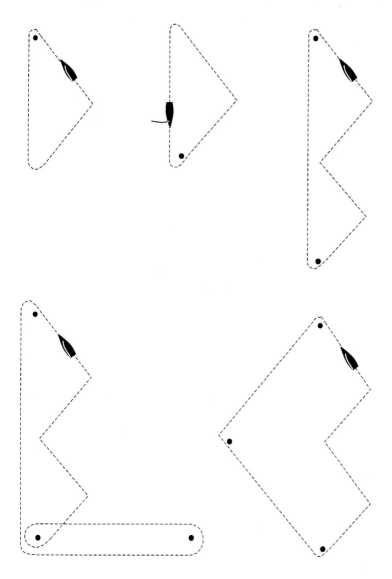

Fig 10.5 Various courses for practicing mark rounding.

or 360° turns soon after rounding each mark will make these short courses even more interesting.

Starting Line Boat Handling Drills

Parking. This "exercise" can be used when you need a break from the high-intensity drills. Simply sail up next to a mark and park your boat there, without inching forward. Ensure that the boom is far out so that the sail does not catch any wind. Try doing this in different currents.

TO DEVELOP
- Boat control on the starting line
- Acceleration off the starting line

NO. OF BOATS
1 or more

SET-UP REQUIRED
1 mark

Sailing Backwards. Point straight into the wind and push your boom out *(fig. 10.6)*. Get used to steering backwards by manoeuvring around some marks. Learn how to get into reverse gear quickly with full control, and how to get out of the reverse gear onto a close-hauled course quickly. This skill is useful when manoeuvring around the starting line and when caught in irons on windy days.

Scalloping. This manoeuvre allows you to "drift" sideways – to windward – in order to create space to leeward. The space created gives you some room to accelerate into at the start, and it also reduces your chances of being affected by backwind from the boat to leeward.

Fig 10.6 Sailing backwards.

On starboard tack, park next to a mark and angle the boat such that it lies between head-to-wind and close-hauled. Push the boom out just enough to catch some wind on the far side of the sail, repeatedly jabbing the tiller to the starboard side in order to prevent the boat from tacking *(fig. 10.7)*. In this case, you are using the rudder to try and bear away rather than propelling the boat forward, so it is legal. You will find the boat drifting slowly to windward.

Start-Stop Drills. Boat speed off the starting line is something every Laser sailor dreams of. Being able to break out in front of the first row means freedom to tack with the shifts and a near-certain top placing at the first mark (provided you do not go speeding off on the wrong tack). Besides accelerating, decelerating the boat is

Starting Line Boat Handling Drills

also a useful starting line skill, as when sailing into a gap in the front row and stopping suddenly to avoid sticking the bow out.

When training alone, practice alternately accelerating and decelerating in different wind conditions. In light winds, heel to leeward and flatten the boat just before you sheet in to get that added surge forward.

When in a group, line up on close-haul evenly across the wind, with about two boat lengths between boats. On the whistle (or a verbal cue if there are fewer than four boats), sheet in and accelerate as quickly as possible. On the next whistle, stop the boat as quickly as possible by pushing the boom out.

Fig 10.7 Scalloping.

Balancing Drills

The next four drills are aimed at improving your balance. In these exercises, sailors tend to fall into the water, so for those training in colder climates - be warned!

Standing Up. At any point of sail, stand up on the side deck and sail from there. This develops your balance, and reduces the risk of embarrassing falls when you stand up to look for wind before the start or during the race.

The Windsurfing Tack. Here is a chance to show the boardsailors that you know how to windsurf too! Start by sailing close-hauled, standing up. Cleat the mainsheet, heel the boat a little to leeward (to give you more time to run across), and push your tiller across. Quickly run across to the other side via the front of the mast, keeping your weight close to the rig. Once you are on the other side, grab hold of the tiller extension and mainsheet to regain control (*fig. 10.8*).

TO DEVELOP
- General boat handling skills
- Balance
- Steering with the bodyweight

NO. OF BOATS
1

SET-UP REQUIRED
Nil

Balancing Drills

Fig 10.8 Tacking windsurfing style, by running across the front of the mast.

The Windsurfing Gybe. This is yet another chance to impress the boardsailors! While sailing on the run, stand at the edge of the transom. Bear away and gybe by pulling on the mainsheet from the aft boom block (*fig. 10.9*).

Fig 10.9 Gybing windsurfing style, by standing behind the sail.

Fig 10.10 Rocking the boat from the front of the mast.

Rock & Roll Your Way Home. This is a useful skill to have, especially if you do not want to be stranded out at sea. Practice this on your way in during one of those windless days. Raise your centreboard halfway and your rudder fully. Next, leaving your mainsheet cleated with the boom at about half a metre from the block-to-block position, stand in front of the mast and rock your boat back and forth to fan the sail (*fig. 10.10*). Steer by adjusting the heeling angle.

Group Games

These two games are ideal for breaking the monotony of training, and they provide opportunities for sailors to have fun and interact in a less serious setting.

Follow the Leader. The slowest boat should be the leader, followed by progressively faster boats. Form a line behind the leader, and do whatever he or she does. Concentrate on the boat immediately ahead and keep a fixed distance between boats. As the group improves, the leader can perform tacks, gybes, stops, and accelerations at shorter intervals.

Ball Tag. Drop four marks in the water such that they form a square with sides of about 100 m. All boats are to stay within the boundaries formed. A volunteer starts by being "it," and throws the ball at another boat. The boat that gets hit then becomes "it," and he goes after the nearest boat and so on.

TO DEVELOP
- General boat handling skills
- Tacking and gybing skills
- Acceleration and deceleration
- Speed control
- Fitness

NO. OF BOATS
2 or more

SET-UP REQUIRED
Follow the leader: Nil
Ball tag: 4 marks and a ball (e.g. soccer ball)

Group Games

SPEED

All-round speed is important, but downwind speed seems to differentiate the top sailors these days. During training, the norm is to spend more time going upwind than downwind, since it takes a longer time to beat up than to run down. Try to correct for this by sailing long downwind or reaching legs, and get towed back upwind if necessary. Triple World Champion Glenn Bourke even had his boat picked up by car at a downwind location along the coast.

Straight-line speed requires a well-tuned rig and fast techniques, and they present good opportunities for working those hiking muscles, especially when sailing upwind.

One-Boat Speed Training

Sail on *long* upwind, reaching, or downwind legs. Focus hard on one area (e.g. steering, torqueing, hiking technique, surfing) at a time. Catch up on areas that you are lagging behind relative to your training group, so that you will benefit more from the group training sessions.

TO DEVELOP
- Straight-line speed (technique)
- Hiking fitness (when beating and reaching)

NO. OF BOATS
1

SET-UP REQUIRED
Nil

One-Boat Speed Training

It is not easy to concentrate when sailing alone on long legs. Grading your performance for each element of the straight-line sailing on a scale of 1-10, and working to move up the scale is one way of maintaining focus during the session. Another way is to use a speedometer, which serves to keep you conscious of your speed. The PRO•TRIM® dinghy speedometer, which has a small display unit that is mounted on the cunningham eye, is accurate to 0.1 knot.

Long upwind and reaching legs are a good way of conditioning those lazy hiking muscles, especially when you have just come back from a break.

Two-boat Speed Testing (Drag race)

Upwind Speed. Pair up, and line up equally across the wind, about two boat lengths apart. If the two boats are too far apart, then they might be sailing in different winds; if they are too close, they will soon interfere with each other's wind. Sheet in at the same time and sail at full speed (*fig. 10.11*). When one boat is clearly ahead, stop. The slower boat re-tunes his sail while the faster boat keeps the same setting. Start over again, and note the difference. When tuning the sail, it is a good idea to adjust only one of the sail controls at a time, so that you will know which control to attribute the increase or decrease in speed to.

TO DEVELOP
• Straight-line speed
• Hiking fitness
• Sailing tuning

NO. OF BOATS
2 or more of similar speed

SET-UP REQUIRED
Nil

Two-boat Speed Testing

Fig 10.11 Upwind speed testing.

Reaching Speed. Two or more boats can start close to each other, taking care to avoid disturbing each other's wind at the start. Decide on a mark or landmark to head for, and start sailing. The objective is to overtake each other, focusing on the waves. If one boat is distinctly faster, and you do not think it is due to the waves or wind, then the slower boat should re-tune the sail and start over again.

Downwind Speed. Look for a landmark or marker that is directly downwind. Sail on a beam reach, forming a line. Bear away at the same time to start, aiming for the predetermined destination. Try to pass each other. As on the reaches, the variables are the waves, gusts, technique, and sail settings.

JUDGEMENT

Ever wondered how some sailors manage to start a boat length or more ahead of the first row? Being able to judge the starting line and the lay lines to the top mark accurately takes experience and practice.

Other than the on-water drills described below, a simple way of learning how to judge the starting line (in case you do not have a transit) is to attempt to stand exactly on an imaginary line between two trees at a variable distance apart. When you think that you are on the line, ask a friend to stand an one end and tell you if you are actually on the line and if not, how far in front or behind you are.

Time-Distance Judgement Calls

Drop a mark in the water. From a position 2-5 boat lengths away from it, make a call on how long you think it would take to get to the mark from the time you start sheeting in (*fig. 10.12*). Accelerate towards the mark on starboard tack, and see if your estimation was accurate. A variation is to fix the time instead, at say five seconds, and position yourself such that you are 5 seconds away from the mark. Accelerate towards the mark and see if you are right.

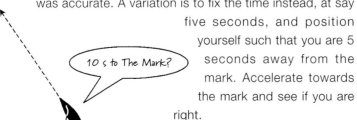

10 s to The Mark?

Fig 10.12 Position at start of time-distance drill.

TO DEVELOP
- Ability to estimate how long the boat takes to get to a mark or line
- Ability to reach a mark or line at a specific time

NO. OF BOATS
1

SET-UP REQUIRED
1 mark, or a starting line

Time-Distance Judgement Calls

To make the drill even more difficult and race-specific, use a starting line instead of a solitary mark. Your coach sights down one end of the line with a video camera. At your own time, cross the line on starboard tack as if starting, and raise your hand in the air at the point in time when you think you are on the line. The video playback often brings about some surprised faces. Instead of a video camera, the alternative is for the coach to blow his whistle when you cross the line.

Judging the Lay Lines

TO DEVELOP
• Ability to call a lay line accurately

NO. OF BOATS
1

SET-UP REQUIRED
1 mark

Drop a mark in the water, and start about 50 m downwind from the mark. Sail towards one of the lay lines and tack when you think you are exactly on the lay line. Round the top mark to port to see if your call was accurate, and go down to start again. Starting further down from the top mark can increase the level of difficulty. Of course, several boats can do this drill together, provided they do not disturb one another's wind on the approach to the mark.

AWARENESS

Too often you see sailors who are so engrossed with what is going on in their boats that they forget what is happening outside. Once you have your boat handling and speed up to a reasonable level it should become second nature to keep the boat moving optimally. You can then have time to think more about tactics and what is going on around you. Top-level sailors have the ability to plan ahead and anticipate situations as they develop.

Where's the Top Mark?

TO DEVELOP
• Awareness of what is happening outside the boat

NO. OF BOATS
1 or more

SET-UP REQUIRED
1 mark and coach

Without a windward mark in position, do a line start. The coach leaves the mark on his boat and drops it at any time as he moves slowly upwind. This will force the sailors to keep their heads out of the boat and stay away from the corners. By being aware of what is happening around and ahead of you, you can learn to become a more proactive sailor, rather than reacting to situations as they happen.

TACTICS

To work on tactics, it is best to have the boats close together, so get all your training partners down and use small courses. Upwind tactics are the most difficult, so spend more time beating to the top mark.

Starts

Practice actual starts frequently, as your starts have a big influence on your results. Go through the whole pre-start routine recommended in *chapter 9* until it becomes ingrained. From the start, you can either beat up to a mark 100 m to windward and return, or return when the coach blows his whistle. Premature starters must return.

Use this opportunity to practice high-risk strategies which you rarely have the courage to attempt during regattas, so that you can eventually overcome the fear. Such strategies include starting right next to the pin or the starting boat, and port tack starts.

Use short starting lines to force everyone to work hard to get into the front row. The line might be biased intentionally to help sailors to practice strategies for coping with such situations. To practice parking skills, all boats must be lined up with one minute to go.

Short Course Racing

Do a proper start, and race round a short course, with the top and bottom marks about 200-500 m apart, depending on the wind. To keep the fleet together, the first boat to round each mark might want to do a 360° or 720° turn. This is racing in "quick time," so there is less time to make decisions. There is less focus on wind shifts and gusts, and more on boat-to-boat tactics.

Match Racing and Team Racing

Match Racing. Here, two boats fight it out even before the start. Set a course and get your coach to do the start sequence. At the preparatory signal, each boat (one at each end of the start line) crosses the start line from the on-course side to the pre-start side, and the race practically starts from here as the pair fights to win the start.

TO DEVELOP
- Starting tactics and strategy
- Start line judgement
- Boat handling (parking, acceleration)
- Speed

NO. OF BOATS
2 or more

SET-UP REQUIRED
Starting line with coach

Starts

TO DEVELOP
- Tactics
- All sailing skills
- Fitness
- Racing Rules

NO. OF BOATS
2 or more (the more the merrier)

SET-UP REQUIRED
A complete but short course with a coach to do the starts

Short Course Racing

TO DEVELOP
- Close-quarter tactics
- Boating handling
- Racing rules
- Fitness

NO. OF BOATS
2 or more

SET-UP REQUIRED
A complete but short course with coach to do starts

Match and Team Racing

The Laser's manoeuvrability necessitates quick decisions and demands a thorough knowledge of the racing rules. Occasionally, match racing tactics (especially the pre-start manoeuvres) are used in fleet racing at the tail end of the regatta, when only a few boats are left in contention for the top spots. A famous example would be the epic battle between Ben Ainslie and Robert Scheidt during the 1996 Olympics.

Team Racing. This offers similar lessons and excitement. The equal-sized teams have 2-4 members each, and each team should have some conspicuous form of identification like a ribbon on the mast or boom. Set the top and bottom marks, and get your coach to do a three-minute start sequence. The team which the last place finisher belongs to, loses.

Team racing forces the sailor to keep his eyes out of the boat to note the relative positions of team mates and rivals, raising an awareness of the big picture.

There are a couple of books on match and team racing, but all you need is the simplest one to give you a basic idea (*see Recommended Reading*). Discover the rest of the tricks yourself on the water.

READING WIND SHIFTS

The fastest way to the top mark is to play the shifts and gusts perfectly. If you can do this, there is no tactical offensive that your rivals can use against you, short of preventing you from staying on your chosen tack. Wind shift reading is a critical skill that takes years to develop, so start acquiring it now!

TO DEVELOP
- Ability to read shifts and recognise wind patterns
- Speed
- Fitness

NO. OF BOATS
1 or more

SET-UP REQUIRED
1 mark

Long Beats

Long beats are the best way to learn about wind patterns as they give you time to see trends in the wind direction and strength. Set a top mark, or use anything else that is anchored, or even a landmark. Beat towards the mark, playing the shifts along the way.

If training alone, use a compass so that you can get an idea of how well you are doing. If you missed the shifts or predicted them wrongly, you will naturally feel frustrated; if you are in synchrony with the shifts, you will get a "harmonious" feeling. Training alone minimises distractions so you can fully concentrate on the shifts, allowing yourself to get immersed in the elements. If you are training in a group, the first boat to the top mark obviously played the shifts and gusts well, assuming everyone had equal speed.

Gate Starts

Since most of us do not have a coach available all the time to lay a starting line for the long beats, it is necessary to learn how to do gate starts. A designated "rabbit" sails close-hauled on port tack, and the rest of the fleet crosses behind, on starboard tack, to start (*fig. 10.13*). The tack of the "rabbit" and the fleet can be reversed for the sake of variation. With less experienced sailors, the gate start tends to get messy, so here are two tips to get it right on the first try:

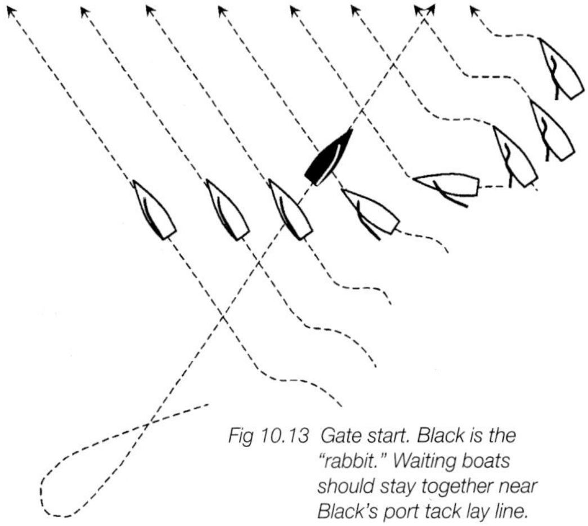

Fig 10.13 Gate start. Black is the "rabbit." Waiting boats should stay together near Black's port tack lay line.

- The "rabbit" has to cross just in front of the fleet, so to make it easier for him to get onto a good lay line, the rest should line up on starboard tack, stay together, and stay still. The "rabbit" cannot get a lay line for the fleet when it is spread out or moving.
- For the "rabbit" to find the lay line, the best way is to sail away from the fleet (on starboard tack) on a course slightly below a beam reach, gybe around, and sail close-hauled towards the fleet.

"That's been a lot harder than the America's Cup racing turned out to be ..."

Dean Barker, former Laser sailor and 2000 America's Cup helmsman, on Team New Zealand's in-house training in the lead up to his victory against Prada.

Chapter 11

Sailing Fitness

content by **Michael Blackburn**
reviewed by **Todd Vladich, Pia Bay, Jacqueline Ellis,
Saratha Bhai Krishnan,** and **Sharifah Shwikar Aljunied**

*S*ailing the Laser requires a high level of fitness: you need to hike hard for extended periods, to work the boat over every wave, and to continually trim or pump the sail. And you need to do all these while keeping your mind on the wind and tactics! One can never be too fit to race the Laser. This chapter discusses how you can use dry-land training to meet the physical demands of the sport.

To get the most out of the Laser, you will need:

- The optimal bodyweight
- Good flexibility
- Good muscular strength and endurance
- Moderate cardio-respiratory endurance
- Moderate anaerobic fitness

To be racing-fit, on-water training is a must. Dry-land training complements this and is a good substitute if we cannot spend enough time on the water, or if we wish to focus on specific elements of fitness that are lacking.

GETTING TO THE RIGHT WEIGHT

The Ideal Weight

Lightweight sailors tend to be overpowered and "thrown around" by the boat. You should be in control of the boat, and not the other way round! On the other hand, excessively heavy sailors weigh the boat down, limiting acceleration and surfing. Being heavy but lean is acceptable as fat-free mass (i.e. muscles) can be made to work for you, whereas fat is simply "dead weight."

So, what is the optimal weight? The 1996 Olympic Laser Medallists' average weight was 78 kg (weight jackets weighing up to 4 kg were allowed then). To be competitive, aim to be about 78–83 kg.

Bulking Up

If underweight, then your objective is to put on lean body mass. A positive energy balance (i.e. the energy or calories consumed exceeds expenditure) through a high calorie diet (*chapter 12*), and

The straight-leg hiking technique and torqueing requires extreme fitness.

stimulation of the muscles to grow through resistance training will achieve this. Both are necessary - alone, neither will deliver the results you desire.

A resistance training programme aimed specifically at muscle hypertrophy will deliver the best results, and this will be discussed later.

Losing Weight

Burning more calories than what is consumed reduces body weight. The trick is to incur a negative energy balance while still having enough energy to sail races and train. This is possible by cutting down on fat intake while increasing carbohydrate intake, since it is carbohydrate and not fat that is the main energy source for sailing. This is discussed in greater detail in *chapter 12*.

While limiting your energy intake, increase your energy output with easy to moderately paced endurance exercises:

Jacqui's Tip for

RADIAL SAILORS

"Radial sailors come in all shapes and sizes, ranging from 55-80 kg. Which weight is best depends on the predominant sailing conditions. Here in Australia we get strong winds most often, so our average competitive Radial weight would be 70-75 kg. In areas where the wind is lighter an average weight of 60-65 kg is best. My recommendation for a good overall racing weight would be somewhere around 70 kg."

Jacqueline Ellis

Types of activity:	Cycling, rowing, running, swimming, deep-water running, windy-weather sailing, etc.
How much: (duration and frequency)	Start with 30 min (less if you are not comfortable with this) three times a week, and increase from there. To lose weight, the key is exercise duration rather than intensity.
How hard: (intensity)	Exercise at around 60-80 % of your maximum heart rate, which is approximately 220 minus your age.

Different activities will burn calories at different rates: those using bigger muscle groups (e.g. running) will tend to burn more calories. Because high training volumes are required to lose weight, it is best to cross-train (i.e. to alternate between the activities listed above) in order to reduce the risk of overuse injuries. If the bodyweight is especially heavy, rely on non-weight bearing activities like cycling, rowing, and swimming in the initial stages, and incorporate a greater proportion of weight bearing exercises later on.

Resistance training can enhance weight loss when combined with aerobic training. It works by building lean muscles, which have a higher metabolism than fat, even at rest. An elevated metabolism burns more calories.

Be patient and aim for a gradual weight loss of not more than one kilogramme a week. Also, aim for fat and not water loss (e.g. spending long hours in a sauna). Water loss or dehydration is detrimental to performance and cannot be sustained.

FLEXIBILITY

Flexibility and Hiking

Flexibility improves technique and agility, while reducing the risk of injury. With straight-leg hiking, hamstring flexibility cannot be overemphasised. When the upper body is upright or leaning in, flexion occurs at the lower back and hip joints. It is the flexion at the level of the lower back, especially when held for an extended period, that leads to back problems. With flexible hamstrings, most of the flexion occurs at the hip joint instead, sparing the lower back, and this is much more comfortable and efficient (*fig. 11.1*).

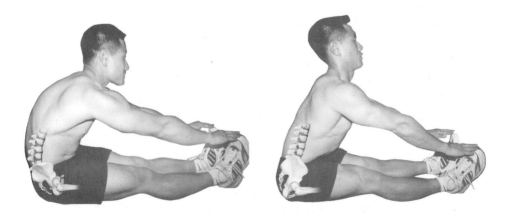

Fig 11.1 Flexible hamstrings allow the lower back to remain straight. Left: Because of the tight hamstrings, flexion at the hip joint is limited and the lower back has to flex to allow the sailor to reach forward. Right: With flexible hamstrings, the sailor is able to reach as far forward through hip flexion alone, while the lower back remains straight. This is more comfortable and efficient.

Stretching

Flexibility is improved through regular stretching. There are three main methods of stretching: static, proprioceptive neuromuscular facilitation (PNF), and ballistic stretches. Static stretches, where the stretch is sustained without jerking, is the safest and is adequate for the sailor's needs. PNF, where the muscle is alternately contracted against a resistance and stretched passively for several repetitions, is effective but it requires a partner and is therefore less practical if alone. Ballistic stretches employ bouncing or jerking movements. They are specific to sports like gymnastics and dancing but not sailing, and are not quite safe for the inexperienced.

Static stretches are thus recommended for sailors. Follow the guidelines below for optimal results:

- Benign as they look, stretching exercises can cause muscle strains. Warm up (e.g. 3-5 min of light jogging) before stretching, and avoid jerking. Also, do not stretch to the point of pain.
- Duration is the key. Hold each stretch for at least 30 s. Muscles naturally tighten at the beginning of the stretch, so hold until the muscles relax spontaneously. In other words, counter the initial spasm by holding longer rather than stretching harder.
- Incorporate stretching sessions into your training and racing routine. Stretch before and after (e.g. while showering) each dry-land or sailing session, and also between races. Make use of the stretching session to collect your thoughts, especially before racing. When performed after the training session or race, stretching may aid recovery.
- Each time you stretch, go through the major muscle groups at least once. If you have the time (e.g. when you get home after training or racing) go through your stretching routine three times.
- Pay special attention to your hamstrings, for the reason stated above. It is important to stretch this muscle before every race or training session. Also, do not neglect your hiking muscles like the quadriceps and hip flexors, as the demands on them are high in Laser sailing, and stretching hastens their recovery.

Stretching to The Rule of 3's

1. *Hold each stretch for 30 s.*
2. *Go through 3 rounds (repetitions) per session per muscle group.*
3. *Stretch 3 times a day – before training, after training, and in the evening.*

Fig. 11.2 and 11.3 illustrate a recommended stretching routine that can be done both on and off the water. The lower body routine (fig. 11.2) is especially important before a race.

Hamstring stretch: Straighten the knee and slowly reach forward, grasping the ankle, toes, or gunwale for leverage. To isolate the hamstrings, keep the lower back straight.

Quadriceps stretch: Keep the trunk upright and pull the heel towards the buttock (you can use your hand instead of the edge of the cockpit). As this also stretches the hip flexors, the stretch should be felt in the front of the hip and thigh.

Hip flexor stretch: Extend the hip joint as shown and feel the stretch in the front of the hip. A variation is to hold the heel against the buttock to stretch the quadriceps at the same time.

Lower back and iliotibial band stretch: Apply firm pressure against the bent knee with the elbow and feel the stretch over the outside of the thigh and buttock.

Abdominal stretch: Try to keep the hips against the deck and feel the stretch in the abdominal muscles.

Bottom stretch: Using the gunwale for leverage, feel a stretch behind the hip.

Fig 11.2 Lower body stretches.

Triceps stretch: *Keep one elbow completely flexed overhead and pull it towards the other side to stretch the triceps.*

Chest and biceps stretch: *Turn the shoulder out and feel the stretch over the biceps and chest.*

Upper back stretch: *Pull one elbow towards the chest to stretch the upper back muscles, especially the rhomboids.*

Forearm flexors stretch: *Extend the wrist fully to stretch out the forearm flexors.*

Fig 11.3 Upper body stretches.

MUSCULAR STRENGTH AND ENDURANCE

Depending on the training variables, muscles can be trained to specifically develop maximum strength, strength endurance, starting strength, explosive strength, and reactive strength capacity. Starting strength and explosive strength are of interest to sprinters, while reactive strength capacity belongs to the realm of jumpers and gymnasts.

For the Laser, *maximum strength* (the highest force that a muscle group can exert) and *strength endurance* (the muscle's ability to sustain a contraction or contract repeatedly) are especially desirable in the muscles used for hiking and sheeting:

- Maximum strength serves as the base upon which other forms of strength, including strength endurance, are built. It also protects against injury resulting from high tensile forces sustained during hiking, torqueing the boat, and various training methods.

- Roughly 25-87 % of the maximum quadriceps strength is used when hiking steadily. If the maximum strength of the quadriceps is increased, then perhaps only 15 % of the maximum strength will be used during hiking. At 15 %, one would expect the quadriceps to take longer to fatigue, thus allowing the sailor to hike longer. In other words, maximum strength is related to, and improves strength endurance.
- Power = Force x Speed. Hence, when maximum strength (i.e. force) is high, explosive strength (i.e. power) is increased even if no specific speed training is done. Developing maximum strength alone thus improves explosive strength (although not as effectively as combined strength and speed training), enabling the sailor to torque the boat more explosively.
- Strength endurance allows the quadriceps and hip flexors to sustain a contraction longer, and this translates to better hiking endurance.

Sailing will develop both maximum strength and strength endurance, but they can be enhanced further through *resistance training*. This is especially true for the development of maximum strength.

Resistance Training Variables
In resistance training, the training variables include:

- Choice of Exercise
- Training load (resistance)
- Training volume
  o Number of repetitions
  o Number of sets
  o Frequency (number of training days per week)
- Inter-set recovery (rest duration between sets)

Depending on the way the training variables are manipulated, the resistance programme can be designed to target muscle growth (hypertrophy), maximum strength, strength endurance, and explosive strength. Of these, we shall focus on hypertrophy and maximum strength (*table 11.1*), as they are most relevant to Laser sailors: hypertrophy training prepares muscles for heavy training loads and is beneficial to underweight sailors; and maximum strength – supplemented by on-water training – improves strength endurance and explosive strength simultaneously.

Table 11.1. Training prescriptions for hypertrophy and maximum strength.

	HYPERTROPHY	**MAXIMUM STRENGTH**
Training Principle	Medium loads High volumes Short inter-set recovery	Heavy loads Moderate volumes Long inter-set recovery
Choice of Exercise	Exercises involving larger muscle groups, where there is greater potential for weight gain.	Exercises involving muscles needed for sailing, especially the hiking and sheeting muscles.
Load	8-12 repetition maximum	4-8 repetition maximum
Sets	6-8 sets	3-6 sets
Frequency	3 or more times a week	3 or more times a week
Inter-set Recovery	30-45 s	1-3 min

Repetition maximum, or RM, is the maximum load that can be lifted a specified number of times. For example, a 10 RM is the maximum load that can be lifted no more or less than 10 times with an all-out effort. As you grow stronger and find that you can perform more repetitions with the same weight, you should increase the load to keep the same RM prescription. Both males and females can use the same RM recommendation as it adjusts for different strength levels, i.e. the 10 RM for the stronger sailor will be heavier than that for the weaker one.

When aiming for hypertrophy or maximum strength, spend a minimum of three weight training sessions per week. Work the whole body during each training session rather than training only limited body parts (i.e. split routines), as a whole-body routine is more sport-specific and timesaving. Later, to maintain your gains (e.g. during the competition phase), resistance training once or twice a week would suffice.

As heavier loads are used to develop maximum strength, it is safer and advisable to spend six or more weeks on a hypertrophy programme to condition the muscles before embarking on a maximum strength programme.

Choice of Resistance Training Exercises

All your muscles can be grouped functionally (*fig. 11.4*) into:

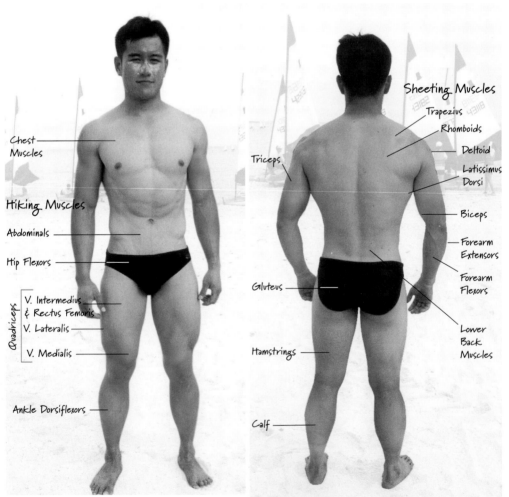

Fig 11.4 Major muscle groups, including the hiking (left) and sheeting (right) muscles.

Muscles for hiking:	Quadriceps
	Hip flexors
	Abdominals
	Ankle dorsiflexors
Muscles for sheeting:	Shoulders & upper back muscles (trapezius, deltoid, rhomboids, latissimus dorsi)
	Biceps
	Forearm flexors (for gripping) and extensors
	Lower back muscles (to stabilize trunk while sheeting)
Other muscles:	Hamstrings, chest muscles, calves, gluteus, triceps, etc.

Although those listed under "other muscles" are not used as much as those in the first two categories, some time should be spent exercising them to achieve a balanced musculature.

For each muscle group, there are various exercises available (*table 11.2*). Base the exercise selection on current priorities. For example, if you find that your quadriceps are not strong enough, but the shoulders are doing fine on the water, then to include two quadriceps exercises (e.g. lunges and wall sits) and only one shoulder / upper back exercise (e.g. bent over rowing) in your programme. Switch to another variation of the exercise every 4-6 weeks, so that the body is continually forced to adapt to a different movement.

Fig 11.5 *Wall sit. Ensure that the VMO (arrow) is activated.*

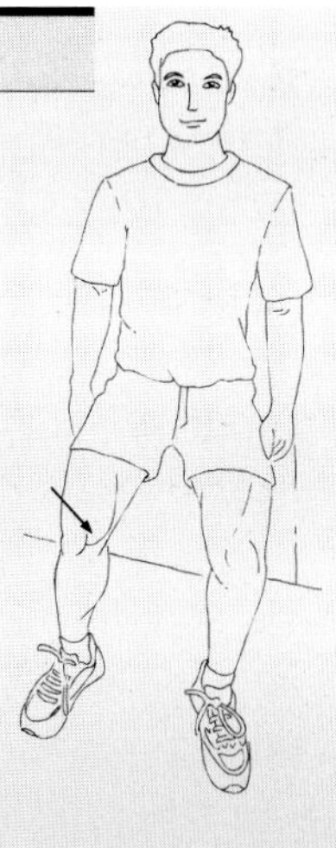

Table 11.2 Exercises categorized according to muscle group.

EXERCISE	DESCRIPTION	
Quadriceps		
Wall Sit (fig. 11.5)	Stand with the back against a wall then slide down until the knees are bent to around 90°-130°. Aim for a total duration of 10-30 min, with short rest pauses. To reduce the risk of knee pain, make a conscious effort to contract the vastus medialis oblique (VMO) muscles.	

Knee Extension - machine	Using the knee extension machine in the gym, work either one or both knees at a time. Point the toes directly upwards or slightly outwards, and hold momentarily at the top. To make this exercise more specific for hiking, hold the knees in extension longer (e.g. for 10 s).
Leg Press - machine	Using a leg press machine, position the feet hip-width apart, toes pointing slightly outwards. Bend the knees to 90°, and push from there. Keep the knees in line with the toes and the lower back in contact with the support at all times.
Walking Lunge - free weight *(fig. 11.6)*	Holding a pair of dumbbells by the side, step forward and lower the back knee close to the ground, get up, and then "walk" one step forward and lower the other knee. Keep the torso upright at all times, and consciously activate the VMOs. Take 10 steps to complete a set. (If there is any difficulty, then perform static lunges instead, and progress to the walking lunge later.)

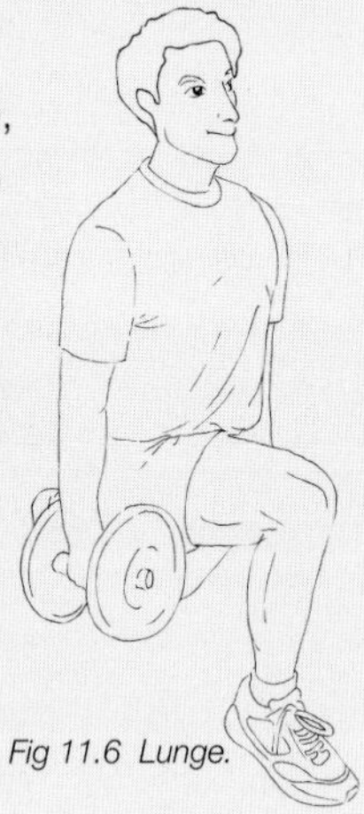

Fig 11.6 Lunge.

Half Squat – free weight	This is an effective hypertrophy and maximum strength exercise as it stimulates large muscle groups with heavy loads. However injuries are common with poor technique, so consult an experienced instructor if unfamiliar with this exercise. Full squats are not specific for sailors, as the functional range of knee motion during sailing is the last 30° of extension.

Abdominals and Hip Flexors

Crunch *(fig. 11.7)*	Lie face up on the mat with knees bent to 90°, feet planted on the ground, and fingers cupping the ears. Raise the upper back as high as possible above the ground, hold momentarily, then lower slowly. Feel the abdominals tighten with every controlled repetition. Try 3 sets of 20 repetitions with a minute's rest between sets and gradually work up to 6 or more sets over the next few weeks.

Fig 11.7 *The basic crunch exercise.*

Variations:

- Repeat the above, but with feet in the air, and knees and hips bent at 90°.
- With feet either on the ground or in the air, bring the left elbow towards right knee and vice versa.
- With both lower limbs pointing to the sky (knees almost straight), reach up and touch the toes, and then slowly lower the shoulders back to the mat.

Sit-Up

Start with 2 sets of 20 repetitions and gradually work up to 6 or more sets over a few weeks. As you get fitter, hold a light weight against the chest to add more resistance, or increase the repetitions.

Reverse Sit-Up

Lying face up with the knees straight, raise the feet until the lower limbs are vertical, then lower slowly with control and repeat before the heels touch the ground. Keep the lower back in contact with the ground at all times by tightening the abdominals and lower the feet only to the level before the lower back arches upwards. As the abdominals get stronger, the feet will eventually be able to reach within an inch of the ground without lifting lower back off the ground.

Hiking Bench
(fig. 11.8)

Short of being on the water, the hiking bench offers specificity. Stay flat out for progressively longer durations.

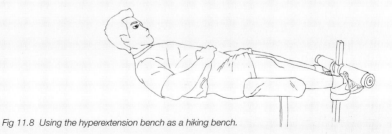

Fig 11.8 *Using the hyperextension bench as a hiking bench.*

Advanced Hiking Exercises

These exercises should be introduced only after many weeks of the more basic exercises.

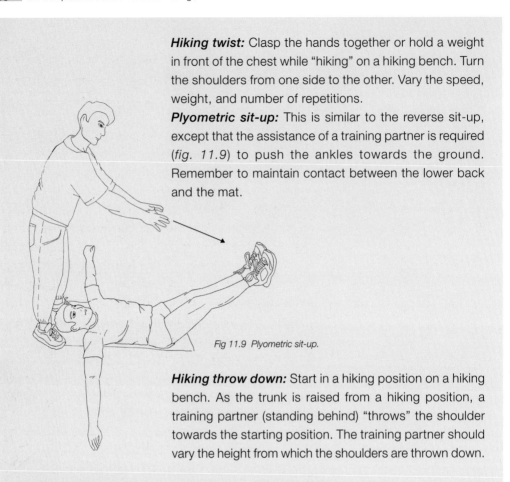

Hiking twist: Clasp the hands together or hold a weight in front of the chest while "hiking" on a hiking bench. Turn the shoulders from one side to the other. Vary the speed, weight, and number of repetitions.

Plyometric sit-up: This is similar to the reverse sit-up, except that the assistance of a training partner is required (*fig. 11.9*) to push the ankles towards the ground. Remember to maintain contact between the lower back and the mat.

Fig 11.9 Plyometric sit-up.

Hiking throw down: Start in a hiking position on a hiking bench. As the trunk is raised from a hiking position, a training partner (standing behind) "throws" the shoulder towards the starting position. The training partner should vary the height from which the shoulders are thrown down.

Shoulder Muscles

Shoulder Press Seated with the trunk upright, hold a dumbbell in each hand, palms facing forward. Starting at shoulder level, push directly overhead, then lower slowly.

Standing Lateral Raise Standing with the dumbbells by the side in each hand, raise the weights laterally to shoulder height and hold momentarily before lowering slowly.

Bent-Over Lateral Raise Sitting on one end of a bench with a dumbbell in each hand, bend over so that the head is above the knees. Raise the weights sideways until horizontal, hold momentarily, then lower slowly.

Upright Row
- free weight

Standing, hold a barbell with hands less than shoulder-width apart, and raise the bar towards the chin (without knocking out your teeth), elbows out to the sides. Hold it there momentarily before lowering slowly.

Upper and Lower Back Muscles

Seated Cable Row
- machine

Using the low pulley from the appropriate machine, sit with the lower limbs straight (bend the knees slightly if the hamstrings are not flexible enough yet). Keeping the torso upright, grasp the handle with two hands, and pull towards the lower chest, arching the shoulders backwards in the process. Use the upper back (i.e. attempt to squeeze your shoulder blades together) rather than the biceps. For variation and specificity to sailing, perform with one arm.

One-Arm Dumbbell Row
- free weight
(fig. 11.10)

With one knee and hand on a bench such that the torso is horizontal as shown, grasp a dumbbell with the other hand and pull it towards the shoulder from ground level, knuckles facing forward. Again, use the upper back rather than biceps to pull.

Fig 11.10   One-arm dumbbell row.

Pull-Up (Chin-Up)

Vary the width of the grip, and the grip itself by facing the palms in or out. For each set, attempt as many repetitions as possible to the point of fatigue. After a minute's rest, attempt another all-out set. Keep going until the total repetitions (i.e. adding the repetitions from all the sets) reaches 15. Progressively increase the total repetitions for the session to 40. When a 40-repetition total can be achieved within three tries, then put on a weight belt to provide more resistance.

Biceps [1]

Standing Barbell Biceps Curl - free weight	Hold the barbell in front with palms facing forward and hands shoulder-width apart. Lift the bar towards the chest without allowing the elbows to move backwards or sideways.
Seated Dumbbell Curl - free weight	Sitting upright on one end of a bench and holding a dumbbell in each hand with the palms facing forward, alternately lift the weights towards the shoulders. Keep the elbows tucked to the side of the body.

Forearm Flexors and Extensors

Wrist Flexion - free weight	Holding a barbell, support both forearms horizontally on a bench, with the hands and wrists hanging over the edge of the bench, palms facing up. Flex the wrists to lift the bar as high as it can go, and then lower slowly, ensuring that the forearms remain in contact with the bench throughout.
Wrist Extension - free weight	Same as above, except that the palms are facing down, and a lighter weight will have to be used.

Lower Back

Superman	Lie face down on a mat with your upper limbs outstretched, as if flying like Superman. Without lifting the head, raise one upper limb and the opposite lower limb off the ground, and then lower both. Keep the limbs straight. Now do the same for the other limbs. Alternate sides, until 20 repetitions are completed. Progressively increase the number of sets.
Hyperextension *(fig. 11.11)*	Adjust the hyperextension (Roman) bench such that the hips are able to flex fully, unhindered by the supporting pad. The starting and finishing positions are as shown. Hold momentarily at the top and pause at the bottom before starting the next repetition.

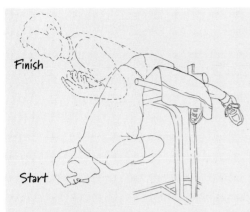

Finish

Start

Variations:

- At the top, twist the upper body to one side and then the other.
- If 20 repetitions can be performed effortlessly, then increase the resistance by holding a light weight (e.g. 5 kg) against the chest.

Fig 11.11 Start and finish positions of the hyperextension exercise. When more proficient, hold a weight to the chest.

Chest [2]

Flat / Incline Bench Press - free weight

Lie on a flat / incline bench and grasp the bar slightly greater than shoulder-width apart, such that the forearms are vertical. Lower slowly, approximately to the nipples, then drive bar upwards.

Flat Dumbbell Bench Press - free weight

Lie on a bench and grasp a dumbbell in each hand. Start with the dumbbells lowered to chest level, and drive upwards, keeping the forearm vertical throughout the movement.

Hamstrings

Leg Curl - machine

Lying face down on the machine with ankles against the rollers, curl the legs towards the buttocks and release slowly to the starting position. Exercise both or one side at a time.

Calf

Calf Raise

Stand with the front half of the feet on the edge of a step. Starting with the heel below the level of the forefoot, push up onto a tiptoe position, hold momentarily at the top, and lower slowly.

Single-Leg Calf Raise

As above, but standing on one foot.

---

1 It is not absolutely necessary to do specific biceps exercises since the biceps are used, to a certain degree, in other exercises like the upright row, seated cable row, one-arm dumbbell row, and pull up. However, if your biceps tend to fatigue when steering in heavy air, then you might need to add these specific exercises to your programme.

2 Chest exercises develop muscles to balance the strong upper backs that sailors tend to have from all the pulling actions, and contribute some lean mass to increase righting moment. The triceps are also exercised at the same time.

When performing the above exercises, take the following precautions:

- It is important to get the technique right: if unsure, do not hesitate to clarify with a qualified strength and conditioning coach. Poor technique may lead to injuries and do not deliver the desired results.
- Breathing: exhale as you exert.
- Warm up (e.g. rowing) and stretch before commencing resistance exercises. The recommended sequence is: 3-5 min of warm up ➤ stretch ➤ resistance training ➤ stretch
- In addition, do a warm up set by performing 10 repetitions at half the usual training load for each exercise.
- Muscle soreness tends to be delayed by about a day, so you might feel fine during the session and ache only afterwards. For optimal results, you should be aching only slightly: if you feel so stiff that it is an effort to move about, then you have overdone it.
- Resistance training supplements on-water training – it cannot fully replace the time spent on the water.

Sample Resistance Training Programme for the Beginner

If you have never done any resistance training before, select a lull period on the racing calendar to start your dry-land training programme. *Table 11.3* is a simple programme to start off with.

The sample programme is divided into four phases. The *familiarisation phase* allows you to get accustomed to the exercises, and is not intended to be strenuous. Here, it is acceptable to do submaximal sets, i.e. you can do say, 10 repetitions using your 15 RM load. The *hypertrophy phase* conditions the muscles and increases lean mass, while the *maximum strength phase* is designed for maximum strength development. The *maintenance phase*, where only a handful of exercises are performed once a week during the racing season, is intended to help preserve your hard-earned gains from the previous phases. After completing this training cycle, commence a new cycle with a programme containing additional exercises from *table 11.2* and step up the volume and intensity for each exercise. For each phase, you do not have to perform the exercises corresponding to the empty rows in the table.

Table 11.3 Sample resistance training programme for beginners.

EXERCISE	FAMILIARISATION 2 weeks				HYPERTROPHY 8 weeks				STRENGTH 8 weeks				MAINTENANCE (racing season) 12 weeks			
	Load	Reps	Sets	Freq	Load	Reps	Sets	Freq	Load	Reps	Sets	Freq	Load	Reps	Sets	Freq
Leg press	15 RM	10	2	2	10 RM	10	3	3	6 RM	6	3	3	6 RM	6	3	1
Seated cable row	15 RM	10	2	2					8 RM	8	3	3	8 RM	8	3	1
Knee extension	15 RM	10	2	2	10 RM	10	3	3								
Pull-up (chin ups)					BW	15	–	3	BW	20	–	3				
Flat bench press	15 RM	10	2	2	12 RM	12	3	3	8 RM	8	3	3	8 RM	8	3	1
Leg curl	15 RM	10	2	2	12 RM	12	3	3	8 RM	8	3	3				
One-arm dumbbell row	15 RM	10	2	2	12 RM	12	3	3								
Standing lateral raise	15 RM	10	2	2	12 RM	12	3	3	8 RM	8	3	3	8 RM	8	3	1
Hyperextension	BW	10	2	2	BW	12	3	3	BW	12	3	3	BW	12	3	1
Crunch	BW	20	2	2	BW	20	3	3	BW	20	3	3	BW	20	3	1
Sit-up					BW	20	3	3	BW	20	3	3				

RM = repetition maximum; BW = body weight (i.e. no added resistance); Reps = repetitions; Freq = frequency

At each session, exercise the bigger muscle groups first while alternating the upper and lower body exercises. The exercise order as shown in the sample programme has already been arranged in accordance with this principle. Ease into the prescribed load and number of sets for each phase progressively, as sudden increases in volume (e.g. at the beginning of the hypertrophy phase) or intensity (e.g. at the beginning of the strength phase) can be counterproductive. The sets prescribed in the table do not include the warm-up set. Consult a qualified strength and conditioning coach if unsure.

Core Stability

The effectiveness of upper body movements is dependent on a stable base, that is, the lower body. Connecting the upper and lower body is the lower back and abdominal area, and this tends to be the weak link between the two. Without stability in this area, forces cannot be transferred effectively between the upper and lower body, as when torqueing the boat. Also, back problems may result.

The reason for this weak link is that the body tends to rely more on stronger muscles and less on the weaker ones to execute a movement. Over time, this motor pattern is reinforced, leading to muscle imbalances and potential injury. Muscles that are prone to this are the abdominal muscles, especially the transversus abdominis, and the lower back muscles. Core stability training aims to appropriately activate these "lazy" muscles during functional movement patterns.

Exercises are initially performed without resistance. As a start, lie facing up on the ground with the knees bent. Now, pull the belly button in towards the spine by contracting the abdominal muscles (especially the lower abdominals) and feel the lower spine coming into contact with the ground. There should be no gap between the lumbar spine and the ground for your hand to pass through. In this position, the core is strongest since the increased intra-abdominal pressure gives added support to the spine. As you improve, dynamic movements like raising the legs are added. Even later, training aids like Swiss balls and medicine balls are used to increase the level of difficulty. For example, you might do push-ups with your feet resting on the Swiss ball, which provides an unstable support, making it more difficult for you to hold the ideal trunk posture. A conscious effort is necessary to sustain this initially, but the idea is to ultimately do this "automatically." Learn how to breathe and go about all your activities with this posture, even when upright. When you are walking, talking, eating, doing bench presses, performing squats, sailing, etc. – remember to pull the belly button towards the spine and reduce the arching (lordosis) of the lumber spine.

CARDIO-RESPIRATORY ENDURANCE

Cardio-respiratory (aerobic) fitness is crucial to marathon runners. But what can it offer to the competitive sailor, whose race is of a different nature?

- Aerobic fitness hastens recovery after a burst of high-intensity activity (e.g. starts, tacks, mark roundings).
- When sailing upwind, 40-60 % of our maximal aerobic capacity is utilised, indicating that a moderate level of aerobic fitness is necessary. With aerobic fitness, you will feel less breathless and concentrate better.
- Hiking involves sustained contractions of the quadriceps and hip flexors, and this impedes blood flow through the muscles, starving them of oxygen and other nutrients. Aerobic training increases capillary growth around the muscle fibres, thus increasing much needed blood flow.
- During hiking, the blood pressure rises sharply. Aerobic training conditions the heart and blood vessels to withstand the high blood pressures associated with hiking. Furthermore, it reduces the rise in blood pressure that tends to occur with age.
- If you are too heavy for the Laser, cardio-respiratory endurance training is an effective way of burning calories.

Mode of Activity

Aerobic training is simple. It involves performing any activity that uses large muscle groups, that can be maintained continuously, and that is rhythmical and aerobic in nature. Of the many activities to choose from, the main ones are:

Cycling   Three-time Laser World Champion, Glenn Bourke, was frustrated at being a weak hiker and decided to get out of sailing for a few years to participate in competitive cycling. When he returned to the sport, he found hiking a lot easier. Cycling is specific to the thigh muscles and is not as damaging as running, especially for heavier individuals.

Rowing

This works both the upper and lower body at the same time, and is easy on the joints (*fig. 11.12*). Olympic Boardsailing Gold Medallist, Lee Lai Shan, uses a rowing ergometer for her aerobic training. (*See Recommended Reading on Concept2 Indoor Rower for training information*.)

Fig 11.12 The rowing ergometer works both the upper and lower body.

Running

As a weight-bearing exercise, running poses a problem for some, especially those who are heavier and those with knee or ankle injuries. However, it is a convenient exercise that can be done at any regatta venue.

Swimming

Swimming utilises the upper body more than the lower body and serious injuries rarely occur. Training with flippers is an excellent way to develop the hip flexors and knee extensors. However the training heart rate tends to be lower compared to running, and those who do not have access to a pool find it inconvenient.

Windy-Weather Sailing

This is of course the most specific to the sailor. You can rely on sailing for aerobic training during the in-season, and use other activities during the off-season.

Cross training (i.e. alternating between activities rather than relying only on one type of activity) is a good way of preventing staleness and overuse injuries, especially since aerobic activities tend to be prolonged.

Training Intensity and Volume

Training intensity (i.e. how hard you train) can be gauged by your exercise heart rate. Your target training heart rate should be 60-90 % of your maximum heart rate, where:

Estimated maximum heart rate (beats per min) = 220 – Age

If you are 20 years old, and you intend to exercise at 60 % of your maximum heart rate, then:

Age-related maximal heart rate = 220 – 20 = 200 beats per min
60 % exercise intensity = 0.60 x 200 = 120 beats per min

Training duration is dependent on the intensity: lower-intensity activity should last at least 45 min while higher intensity activity should take at least 30 min. Aerobic training 3-5 days per week is preferable as it has been shown that training fewer than 2 days a week, at less than 60 % of maximum heart rate, for less than 10 min is inadequate for developing and maintaining cardio-respiratory fitness.

Circuit Weight Training

Circuit weight training involves a series of resistance exercises performed in rapid succession (15-30 s of rest between stations) to keep the heart rate elevated. This is a compromise between aerobic endurance training and strength training. Although it has some value in increasing muscular strength in untrained subjects, improvements in cardio-respiratory endurance are minimal. It is a satisfactory training method for the beginner but as aerobic fitness improves, circuit training becomes an inadequate stimulus for further improvements. Its time-efficiency is an advantage, and it can be used to add some variation to the usual gym routine.

ANAEROBIC CAPACITY

A sailing race tends to be interspersed with short bursts of high-intensity activities like all-out hiking during the first 100 m, tacking, mark roundings, and penalty turns. These activities are fuelled by anaerobic metabolism, so the capacity for performing such activities is enhanced by anaerobic training.

Tacking drills, short courses, and all-out hiking are forms of anaerobic training. Interval training is the dry-land version. If you cannot get onto the water for some reason, you might want to incorporate interval training into your dry-land programme as an alternative. In interval training, short bursts of activity are interspersed by recovery periods of partial or complete rest. It can be applied to various activities like road cycling (using hilly terrain), stationary cycling, rowing on the ergometer, running, and swimming.

Guidelines for work : rest ratios are found in *table 11.4*. It is best to vary the work : rest ratios every few weeks. Effort during the duration of load should be maximal. During the recovery period, you can either rest partially (e.g. a 30 s rowing sprint followed by 90 s of light rowing) or completely (i.e. stop rowing during the recovery period). Partial rest is preferable as it simulates sailing more closely. Interval training is stressful to the body, so in order to allow adequate recovery between sessions, no more than 2-3 interval training sessions should be performed each week.

Table 11.4 Interval training guidelines.

	TRAINING FOR SHORT BURSTS (e.g. double-tacks)	**TRAINING FOR MEDIUM BURSTS (e.g. hiking off the start line)**	**TRAINING FOR LONG BURSTS (e.g. windy reach)**
Duration of load	10-30 s	30-120 s	120-300 s
Duration of recovery	30-90 s	60-240 s	120-300 s
Work : rest ratio	1:3	1:2	1:1
Repetitions	20-30	10-20	3-5

ON-WATER FITNESS TRAINING

Do not forget that we can also increase our fitness while sailing. Often, too much emphasis is placed on land-based training routines to the detriment of developing on-water skills and capacities. Sailing skills can be developed at the same time as fitness using drills like:

- Working on upwind boat speed and sail trim in windy conditions.
- Close reaching.
- Laps around a very short course when windy.

- Tacking every 15 m in a race against a training partner.
- Long upwind hiking stints.
- Applying a very close cover to another boat upwind (tacking duel).
- Beating and reaching with the ratchet block off.
- Placing extra load on the thighs by not wearing hiking pants.
- Wearing heavier clothing on the trunk to increase the work done by the hiking muscles during the above activities.

On-water sailing is best for fitness development because the gains in fitness are exactly in the right areas. Therefore, the training will be of higher quality and more efficient despite the extra time spent rigging, unrigging, getting changed and so on. Another advantage over dry-land training is discovering things that do not happen very often especially in terms of the weather, waves, and boat handling due to the longer hours spent on the water. Besides, sailing in a good breeze is more fun than being in the gym.

A long reach in a good breeze provides an excellent cardio workout.

HOME FITNESS TEST

It is a good idea to monitor your fitness to track your progress and see if your training programme is effective. Below are five easy tests which you can use, together with targets to work towards. The tests should be done at regular intervals, say every three months, so that you can plot your progress. For reliable results, they should be performed in the same order each time and the measurement procedure should be consistent.

Bodyweight

Using an accurate set of scales, weigh yourself with minimal clothing in the morning, after waking up and going to the bathroom, but before breakfast.

Target: Standard rig: 78-83 kg
Radial rig: 60-75 kg

Resting Heart Rate

A lower heart rate at rest indicates good cardio-respiratory fitness. Count the number of beats over one minute, using either the radial or carotid pulse. This should be done on waking, before getting out of bed.

Target: < 60 beats per min

Sit and Reach Test

This monitors hamstring flexibility. Sit on the floor with the lower limbs straight in front, without shoes and toes pointing up. Place one hand over the top of the other, fingers overlapping, elbows straight. Lean forward as far as possible, sliding the hands towards or past your heels, while keeping the knees straight. The full stretch must be held for 3 s, with no bouncing allowed. Measure the distance between the fingertips and the soles of the feet with a ruler placed on the floor. If the fingers cannot go beyond the heels, a negative score is recorded.

Target: Club sailor: +6 cm
National level: +12 cm
International level: +18 cm

Crunch

The number of crunches performed reflects the endurance of the abdominal muscles. Lie on the floor with the knees bent to 90° and the feet flat on the floor. Start with the arms straight, hands resting on top of the thighs, head on the floor. Slowly curl up so that the fingertips just touch the bottom of the kneecaps then return to the starting position. Complete the crunches slowly with strict form, at a rate of one every 3 s. Record the maximum you can do.

Target: Club sailor: 20 reps
National level: 40 reps

Pull-Up (Chin-Up)   Pull-ups will give an indication of the strength endurance of the back muscles. Use an overhand, shoulder-width grip. The chin must touch the bar for the repetition to count. The elbows must be straight before commencing the next repetition, and there should be no swinging. Record the maximum repetitions completed.

Target: Club sailor: 2 reps
National sailor: 6 reps
International level: 12+ reps

"*It took a number of years of good training to be fit enough ...
... the fastest techniques in small boat sailing involve more activity
than before: The trunk is leant back further and thrown forward
and/or backwards in response to every wave; the sail is trimmed
almost as regularly to keep it at the optimum angle to the wind
and every chance to surf the boat down a wave is leapt upon ...*"

Michael Blackburn

Chapter 12

Sailing Nutrition

content by **Gary Slater**

*T*he modern athlete must be aware of the wide range of factors that can influence his performance, and nutrient needs is one of these factors. What you eat and drink will have an impact on performance and thus demands its own planning and preparation. The Laser sailor must have suitable nutritional strategies to deal with unique challenges like spending upwards of six hours on the water with limited storage space for food and water. Racing over several days requires consideration of recovery strategies while a narrow optimal weight range imposes further challenges.

TRAINING DIET – THE CENTREBOARD OF GOOD NUTRITION

No one magic food exists with all of the nutrients we need in the correct proportions. Rather, you need to select a wide variety of foods to provide the nutrient needs of everyday training. Training brings with it additional demands for energy and nutrients such as carbohydrate, protein, and fluid. The energy content of food is measured in kilocalories (kcal or Cal) or kilojoules (kJ) were 1 kcal = 1,000 calories = 4.2 kJ. Calories are provided by the carbohydrate, fat, and protein in your diet. Alcohol too has calories, but it also brings with it the risk of dehydration and other detrimental effects. The amount of energy contained in each varies:

- Carbohydrate   4 kcal/g or 16 kJ/g
- Protein   4 kcal/g or 17 kJ/g
- Fat   9 kcal/g or 37 kJ/g
- Alcohol   7 kcal/g or 29 kJ/g

Sitting idle or during very low intensity exercise, the body uses a combination of both carbohydrate and fat as fuel, but as exercise intensity increases, so too does the reliance on carbohydrate - primarily from muscle and liver glycogen (the storage form of carbohydrate in the body) plus blood glucose. At near maximal intensity exercise, carbohydrates are used almost exclusively. While even the leanest athlete has adequate fat stores, carbohydrate reserves can be readily depleted.

Carbohydrates
A carbohydrate-rich diet offers many advantages. It keeps muscle and liver glycogen stores elevated, providing fuel for training and competition. Additionally, carbohydrate-rich foods are also generally

nutrient-dense, contributing to a large part of the daily vitamin, mineral, and fibre intake. Many carbohydrate-rich foods also contribute moderate amounts of protein. They tend to satisfy the appetite best and are generally low in fat, helping to control body fat levels. For these reasons, carbohydrate-rich foods should form the basis of your meal plan. *Table 12.1* provides a list of nutritious carbohydrate-rich foods and the amount of each food required to obtain 30 g of carbohydrate.

How Much Carbohydrate? While many athletes appreciate the value of a high-carbohydrate diet, few understand their absolute carbohydrate needs and how this can be achieved. Individual carbohydrate requirements will vary depending on bodyweight and activity levels. However, you should aim for a daily carbohydrate intake of 6-10 g per kg of bodyweight. Days involving only 1-2 hours of dry-land cross training may require a carbohydrate intake of 6-8 g/kg bodyweight. While racing, carbohydrate intake goals increase to 9-10 g/kg, matching the greater amount of carbohydrate fuel burnt during a full day of sailing. Carbohydrate intake may need to increase to 65-70 % of total energy intake to achieve this goal. Such a high carbohydrate requirement while sailing creates the unique challenge of increasing the intake when space for storage and opportunities to eat and drink are restricted. This will be discussed in greater detail in the competition preparation section.

Calculating Carbohydrate Requirements. Take for example an 80 kg male Laser sailor, training five to six days a week. Assuming he trains 1-2 hours per day during the week, carbohydrate requirements equate to 480-640 g per day (6-8 g/kg x 80 kg) or 16-21 x 30 g serves of carbohydrate-rich food from *table 12.1*. While racing,

Table 12.1 Carbohydrate-rich foods. A serve from any of the options specified provides approximately 30 g of carbohydrate.

FOOD/FLUID	SERVE
Nutritious Carbohydrate Foods	
Rice	½ cup
Noodles / Pasta	⅔ cup
Bread / Fruit Loaf	2 slices
Bread Roll	1 medium
Crumpet	1½
Muffin (English)	1
Muffin (baked)	½ large
Rice Cakes	3 slices
Potato	2 medium
Corn	1 cup
Breakfast Biscuit	3 biscuits
Flake and Fruit Cereal	1 cup
Oats – cooked	1½ cups
Kidney / Baked Beans	1 cup
Cereal Bar	1 bar
Muesli Bar [1]	1½ bars
Fruit Salad	2 cups
Apple / Pear	2 medium
Orange / Mandarin	2 large
Banana	1 medium
Dried Fruit	½ cup
Milk [2]	2½ cups
Yoghurt – Fruit [2]	200 g
Fruit Juice	1½ cups
Refined Carbohydrate Foods	
Jam / Honey / Syrup	2 Tbsp
Sugar	1½ Tbsp
Chocolate [1]	50 g
Ice Cream [1]	6 scoops
Potato Chips [1]	1 cup
Jubes / Jelly Beans	50 g
Jelly	¾ cup
Soft Drink	1 can (335 ml)
Cordial	1½ cups
Ice Block	2
Sports Nutrition Supplements	
Sports Drink	2 cups
Carbohydrate Gel	1-1½
High Carbo. Drinks	⅔ cup
Sports Bar	⅔ bar
Carbo. Loader Powder	1½ Tbsp

Source: NUTTAB 1995, Australian Department of Community Services and Health
[1] *Higher fat choice,* [2] *Preference for low-fat varieties*

carbohydrate requirements approximate 720-800 g per day or 24-27 x 30 g carbohydrate serves. The following meal plan, illustrated in *fig. 12.1*, provides 600 g of carbohydrate or 20 serves:

Meal	Food and Fluid	Carbohydrate Serves
Breakfast	2 C breakfast cereal plus 1¼ C milk 1 x banana and 1½ C orange juice	**4½**
Mid-morning	200 g tub low-fat flavoured yoghurt ½ C dried fruit	**2**
Lunch	Noodle soup with 2 C noodles Apple	**3½**
Mid-afternoon	Sandwich with jam / honey	**2**
Evening training	1,000 ml sports drink	**2**
Dinner	Stir-fry with lean meat[1], vegetables[1] 2 C cooked rice, 1 C cordial	**5**
Supper	2 C fruit salad and 1 scoop ice cream	**1**

Fig 12.1 *Example of a meal plan providing 600 g of carbohydrate. Add some lean meat, chicken, or seafood (or vegetarian alternative) and plenty of vegetables for a nutritionally complete intake over the day.*

1 *While the meat and vegetables do not contain much carbohydrate, they provide many other nutrients essential to a well-balanced meal plan. Include animal flesh or vegetarian alternatives and vegetables daily for a well-balanced and nutrient-dense meal plan.*

Check your current carbohydrate intake against recommendations

Follow the same process as above to calculate your current intake:

- *Record all food and drinks consumed in 1 day.*
- *Calculate the number of carbohydrate serves from each meal / snack. Multiply this figure by 30 to obtain your total carbohydrate intake in grams.*
- *Compare this with your recommended intake as per the example.*

Meeting Your Carbohydrate Requirements. Failure to meet your carbohydrate requirements will decrease glycogen stores, promote early fatigue, and delay recovery. Use the following tips to help avoid this:

- Base all meals and snacks on nutritious carbohydrate-rich foods like noodles, rice, pasta, bread, and other flour-based foods, cereals, fruit in all its forms, legumes, and starchy vegetables. These foods should take up most of the room on your plate. It is best to serve these up first at a meal, ensuring they take up at least half of your plate.
- Vegetables are very nutritious but only potato and corn contain significant amounts of carbohydrate. Thus you should accompany a vegetable-based dish with some carbohydrate-rich food e.g. rice, noodles, and bread.
- Include carbohydrate-rich snacks in your meal plan each day. It can be very difficult to achieve carbohydrate requirements from just three meals a day. Snacks such as sandwiches, fruit bread, cereal bars, fruit yoghurts, fresh and dried fruit, low-fat fruit smoothies, pancakes, and scones are excellent choices.
- Include small serves of refined carbohydrate foods like jam and honey. As a very concentrated source of carbohydrate, they can increase the total carbohydrate intake without adding to the bulk of a meal. These are especially good choices for athletes with very high carbohydrate requirements, e.g. during the hypertrophy phase of your resistance training programme.
- Make use of carbohydrate drinks like sports drinks and diluted cordials. They can be especially useful while exercising, helping to achieve both carbohydrate and fluid needs.

Carbohydrate intake before, during and after exercise is also critical to maximising your performance. This will be addressed in the section on competition preparation.

Protein

Protein is a normal part of your diet, a nutrient widely distributed among animal and plant foods. It was previously a common belief that protein was the major fuel used during exercise. We now know that carbohydrate and fat are our main energy sources, yet protein has many essential roles in the body. Dietary protein has two possible fates – it can be either used in growth and repair of body tissues or burnt for fuel like carbohydrate and fat. Growth and recovery are essential to the hardworking Laser sailor looking to improve his boat speed.

Each protein is made up of differing combinations of amino acids. In fact, our dietary need for protein is actually a need for amino acids. Twenty amino acids make up all of the proteins in our diet. Eight of these are essential amino acids - the body cannot make them, so they must come from the diet. Protein from animal food contains all the essential amino acids (complete protein) while plant protein does not (incomplete protein). Choosing a wide variety of protein-containing food ensures that both vegetarians and non-vegetarians obtain adequate amounts of essential amino acids. While meat and dairy foods are especially good sources of protein, many plant foods also contain significant quantities of protein (*table 12.2*).

Table 12.2 Sources of animal and plant proteins. Each serve contains 10 g of protein.

Animal	Plant
70 g cottage cheese	100 g wholemeal bread (about 3 slices)
40 g cheese	90 g breakfast cereal
2 medium eggs	220 g baked beans
30-35 g beef, lamb or chicken	300 ml soy milk
50 g fish	150 g lentils
150 ml liquid meal supplement	120 g tofu
200 ml yoghurt	2 cups steamed rice
300 ml milk	50 g nuts

Source: NUTTAB 1995, Australian Department of Community Services and Health

How Much Protein? Muscle protein is constantly being made and broken down. Some of this protein is recycled in the body while the remainder must come from the diet. The recommended dietary intake (RDI) for protein in the general population is 55 g a day or just under 1 g/kg bodyweight daily. Both strength and endurance athletes have greater protein needs than inactive people, with strength athletes requiring 1.6-1.7 g/kg/day (nearly twice the RDI) and endurance athletes about 1.2-1.4 g/kg/day (about 1.5 times the RDI). With many sailors undertaking a combination of both strength and endurance training, a protein intake of 1.4-1.6 g/kg/day will more than adequately meet your daily needs.

Fortunately, the high food intake of most athletes ensures a generous protein intake that is usually well above requirements. As food intake is increased with the additional energy needs of training, the additional protein needed is easily achieved from a diet providing 12-15 % of total energy as protein. Take for example, Tim, a national-level Laser sailor:

Weight:	80 kg
Energy needs:	16,000 kJ (3,820 kcal) per day
Protein needs:	A typical diet provides 12-15 % of his energy (1,920-2,400 kJ) from protein. As one gram of protein contains 17 kJ, this equates to 113-141 g protein (1,920 ÷ 17; 2,400 ÷ 17) or 1.4-1.8 g protein/kg body mass, adequately meeting his increased protein needs.

A high-carbohydrate, moderate-protein diet meeting all nutrient requirements can easily be achieved with sensible food selection. Many protein-rich foods are also excellent sources of minerals like calcium (milk, cheese, yoghurt) and iron (meat, fish, chicken). Try to include a small serve of protein-rich food at each meal and snack. For example milk on cereal, a tub of yoghurt, lean cold meat or cheese in a sandwich, and lean meat, fish, chicken or vegetarian alternative with your evening meal. Following this simple guideline will help to ensure an adequate protein intake.

Inadequate protein intake may cause loss of muscle, slow recovery, and serious health consequences if continued for some time. Few athletes are at risk of eating too little protein. However, some ill-informed athletes may put themselves in this situation by replacing protein-rich foods with extra carbohydrate foods. Those following low-calorie diets are also at risk of eating inadequate protein, and whatever they consume is more likely to be used as muscle fuel, leaving little for muscle repair and growth.

While heavily training sailors have greater protein needs than inactive people, the very high protein intakes by some (who are possibly influenced by ill-informed bodybuilders and magazines) are unnecessary and unlikely to enhance athletic performance. Diets that are excessively high in protein may promote dehydration and calcium loss from the body and displace other important nutrients from the diet. Protein-rich foods are also generally more expensive and some can be a major source of artery-clogging saturated fat. The excess protein is not stored; rather it is used as an energy source, similar to carbohydrate and fat.

Fat

Dietary fat is one of the most commonly discussed yet poorly understood nutrients. With approximately twice the energy of carbohydrate and protein per gram, fat is a very concentrated source of energy which provides essential fatty acids and fat-soluble vitamins essential for maintaining health. Fat also enhances the flavour and texture of many foods and simplifies the cooking process. It is an essential component of a well-balanced meal plan.

How Much Fat? For most people, it is not the lack of fat in their diet but the excess that is a concern. Ingesting too much fat carries with it the potential of becoming overweight and developing lifestyle related disorders like cardiovascular disease and some cancers. Of more immediate concern to the athlete is that high-fat diets limit carbohydrate intake. Choosing a diet with less than 30 % of energy coming from fat will help ensure that nutrient needs for fat and its associated nutrients are met without compromising carbohydrate intake. The following tips will help to limit excessive fat intake:

- Choose low-fat methods of cooking such as grilling, dry or light frying, baking on a rack, microwaving, steaming, or poaching. All these techniques require little or no added fat or oil. When light frying, choose a non-stick pan and use an oil spray.
- Choose lean cuts of meat and chicken. Trim off all the fat and remove the skin from chicken prior to cooking. When buying meat, look for the cuts without marbling.
- Be aware of the fat added to many foods: butter, margarine, or mayonnaise on bread; oil-based dressings on salad; oil in tinned fish and meat; or cream (coconut or dairy) in sauces. Use these sparingly or try low-fat alternatives, e.g. oil-free dressings, low-fat mayonnaise, evaporated skim milk with coconut essence, and tinned fish in water or brine.

- Use low-fat varieties of foods that are now readily available, e.g. low-fat dairy products.
- Beware of misleading claims or food labels like "Cholesterol-free," "Reduced Fat," or "Light". Learn how to read food labels so better choices can be made.
- When dining out, choose lower fat options. This will be especially important if you are racing overseas or if you lead a busy lifestyle and rely heavily on takeaways. Look for options that are based on noodles, rice, or pasta with a healthy serve of vegetables and some lean meat, fish, or chicken. Avoid deep-fried choices, creamy or satay sauces, and options with lots of added oil.
- High fat snacks like potato or corn crisps, nuts, chocolate, biscuits, and cakes should only be enjoyed in small quantities. They should not form the bulk of your mid-meal snacks. Instead, take high-carbohydrate, low-fat snacks like sandwiches, fruit bread, fruit, cereal bars, scones, low-fat muffins, and low-fat fruit yoghurt.

Hydration

Despite exercising in an aquatic environment, total sweat production and thus fluid requirements can be high for sailors over the course of a day. This is especially so during the hot summer months or during windy days when work rates are high. Even before sweat losses from exercise are considered, the average person requires about 2 L of fluid per day. Sweating is the body's most important method of dissipating excess body heat and it is influenced by exercise intensity and environmental conditions. Basically, the hotter it is and the harder you work, the more you sweat. While sweat rates vary between individuals, it is the ability to match these rates with adequate fluid intake that is most important. Failure to do this results in dehydration, where the fluid content of the body drops below normal. Dehydration compromises:

- Endurance exercise performance.
- Thermoregulation (ability to regulate body temperature), increasing the risk of heat cramps, heat exhaustion, and heat stroke.
- Mental function and skill co-ordination, and increases the perception of effort.

- Gastrointestinal function, increasing the risk of nausea / vomiting and slowing the rate of fluid absorption. Thus, as you become dehydrated it becomes increasingly difficult to reverse the fluid deficit!

Even mild dehydration (< 2 % bodyweight reduction) can negatively affect exercise performance, and the more dehydrated you are, the more your performance suffers.

The voluntary fluid intake of many athletes replaces less than two-thirds of sweat losses. Possibly this is because most people rely on thirst – a very poor indicator of fluid requirements – to gauge their fluid needs. Often you will not become thirsty until some degree of dehydration is present.

How Much Fluid? A recent study by the Sports Medicine and Research Centre, Singapore, looked at the practices of club sailors in warm and humid conditions (29-31 °C, 73-82 % humidity, average wind speed 6 knots). The group averaged 1.6 % dehydration during 6 1/2 hours on the water, of which only 3 1/2 hours involved racing. Furthermore, almost 30 % of the group incurred dehydration in excess of 2 % body mass, certainly enough to significantly impair performance. The dehydration observed was most likely due to the low fluid intake of just 900 ml (range 0-2,500 ml) for the day. All this in the calm conditions of a 6-knot breeze. An increase in wind strength would certainly increase work rates and hence sweat losses and the potential for even higher levels of dehydration.

Fig 12.2 A sailor takes time out to replace fluid losses between races. Small amounts of fluid taken regularly (e.g. 150-250 ml every 15 min) will maximise fluid absorption and reduce abdominal discomfort.

Meeting Fluid Requirements. Remaining well hydrated throughout a day of sailing requires a suitable strategy, one that takes into consideration your limited opportunities to drink while racing and the lack of storage space. Use the following guidelines to assist you in remaining well hydrated while sailing (*fig. 12.2*):

- Start each sail well hydrated, making sure you have replaced fluid losses from the previous session. Experiment with a moderate volume of fluid (about 5 ml/kg body mass or 400 ml for 80 kg sailor) in the 15-30 min prior to racing. This will maximise the rate of fluid absorption. Sports drinks contain a small amount of salt that will help improve the absorption and retention of the ingested fluid.

- Start drinking early and at regular intervals in an attempt to match fluid intake with sweat rates. With a little training you should be able to tolerate 600-1,000 ml of fluid per hour or 150-250 ml every 15 min. Take advantage of the period prior to the start and the break between races. If the conditions are such that it is impossible to drink while racing, the interval between races becomes even more critical. You should be able to tolerate 300-500 ml of fluid during this time.

- Ensure you have sufficient fluids for an entire day of sailing. Carrying a 750-1,000 ml drink bottle with you while racing is an excellent idea. Besides ensuring a ready supply of fluid, seeing the bottle is a constant reminder to drink. The remainder of your fluids should be carried on your support boat.

- Make use of sports drinks - they help to achieve both fluid and carbohydrate needs simultaneously. Furthermore, most find sports drinks more palatable than water and this ensures more fluid is consumed, reducing the potential for dehydration. The small amount of sodium in sports drinks enhances palatability, maintains the drive to drink, and promotes retention of the fluid consumed. Keeping drinks chilled (15-22 °C) in a cooler is another way of improving palatability.

Monitoring hydration status.

- Monitor your weight before and after sailing. Any weight loss during a session reflects an accumulated fluid deficit. For example, 2 kg weight loss equates to a fluid deficit of 2 L. Always attempt to keep the fluid deficit to less than 1 kg. During recovery, any fluid deficit should be matched with an amount of fluid equivalent to 150 % of losses. This accounts for continuing sweat losses and urine production.

The same guidelines are applicable to dry-land training. As with any new dietary intervention, experiment with your fluid intake during training. This will give you insight into the amounts of fluid you can tolerate.

COMPETITION PREPARATION

Pre-race Nutrition

What you eat and drink prior to a day of racing will have a real impact on performance and thus demands special consideration. The goal of your pre-race diet should be to optimise fuel stores and hydration levels while limiting abdominal discomfort. The emphasis should be on meals that meet the following guidelines:

- Rich in carbohydrate.
- Low in fat.
- Based on food and fluids you are familiar with and enjoy.
- Low in fibre.
- Include plenty of fluid.

Eating prior to a full day's racing is essential. This helps to top up muscle and liver glycogen stores and optimise hydration while helping maintain blood glucose levels. Larger meals are best consumed 3-4 hours before launching while smaller snacks can usually be tolerated 1-2 hours before launching. A meal containing 2-4 g/kg bodyweight of carbohydrate may help to reduce fatigue by increasing carbohydrate availability while racing. Experiment during training to identify choices and quantities you feel most comfortable with.

If racing gives you butterflies, liquid meal supplements or home-made shakes may be the best choice as they are absorbed from the intestine faster than solid foods. *Table 12.3* provides examples of suitable pre-race meal and snack ideas. The amount of carbohydrate ingested will depend on the quantity of food and fluids consumed. Refer to *table 12.1* to calculate the carbohydrate content of your pre-race meal.

Your glycogen stores and hydration status are the result of eating and exercise practices from the previous 24-36 hours. Thus, an increase in carbohydrate intake which coincides with a reduction in training volume (tapering) 1-3 days prior to racing will help to load up your fuel stores. Aim for a carbohydrate intake of 9-10 g/kg bodyweight during the few days prior to a regatta.

Table 12.3 Low-fat, high-carbohydrate options for pre-race meals and snacks.

Breakfast cereal / porridge with low-fat milk and fruit

Bread / toast / muffins / crumpets with jam / honey / syrup and fruit juice

Pancakes with maple syrup / jam / lemon / honey and fruit juice or smoothie

Baked beans[1] / tinned spaghetti on toast

Fruit smoothie based on low-fat milk / soy milk, fruit, and low-fat yoghurt

Liquid meal supplement

Sandwiches or rolls with low-fat fillings, e.g. banana / jam / honey

Rice / noodle / pasta dish with low-fat sauce, e.g. napolitana (tomato)

Cereal bar / sports bar and sports drink

Fresh fruit and low-fat fruit yoghurt

[1] High fibre choice

Making use of compact, low-bulk / low-fibre carbohydrate foods and fluids during this time can help to achieve higher carbohydrate goals while small and frequent meals will help minimise any gastrointestinal discomfort. Carbohydrate-rich drinks (e.g. fruit juice, sports drinks, cordial, soft drinks, or commercially available carbohydrate loading powders) can be especially useful for boosting carbohydrate and fluid intake at the same time. It may also help to reduce the servings of low-carbohydrate foods (e.g. protein-rich options like meat or non-starchy vegetables) during the final few days prior to a regatta. Carbohydrate-rich foods must remain the priority.

For our 80 kg sailor, carbohydrate requirements while racing equate to 720-800 g carbohydrate per day or 24-27 x 30 g carbohydrate serves from *table 12.1*. The addition of:

- 1½ C fruit juice (1 x 30 g Carbohydrate serve)
- A can of soft drink (1 serve)
- 50 g of jelly beans (1 serve)
- A more generous serve of jam or honey on the sandwich (1 serve)
- 4½ Tbsp of a carbohydrate loader powder (3 serves)

over the course of a day would increase carbohydrate content of the sample meal plan previously described from 600 g (20 serves) to 800 g (27 serves) without causing a significant increase in total food volume.

Eating on the Water

Muscle glycogen stores can be depleted after just 90-120 min of high-intensity dry-land exercise. While it is likely that carbohydrate stores are depleted at a slower rate while sailing, the threat of 'hitting the wall' while racing is still an issue. The provision of additional carbohydrate while on the water is essential if you are to minimise the performance-sapping effects of fatigue.

Plan to ingest 30-60 g of carbohydrate for every hour raced. Both solid and liquid forms are suitable. Drinking 900-1,000 ml of sports drink per hour provides 50-60 g of carbohydrate plus plenty of fluid to keep you adequately hydrated. While solid food may cause intestinal discomfort while racing, small amounts will help top up

carbohydrate intake and stave off feelings of hunger. Solid forms of carbohydrate are also more compact (e.g. cereal bars, sports bars, and carbohydrate gels) and can be easily packed away on a support boat, under a buoyancy vest or taped to the mast for access at any time (*fig. 12.3*).

Ensuring you have sufficient carbohydrate supplies in between races requires planning – calculate your requirements in advance and bring suitable food and fluids with you (or your support boat) on the water (*fig. 12.4*).

A study on club-level Laser sailors in Singapore revealed that the nutritional practices of the sailors fell short of current sports nutrition recommendations. During the 6½ hours on the water (3½ hours of which was actual racing), carbohydrate intake averaged 17 g (range 0-110 g) or just 3 g per hour - well below the recommendation of 60 g per hour! Over half the sailors ingested no carbohydrate-containing food or fluids while on the water,

Fig 12.3 Taping carbohydrate-rich foods to the mast of your boat ensures ready access to fuel foods between races.

even though the racing day stretched from mid morning to far beyond lunchtime. Such practices would certainly compromise performance by aggravating fatigue and limiting the potential for recovery between races.

Recovery

Refueling and rehydrating your muscles before the next day's races is critical to consistent results. Take plenty of carbohydrate-rich foods and fluids soon after the completion of a day's racing to ensure glycogen and fluid levels recover in time for the next day's racing.

Fig 12.4 The food and drinks shown provide 420 g of carbohydrate, an amount similar to what a sailor may aim for when on the water for upwards of seven hours. All these choices are very concentrated sources of carbohydrate, taking up minimal space and come in waterproof, nonperishable packaging.

The most critical factor when attempting to restore muscle and liver glycogen levels is total carbohydrate intake. Aim for a total daily intake of about 8-10 g/kg body mass. Timing of carbohydrate intake is also important. Rates of glycogen synthesis remain low until carbohydrate is consumed, so ingest a carbohydrate-rich snack as soon as possible after each race. Sailing back to shore can be an excellent time to initiate the recovery process. Instead of heading straight to shore after the last race of the day, drop by your support boat to grab some food and water and consume them on the way in. If this is not possible then start replenishing your carbohydrate stores as soon as you get back to shore. It is natural not to have an appetite after physically exerting yourself, so make use of compact, low-bulk carbohydrate-rich foods and drinks (e.g. sports drinks, cordial, soft drink, prepared liquid meal supplement or carbohydrate loader powdered drink, cereal or sports bars, sugar based confectionery, etc.).

The choice of fluid may vary with individual preferences but sodium- or salt-containing options like sports drinks may be particularly useful in recovery, enhancing the rate of rehydration. Use the following tips to help maximise recovery between sailing sessions:

"Immediately after the race we'd eat a lot of carbos and fluids. It's most important to have some right after the race—that half an hour is the best time to recover. After that we'd have dinner"

Greg LeMond, three-time winner of the Tour de France

- Maintain a high-carbohydrate intake throughout the day. Aim for a carbohydrate intake of about 8-10 g/kg bodyweight.
- Ingest carbohydrate-rich food and / or fluids as soon as possible after the completion of exercise. Aim to ingest 1-1.5 g carbohydrate/kg bodyweight in the first 30 min following the completion of exercise and repeat this every 2 hours until your appetite returns and normal eating patterns resume.
- Make use of compact, low-bulk carbohydrate foods.
- Do not rely on thirst. Calculate your fluid deficit and match this with an amount of fluid equivalent to 150 % of losses. Alternatively, drink till your urine becomes clear.
- Make use of sodium-containing foods and / or drinks if dehydrated. While sports drinks contain small amounts of sodium, the salt does not have to come from the fluid. It may be derived from ingested food. Examples of recovery snacks with adequate carbohydrate, sodium, and fluid include:
  - Fruit, yoghurt, and sports drink.
  - Sandwiches with lean meat / low-fat cheese plus soft drink or water.
  - Noodle / rice / pasta dish with vegetables, meat, and sauce plus cordial or juice.

  Each of these options also contains a small amount of protein to assist recovery and contribute to your daily requirements. While carbohydrate intake remains the focus, daily protein requirements must still be achieved. The addition of a small serving of protein-rich food to your recovery snacks / meals will help ensure all nutrient requirements are met.

- Alcoholic and caffeinated beverages (cola drinks, tea, coffee) exacerbate fluid losses and should be avoided during recovery.
- Incorporate recovery snacks into the balance of foods and fluid available to you while on the water so that recovery can be initiated on the sail back to shore.

Sailing clubs are unlikely to provide food and fluid choices that are in line with your recovery goals, so you many have to pack appropriate recovery snacks for yourself.

WEIGHT LOSS AND WEIGHT GAIN

Most athletes are required to modify their bodyweight at some stage of their career. For some it may be an attempt to lose weight following injury or an off-season break. Others may need to gain weight and increase size, strength, and power. Laser sailors are no exception. Despite what is written about both weight loss and gain in promotional material, the basic principles are simple. Weight loss or gain is a result of the balance between energy intake from food ingested and energy expended through daily activities. When intake is less than expenditure, bodyweight decreases. Conversely, if energy intake exceeds expenditure, bodyweight will increase.

Losing Weight / Body Fat

The focus of any weight loss plan should be on body fat reduction. This requires a suitably designed physical training programme and a well-balanced meal plan that primarily focuses on food quality rather than reducing the absolute amount of food ingested. Nutritious carbohydrate-rich foods must still form the base of your diet, providing adequate fuel for training and racing. Protein requirements remain the same during weight loss. Therefore a reduction in energy intake should come from a reduction in dietary fat and alcohol intake. Fats are the most concentrated source of energy in the diet, so a small reduction in fat intake can cause a significant reduction in total energy intake without influencing the total amount of food ingested. Additionally, fats have a low satiety rating, i.e. they do not satisfy your appetite for long. Look to the section on fat in this chapter for tips on how to reduce dietary fat intake.

In addition to controlling dietary fat intake, the following tips will help to reduce body fat levels:

- Maintain a high intake of fresh fruit and vegetables. Both are rich sources of vitamins and fibre, and they fill you up for very few kilocalories. Aim for two or more pieces of fruit and two or more cups of vegetables per day.
- Limit alcohol consumption. Alcoholic drinks are rich in energy but provide very few essential nutrients.
- Do not quench your thirst with energy-containing drinks like fruit juice, cordial, soft drink, smoothies, milk, and sports drinks. While all are fat-free, these drinks are easily overconsumed, providing a large number of kilocalories. Sports drinks may be required during prolonged training sessions. At other times, use water.
- Get organised. Plan the day's food intake so suitable choices are readily available. Keep a bowl of fruit on your desk at work and low-fat flavoured yoghurt in the fridge. Always ensure suitable food options are available to you.
- Have your progress monitored. Seek the support of a qualified anthropometrist – someone who can systematically assess what is happening to your body fat levels with the aid of skinfold callipers. It does not hurt and will help to identify if the plan implemented is working. Many exercise physiologists and sports dietitians now have these qualifications.
- Distribute your food intake evenly throughout the day. Include three main meals and 2-3 snacks per day. This will help to maintain "energy levels" and prevent you from getting hungry.
- While energy intake must be less than energy expenditure on a daily basis, *do not count calories*. Stick to the basics – a diet rich in nutritious carbohydrate foods, adequate in protein and low in fat!
- Combine your eating plan with a suitable exercise programme, like the one recommended in *chapter 11, pg 175*.

Aim for a weight loss of no greater than 0.5-1.0 kg per week. This ensures that almost all the lost weight is from body fat. Faster rates of loss come from a combination of fat and muscle mass.

Gaining Weight / Muscle Mass

Underweight sailors need to bulk up in order to keep the boat flat and remain competitive in windy conditions. Fat mass does not improve performance, so the intention should be to increase muscle mass. Besides helping to keep the boat flat, muscle mass also improves strength. To ensure that what you are gaining is lean body mass rather than fat, muscle growth needs to be stimulated through a well-designed resistance training programme while consuming an energy-rich, moderate-protein meal plan to feed the growing muscles.

Some sailors may have difficulty increasing their energy intake. Frequent and prolonged training sessions can limit the opportunities for meals and snacks while intense sessions on the water and in the gym may suppress the appetite. Energy-dense snacks and drinks may be required to overcome such obstacles.

Use the following tips to increase the energy content of your meal plan:

- Increase meal / snack frequency. It is generally more comfortable on the stomach to eat more frequently than to increase the size of existing meals. Look to include three main meals and 2-3 snacks a day, even when busy.
- Make use of energy-dense drinks (e.g. smoothies, milk shakes, powdered liquid meal supplements, fruit juice, cordial, soft drink, sports drinks) and carbohydrate-rich foods (e.g. jams, honey, cereal bars, dried fruit / trail mix). Skim milk powder can be added to home-made milk drinks for extra protein and energy.
- Moderate the intake of high-fibre options. Look to replace some wholegrain options with refined or 'white' choices. Low energy fruit and vegetables, while a great source of nutrients, may also need to be reduced, allowing more room for energy-dense and nutrient-rich options.
- Plan the day's intake of food – what and when. This will assist you in ensuring that suitable food and drinks are at hand when required. A ready supply of non-perishable snacks in your training bag can be a great idea (e.g. tetra packs of UHT flavoured milk / fruit juice, cereal bars, powdered liquid meal supplements, and sports drinks).

Protein and Energy Booster Smoothie
(1,708 kJ or 408 kcal; 78 g carbohydrate; 19 g protein; 3 g fat)

- 1 cup Low fat milk
- 1-2 Tbsp Skim milk powder
- 1 Banana
- 2 Tbsp Caramel flavoured ice cream topping
- ½ cup Low fat vanilla flavoured yoghurt or 2 scoops ice cream

Combine all ingredients in blender and mix for 20-30 s. An excellent between-meal or recovery snack.

The higher food intake usually ensures that adequate proteins are consumed to meet the increased protein requirements. A specific protein supplement is usually not necessary. (*See the section on protein intake for tips on an adequate protein diet.*) You should focus on increasing the overall energy intake, and not just boosting the protein intake.

The preparation phase of your training cycle (*chapter 15*) is the ideal time to gain muscle mass. A hypertrophy (muscle building) phase needs to be incorporated into your resistance training programme (*chapter 11*) to encourage the muscles to grow. Include at least three resistance training sessions a week while keeping the overall training volume low. If you tend to have problems putting on weight, you might want to limit your conditioning sessions (i.e. aerobic training) as they use up a lot of calories and limit any increase in muscle mass.

Ensure that your short and long-term weight gain goals are realistic. An increase in bodyweight of 0.25-0.5 kg per week is appropriate, but the actual figure depends on your genetics and resistance training history. The longer you have been doing resistance exercises, the closer you are to your potential, and hence the smaller the gains expected. Gains of more than 0.5 kg per week are likely to include body fat that may have to be reduced at a later stage.

Also ensure that your overall body composition goals are realistic. Far too many athletes want to increase muscle mass and reduce body fat simultaneously. This is not achievable for most athletes as the two goals are mutually exclusive; one demanding an increase in energy intake while the other requires a reduction in energy intake. Priorities must be set and your diet and exercise programme applied accordingly.

As with weight loss, monitoring body composition during a hypertrophy phase is a useful tool for assessing progress. It helps identify if energy intake is adequate and may alleviate fears of body fat gain for those who are weight conscious. Measurement of bodyweight, skinfolds, and girths will generally provide an accurate indication of any changes in body composition. Seek the assistance of a qualified anthropometrist to monitor changes in body composition.

SPORTS SUPPLEMENTS

Sports supplements are one of the most visible examples of sports nutrition. *Fig. 12.5* shows the almost endless array of pills, powders, gels, drinks, formulas and bars that greet the eager consumer. Emotive labelling on products promoted in many gyms, sporting magazines and health food stores ensures dietary supplements are very popular among athletes. Do they work? Unfortunately, most products do not live up to expectations. The small percentage of products that do offer some value will only be beneficial if they meet a specific nutritional or physiological need of the individual. There is no magic bullet! A simple classification system has been used to help you better understand sports supplements and identify those that may assist you in achieving specific goals. Products may be classified as either dietary supplements or nutritional ergogenic aids.

Fig 12.5 *The wide array of dietary supplements and nutritional ergogenic aids available at most health food stores.*

Dietary Supplements

These generally contain nutrients in amounts similar to food and help to achieve specific nutrient needs, offering a combination of convenience, practicality, and palatability. Sports supplements that meet these criteria are summarised in *table 12.4*. The value of dietary supplements like sports drinks and other carbohydrate supplements (e.g. carbohydrate gels and powders, sports bars) in the nutrition armoury of a well-prepared athlete have been highlighted throughout this chapter.

Table 12.4 Common sports supplements that may be of value to Laser sailors.

Sports Supplement	Composition	Application
Sports Drink e.g. Gatorade™, 100 Plus™	• 6-7 % carbohydrate • 10-25 mmol/L sodium	• Fluid and carbohydrate source while exercising • Recovery of fluid balance and glycogen levels post-exercise
Liquid Meal Supplement e.g. Gator Pro™, Sustagen Sport™	• 50-70 % carbohydrate • 10-25 % protein • Fortified with vitamins and minerals • Available as liquid or powder	• Concentrated source of energy to assist weight gain • Compact source of nutrition while sailing • Recovery snack, especially beneficial if appetite is suppressed post-exercise • Convenient and familiar snack when travelling overseas
Carbohydrate Loader Powders e.g. Ultrafuel™, Maxim™, Gatorload™	• 100 % carbohydrate generally in form of glucose polymers	• Maximising glycogen stores in preparation for competition • Recovery of glycogen levels post-exercise
Carbohydrate Gels e.g. Power Gel™, Gu™, Carbo Shotz™, Lepin™	• 20-30 g carbohydrate per sachet • Numerous additional ingredients e.g. amino acids, chromium, caffeine / guarana, Vit. C and E	• Concentrated source of carbohydrate while on the water • Presented in small sachets easily stored in buoyancy vest • Consume with fluid
Vitamin and Mineral Supplements e.g. Centrum™ - MVM supplement, Fefol™ - iron supplement, Caltrate™ - calcium supplement	• Multi-vitamins (MVM) meeting 100 % of recommended dietary intake or • High dose of specific vitamin or mineral	• Low energy consumers • Restrictive eaters or athletes competing in countries where food quality is compromised • Treatment of diagnosed deficiency • Use only under the guidance of a sports dietician / physician
Sports Bars e.g. Power Bar™, Clif Bar™	• 40-50 g carbohydrate • 10+ g protein • ± vitamins and minerals	• Concentrated source of carbohydrate while sailing • Easily stored in buoyancy vest

NUTRITIONAL ERGOGENIC AIDS

Ergogenic aids contain nutrients in amounts much greater than typically provided by food. Such products are usually promoted as possessing direct ergogenic or performance enhancing effects, often through a pharmacological (drug-like) mechanism rather than meeting a specific nutrient need. Claims of increased growth hormone production, fat loss, immune function enhancement, energy release, and recovery are often made. However, the purported performance gains from these products are too rarely seen. *Table 12.5* lists some of the most popular nutritional ergogenic aids available and their proposed effects.

It is important to note that the efficacy of many nutritional ergogenic aids have not been validated in sailors. Individual responses may vary. Furthermore, inappropriate use of such products may actually compromise performance or be considered a "doping" offence by the International Olympic Committee / International Sailing Federation. If you are contemplating the use of a product, seek the professional advice of a sports dietitian who can provide you with the latest information on its safety, legality, efficacy, and (if applicable) appropriate dosage regime. While athletes will continue to pursue the 'magic bullet', the focus of your nutrition plan must remain with the proven winning formula of a meal plan that meets your extra demands for energy, carbohydrate, protein and fluid!

"While the optimal nutrition for an athlete must meet his or her increased nutrient requirements, it must also offer convenience, enjoyment, and individuality, being based on the individual's needs and preferences."

Gary Slater

Table 12.5 Commonly available nutritional ergogenic aids and scientific opinion on these products.

Nutritional Ergogenic Aid	Purported Benefits	Scientific Support
Caffeine[1]	Increases fat metabolism and stimulates the nervous system, enhancing performance in both brief, high-intensity exercise and endurance performance.	✓
Creatine	Enhances recovery between repeat efforts of high-intensity exercise.	✓
Glycerol	'Hyper-hydrating' agent, reducing the performance-sapping effects of dehydration by helping athletes to load up with fluid prior to exercise.	✓/✗
HMB	Reduces muscle damage and protein breakdown, enhancing strength and muscle mass development.	✓/✗
Anti-oxidants e.g. Vit A, C, E	Reduces the oxidative damage to muscles caused by exercise.	✓/✗
Colostrum	Enhances immune function, growth factor production, strength and endurance performance, plus recovery.	✗
Fat Metabolisers e.g. L-carnitine	Mobilises dietary fat and helps athletes reduce body fat.	✗
Amino Acids e.g. BCAA's, glutamine	Increases growth hormone production, stimulating muscle growth; reduces fatigue and improves endurance performance; enhances immune function.	✗
Ginseng	Improves stamina during times of physical exertion.	✗
Chromium	Enhances energy utilisation and protein synthesis.	✗

1 Caffeine is considered a restricted substance by the International Olympic Committee, with urinary levels above a certain limit considered 'doping'. While this limit is not easily achieved through "normal" consumption of caffeinated drinks (e.g. coffee, tea, cola drinks), extreme caution must be taken as caffeine excretion rates vary between individuals.

Chapter 13

Practical Sailing Psychology
- The Essential Tool Kit!

*content by **Trisha Leahy***

Thinking Positive !

If you have been working your way through this book, you will have realized by now that sailing successfully in competition is not just a matter of jumping in the boat and enthusiastically heading out to the starting line. There is so much preparation that is necessary in terms of boat preparation and maintenance, boat handling skills, technical and tactical knowledge, nutrition, etc. There is also physical fitness, and mental fitness.

How mentally fit are you? Have a look at these questions:

Do you find that while you perform well in training, you seem to be unable to reproduce the same level of performance in competition?

❏ Yes   ❏ No

Do you find that pre-race anxiety negatively affects your starts?

❏ Yes   ❏ No

Have you ever had trouble concentrating on sailing your boat well, because you cannot stop thinking about what a particular boat in front of you is doing?

❏ Yes   ❏ No

Have you ever found it hard to get back into the race after getting buried at the start, missing a big shift, or hitting a mark?

❏ Yes   ❏ No

Does your performance vary depending on whether you believe your opponents are better than you or not as good as you?

❏ Yes   ❏ No

Does your confidence drop when the race outcome is not as successful as you wanted?

❏ Yes   ❏ No

If you answered yes to any of these questions then you may benefit from some mental fitness training! What you think and what you feel directly affects your ability to sail well. Being mentally fit enables to you control your thoughts and feelings to ensure you can perform at your best, just like being physically fit means that you can control your actions! And, just as physical fitness is a matter of training consistently, so is mental fitness.

Mental Skills and Sports Success

Orlick & Partington (1988) have shown that there is a link between peak performance and mental skills. Canadian Olympic-level athletes were asked to rate their perceived physical, technical, and mental readiness before competition. Those who achieved personal bests, including medallists, gave mental preparation the highest ratings.

Similarly, a study was conducted on Singaporean athletes who participated in the 1994 Asian Games. They were asked to rate their degree of physical, technical, tactical, and mental readiness:

- *Medallists reported greater mental and technical readiness than physical and tactical readiness.*
- *Non-medallists reported their mental readiness to be the lowest even though they felt that their physical preparation was relatively the highest.*

These findings suggest that mental readiness is an important factor associated with high-level performance.

This chapter will describe a basic psychological "Tool Kit" that you can use to begin your mental fitness training. As with all tools, depending on the job that needs to be done, you may use different tools at different times for different purposes. The essential tools in any psychological kit bag are goal setting, mental rehearsal, and positive self-talk.

GOAL SETTING

Goal setting is like creating a clear and detailed map of the race course. If you do not know where the starting line is, it is hard to get started! If you do not know where the top and gybe marks are, how will you know that you are on the right course! There are two types of goals that can be set – outcome and process goals.

Outcome goals, as the name suggests, are about defining outcomes. For example, winning and being selected for the Olympic team are outcome goals. Setting long-term outcome goals is fun and motivating but it will not help you perform well while you are racing. Setting only outcome goals is like knowing where the finishing line is but not knowing where the top mark is. Outcome goals can send you off on the wrong course, because they do not contain the information necessary to perform well. Furthermore, they are not entirely under your control. So, even if you sail as well as you can but someone else sails better on the day, then that person wins or gets selected. You cannot control your opponent's performance but you can control your own.

This is where process goals come in. Process goals answer the question, "How?" How do I get to the outcome I want? Process goals focus your attention on the task at hand, on what needs to be done now, on what is under your control. Process goals can make each training session a quality session if they are specific, realistic, challenging and controllable. Process goals also work well while racing. For example, when sailing upwind against a boat that is just ahead-to-leeward. You are thinking, "OK, my goal is to pass this boat!" (Outcome goal.) You are so busy looking at the leeward boat and focusing on the outcome, "I have to get past, I have to get past!" that suddenly you find that you have been sucked into the leeward boat's dirty air. How did that happen? Well, the outcome goal did not contain any information about what to do to avoid that situation, and so it directed your focus away from the fundamental skills that needed to be performed. That outcome goal was a distraction – not the proper tool for the job. A process goal would have focused your attention on what to do in that situation, on how to cope. Try the following exercise:

Goal-Setting Exercise

Goals for Training

Write down your long-term outcome goals. Have some fun with it – let yourself dream! Now work with your coach on identifying a realistic long-term outcome and most importantly, the long and short-term process goals to take you step by step closer to that outcome. Meeting regularly with your coach to review and reset process goals not only helps keep your focus appropriately directed, it also makes learning and improving an enjoyable, rather than an overwhelming activity.

Goals for racing

Generate a list of "What if's …" For example, "What if I get buried just after the start?" and "What if I am on the wrong side of the shift?" Now, work with your coach to develop specific process goals for racing successfully in these situations.

MENTAL REHEARSAL

Mental rehearsal or imagery is one of the most frequently used mental skills in elite sport. The brain has a wonderful capacity to clearly imagine situations as if they were really happening. Athletes use mental rehearsal to practice new skills, to get "psyched up", to recover from injury, or just to relax. Mental rehearsal can really improve confidence when it is used to practice coping successfully with challenging situations. Let us say, for example, that you have indicated on your "What if …" list that pre-race jitters interfere with getting a good start. You have gone to your coach, and together you have come up with the most appropriate process goals for this situation. Now spend a few minutes every day imagining yourself successfully achieving these goals. For example, mentally rehearse going through - step by step - the pre-start and start routine described earlier in *chapter 9* and see yourself getting great starts. Imagine yourself successfully performing each step under different conditions, such as different wind strengths, port and starboard biased lines, long and short starting lines, etc.

The good thing about mental rehearsal is that it does not require much time to practice - just a few minutes a day. You can practice on the train, on the bus, at the boat park, or even in your boat. Here is a simple mental rehearsal exercise to try:

Mental Rehearsal Exercise

No matter how well prepared your body is, if you are not mentally ready for training, you will not progress as fast as you can. The purpose of this exercise is to get mentally ready for a long day on the water, training in unpleasant weather.

Step 1

Before you even begin your physical warm up, sit down. You can close your eyes if you wish, but it is not necessary. Take a few gentle and deep breaths, and as you exhale focus on the sound of your breath and let yourself relax just a little.

Now keeping aware of the noises around you, turn your focus inwards for a couple of minutes and just do a simple check up on what is going on inside yourself. What are your thoughts and feelings? Are you still thinking about what happened at work or school before you arrived, or about all the things you have to do after training? Are there any problems on your mind that can distract you from your training? Are you letting the weather conditions control your feelings? Do not try to force these concerns out of your mind. Instead, mentally gather them into a bundle and in your mind, put them in your sports bag with your clothes and close the bag tightly. You can get back to these concerns later when you get your bag to change after training!

Step 2

Now once again, take a few gentle and deep breaths, and as you exhale focus on the sound of your breath and let yourself relax just a little. With the same inward focus, think about your process goals for this training session (e.g. steering upwind through the chops) and remind yourself of the long term outcome goal that they will lead to (e.g. good all-round upwind speed). Think about how important these goals are to you. Decide that you will give 100 % commitment to these goals today. Visualize yourself achieving these goals with that level of commitment. Visualize the great satisfaction you can feel at the end of the day.

Now take a few strong, deep breaths and as you exhale let yourself feel energized and ready for action!

POSITIVE SELF-TALK

What you think affects how you feel!
How you feel affects how you perform!

This is one of the key principles in psychology. Your ability to cope in any situation depends not just on the facts of the situation, but also on what you think those facts mean. You cannot change the facts, but your interpretation of the facts is probably not the only one possible. There is usually more than one meaning for any set of facts. Choosing a meaning that facilitates good performance is a key skill for any successful athlete. Look at the example of the two athletes below. They have both made an error. Who do you think will recover more effectively and minimise the losses?

Athlete	Fact	Thoughts	Feelings
Chris	Hit the top mark.	"Do the penalty turn smoothly, catch the next wave, and surf all the way to the next mark."	In control Focused Determined Confident
Joe	Hit the top mark.	"Oh no, how could I do that? I am completely hopeless! I'll never catch up now!"	Unhappy Panicked No confidence

Of course, Chris is mentally in a much better position to recover from that error. Chris is speaking and thinking in a logical, task-oriented, and positive manner – just like a pro! Joe, on the other hand, is thinking in a negative and unhelpful manner and, unfortunately, he is no longer focused on the task at hand. He is not being a good coach to himself! It is almost impossible to make effective decisions under pressure, and to perform complex tasks if your self-talk causes you to feel frustration and panic. There are many exciting examples of sailors who have had so-called "disasters" from which they subsequently recovered to win the regatta! Let us try thinking positively:

Rounding the top mark.

Positive Self-Talk Exercise

Choosing to think and talk positively to yourself in performance situations is one of the most important tools to ensure effective focus and consistent motivation and confidence. Just like you made a "What if …" list of process goals and used mental rehearsal to practice them, now you can make another "What if …" list of potentially challenging situations and write down how you will think and speak logically, positively, and helpfully to yourself in each situation. Mentally rehearse this way of coping regularly and it will eventually become your natural response. Practice positive self-talk in other areas of your life as well - at school, work, or home and notice how your ability to cope and communicate effectively improves.

USING THE TOOLS TO MENTALLY PREPARE FOR COMPETITION

Now that you have the basic tools, you can apply them to any of the challenges that you meet on your road to successful sailing. Use them in a systematic way to develop a planned mental preparation for competition. Some athletes need to feel relaxed, some athletes need to feel more aroused to achieve optimal performance. Working with a psychologist can be really useful for developing the best mental preparation plan for you. But even if you do not have access to a psychologist, you can monitor yourself by keeping a mental skills training logbook. Keep good records of the thoughts, feelings and arousal levels associated with your best performances. Then develop pre-competition routines to facilitate these mental states. For example, many athletes successfully use recordings of their favourite music, statements about their goals, mental rehearsal scripts, and positive self-statements to help them feel focused, confident, and in control at competition time.

Competitive sailing is an area of achievement that can provide enormous enjoyment and satisfaction. But it is a sport that demands peak performance in both mental and physical skills. Successful athletes stay on top of the multiple demands of competitive sailing by training mentally as well as physically. They adopt an approach that identifies both successful and unsuccessful performances as learning opportunities. They are very skilled at using resources from various sources to ensure that on race day they are completely prepared, mentally and physically, to perform at their best.

It takes time to acquire mental skills, so start training now!

"Success is not so much an occurrence as an attitude. If you have the right kind of mental attitude, you will overcome all of the discouraging confrontations throughout your preparation to excel."

Helliksen, former USA Olympic wrestling coach

Chapter 14

Essential Sports Medicine for Sailors

content by ***Ben Tan***
reviewed by ***Tullio Giraldi, Teh Kong Chuan,***
Patrick Goh, *and* ***Saratha Bhai Krishnan***

And Doc said that sailing is a safe sport !

S *ailing a physical boat like the Laser develops cardiorespiratory endurance, anaerobic capacity, strength, flexibility, and agility. Besides these fitness benefits, our sport is also blessed with a relatively low injury rate. Lasers have been raced in 40-knot winds with few incidents, as the water provides a soft landing and the light hull and rig usually do not inflict serious injury.*

Although uncommon, sailors do sustain injuries. The demands of hiking are anecdotally associated with certain overuse injuries, and minor accidents do occasionally occur. This chapter will focus only on the most commonly presented injuries and medical conditions amongst sailors. As the competitive sailor will also have the opportunity to compete internationally and be exposed to doping control, the nebulous issue of doping will also be discussed.

SAILING INJURIES

For dinghy sailors, muscle strains and soreness tend to be the most common injuries, followed by accidental injuries like cuts and abrasions (*table 14.1*). In the Laser, where the boat is relatively devoid of sharp edges, and where the straight-leg hiking is particularly demanding, the injury pattern is likely to be skewed even further towards overuse injuries.

Recently, researchers have focused their attention on the mechanics of the most physically demanding aspect of Olympic yacht racing – hiking (*fig 14.1*). Not surprisingly, hiking was found to be physically stressful to the body: the peak upward force on a Laser's hiking strap was recorded at 828 N (i.e. the force equivalent to that exerted by an 84 kg weight); the isometric nature of hiking reduces blood flow to the muscles, starving them of much-needed nutrients; and the static nature of hiking raises the mean arterial pressure (i.e. blood pressure) by 48%. The joints most commonly affected by the stress of hiking are the lower back, knees, and ankles.

Fig 14.1 Hiking hard.

Table 14.1 Injuries and medical conditions reported by Singaporean sailors from several dinghy classes during the 1998 Asian Games.

	NO. OF CONSULTATIONS	PERCENTAGE OF TOTAL
Injury		
Muscle strains / soreness	23	39.7
Cuts, abrasions, blisters	11	19.0
Contusions	1	1.7
Sprains	1	1.7
Miscellaneous	7	12.1
Medical conditions		
Upper respiratory tract infection	8	13.8
Diarrhoea	2	3.4
Rashes	1	1.7
Miscellaneous	4	6.9
Total	58	100

Lower Back Pain

The lower back is a complex region, with many forces acting on the spinal column. Due to its anatomical and biomechanical complexity, it is difficult to conclusively link a specific pathology to a certain biomechanical factor. However, empirical observations can be made.

Causes of Lower Back Pain. The iliopsoas, abdominals, and quadriceps are the major hiking muscles (*fig. 14.2*). One of the forces acting on the spine is the pull of the iliopsoas muscle. Without strong abdominal muscles and, to a lesser extent, strong quadriceps muscles to assist in flexing the trunk, the iliopsoas exerts an excessive pull on the lower spine, possibly resulting in lower back pain.

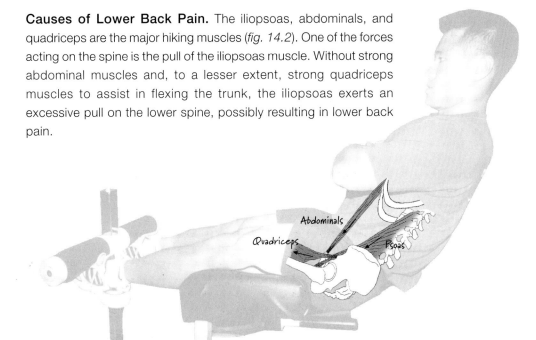

Fig 14.2 Forces (arrows) at play in the major hiking muscles when hiking.

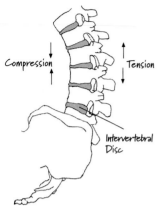

Fig 14.3 A crouching position curves the spinal column forward, leading to excessive compression of the anterior structures, especially the intervertebral discs, and excessive tension on the posterior structures, namely ligaments and muscles.

Another significant stress on the spinal column relates to the weight of the body on the intervertebral discs (structures lying between the vertebrae). Crouching loads the front of the spinal column (*fig. 14.3*), compressing the intervertebral discs. Bumpy seas accentuate the compression force, possibly leading to internal disc disruption and intervertebral disc prolapse (i.e. slipped disc). At the same time, the posterior structures of the spinal column are put under tension, resulting in further sources of pain. Torqueing, or the violent throwing of the torso outwards and backwards while hiking, stresses the joints between adjacent vertebrae.

Prevention. From the injury mechanisms described above, it is evident that trunk stability from well-conditioned muscles around the back and abdomen, and good posture are essential in avoiding lower back problems in sailing. The following preventive measures will help to minimise stress on the lumbar spine:

- *Increase hamstring flexibility.* This allows a greater degree of flexion to occur at the hip joint, so that the lumbar spine can remain straight (*fig. 14.4*), minimising compression force on the intervertebral discs.

Fig 14.4 Flexible hamstrings allow the lower back to remain straight. Left: Because of the tight hamstrings, flexion at the hip joint is limited and the lower back has to flex to allow the sailor to reach forward. Right: With flexible hamstrings, the sailor is able to reach as far forward through hip flexion alone, while the lower back remains straight.

- *Strengthen the abdominal muscles.* Strong abdominals will assist the iliopsoas in flexing the trunk, and also increase the intra-abdominal pressure, adding support to the lower back.
- *Condition the hiking muscles.* Well-conditioned abdominal, hip flexor (e.g. iliopsoas), and quadriceps muscles enable sailors to hike flat-out. A horizontal position is probably

associated with lower compression forces on the spine compared to a more upright or crouching position.

- *Adopt a good back posture at all times.* Avoid crouching while sailing. On shore, the back should be kept straight when flipping the hull over to clean the bottom and when pulling the boat out of the water. Flex the hips instead.
- *Condition the opposing muscles.* It is also important to strengthen opposing muscles to achieve a balanced musculature. The abdominals and hip flexors flex the spine, so their opposing muscle, the paravertebral muscles, should also be strengthened at the same time through back extension exercises.

Patellofemoral Pain

The most common pathology in the sailor's knee is patellofemoral pain. This refers to pain arising from the articulation between the kneecap (patella) and the lower end of the thighbone (femur). When hiking with the knees almost straight, the patellofemoral compression force is estimated at more than double the bodyweight. In this position, the contact area between the kneecap and the thighbone is small, so the pressure exerted is high. Compression force increases with increasing knee flexion angles.

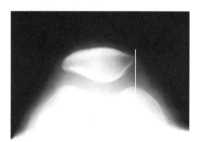

Causes. High compression forces are better tolerated if the kneecap sits nicely in its groove in the thighbone. If not, the joint undergoes excessive wear and tear, leading to pain and potential swelling (*fig. 14.5*). Among other factors, the alignment or tracking of the kneecap is determined by the tightness of the iliotibial band (ITB) and the activity of the vastus medialis oblique (VMO) muscle (*fig. 14.6*). The ITB is a strong band of connective tissue stretching from above the hip to just below the knee, with fibres attaching it to the lateral edge of the kneecap. When the ITB is tight, it tends to pull the kneecap laterally; the VMO muscles pull the kneecaps medially when they are activated. Hence, tight ITB's and weak VMO's cause the kneecaps to be displaced laterally, resulting in excessive friction against the lower end of the thighbone.

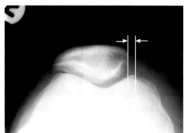

Fig 14.5 "Skyline" view X ray of the knee joint showing the patella (kneecap) and femur (thighbone). Top: The kneecap sits centrally in the groove on the thighbone. Bottom: X ray of an older subject with patellofemoral pain, showing the lateral displacement of the kneecap and early signs of wear-and-tear (osteoarthritis).

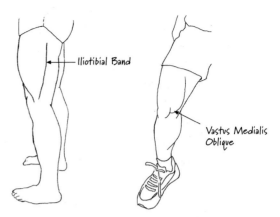

Fig 14.6 Structures associated with patellofemoral pain. Left: The iliotibial band is a strong, broad band of connective tissue stretching from above the hip to the knee. Right: The vastus medialis oblique, or VMO, is attached to the inside edge of the kneecap and it controls its lateral and medial movements.

Iliotibial Band

Vastus Medialis Oblique

Prevention. Following are some pointers for saving your knees:

- *Avoid hiking with the toes pointing in.* The toe-in position activates the outer part of the quadriceps muscles, causing the kneecaps to track laterally rather than in the middle of the groove.
- *Stretch the ITB's and related muscles.* As the ITB's are very strong, it is important to stretch them regularly to overcome the tension. The gluteus, piriformis, and quadriceps muscles are all attached to the ITBs, so they need to be stretched as well. Hamstring stretches allow a fuller knee extension, reducing the patellofemoral pressure. See *fig. 11.2 (pg 178)* for a description of the necessary stretches.
- *Strengthen the VMO's.* These muscles are easier to activate when the feet are in a slight toe-out position. Strengthen them by making a conscious effort to activate them when doing wall sits, knee extensions, squats, and other quadriceps strengthening exercises. Most importantly, ensure that they are activated while hiking.
- *If symptomatic or prone to patellofemoral pain, avoid aggravating activities.* Repetitive knee-bending activities while bearing weight, like running up and down steps, using steppers in the gym, and jumping exercises aggravate patellofemoral pain. If you have patellofemoral pain or are prone to it, cross train with cycling (this involves knee bending but is not fully weight-bearing) and swimming (avoid the breast-stroke) instead.

Extensor Tendinitis in the Ankles

The extensor tendons are found on the front of the ankles, running from the group of muscles just next to the shin bone to the toes. They bend the ankles and toes upwards, and are therefore under tension when hiking.

Causes. Hiking from the toes subjects the extensor tendons to high tensile forces, while hiking from the ankles cause the tendons to be compressed between the hiking straps above and the bones of the ankle joint below. Either way, the tendons tend to become inflamed, especially when sailors hike excessively without prior progressive training.

Prevention. It takes years to be able to hike flat out, on your toes, for prolonged periods. The ankle joints and tendons will adapt to the stress of hiking if the training is stepped up progressively. Rigid boots provide some support and padding, while padded hiking straps provide further cushioning.

Muscle Strains and Soreness

Delayed onset muscle soreness (DOMS) is characterised by muscle stiffness and pain after exercise. It is usually evident one to two days after a hard day's sail and disappears within a week. It may be considered as part and parcel of training, and is acceptable if mild. However, severe stiffness to the extent where it is difficult to get up from a chair, for example, is counterproductive.

Muscle strains are more severe and take longer to recover from. In sailing, strains are usually not as dramatic as the hamstring pull of a sprinter during a dash, and may be noticed only at the end of the day.

Causes. For Laser sailors, peak forces in the quadriceps muscle have been recorded at over 800 N (force roughly equivalent to an 80 kg weight) during hiking; while in the elbow flexors, the peak force exceeded 280 N (force roughly equivalent to a 28 kg weight) while sheeting. Apart from such high forces, the static nature of hiking and holding on to the mainsheet impedes the flow of blood to the muscles at a time when the muscles are under stress. When the load exceeds the muscles' capacity, strains or DOMS occur.

Muscles that are prone to DOMS and strains are the hiking and sheeting muscles (i.e. abdominals, hip flexors, quadriceps, ankle dorsiflexors, lower back extensors, elbow flexors, and forearm muscles).

Prevention. Progressive strengthening of the above muscles from a combination of dry-land training and hiking on the water reduces the risk of injury. When there is a stretch of light wind over several days, keep the muscles conditioned with dry-land training. During periods of high volume and high intensity training, pay more attention to recovery methods like stretching, sports massage, and warm baths.

Cuts, Abrasions, and Contusions

Next to muscle strains and soreness, accidental injuries like contusions, cuts, and abrasions are the next most common complaints. The boom and centreboard appear to be the most "dangerous" parts of the boat, especially for novice sailors.

Causes and Prevention. Most accidents are avoidable, and the key is to anticipate the accident.

- Accidents tend to occur when fatigued. A fatigued sailor tends to be stiff and slow, making him more likely to deviate from rehearsed routines like bending low to get across the boat, resulting in an unpleasant bump on the head. Fortunately the Laser's boom is not as heavy as that of a keelboat! Missing the hiking straps when tacking and losing hold of the mainsheet are also common occurrences when a sailor is fatigued.
- When capsizing, it pays to keep your balance and stay on the gunwale. Falling backwards may cause the sailor to hit the centreboard and become winded. Falling forward onto the sail may be safer, but that damages the sail.
- Trying to stay on the gunwale when capsizing at high speed can present some difficulty. Avoid getting your hands cut by the gunwale as you slide forward, and when flung forward in a capsize, beware of the mast.
- Avoid sheeting the mainsheet with your teeth and holding the mainsheet with several turns round the hand.

- Do not put your fingers on the gunwale when coming alongside the coach boat or another Laser.
- Getting in and out of the water presents significant injury risks. On slipways, boats are not the only things that slip into the water! Many are either slippery or covered with sharp barnacles. Falling over the edge of the slipway is common and unnecessary. When dragging the boat out of the water, keep your back straight and use your hips and not your back to pull.

Treatment. Seawater harbours certain organisms (e.g. *Vibrio vulnificus*, *Mycobacterium marinum*) that have a tendency to cause nasty infections in open wounds. To keep an open wound clean and reduce its risk of becoming infected, hydrocolloid dressings (*fig. 14.7*) are appropriate for sailors who need to continue to race or train, as they:

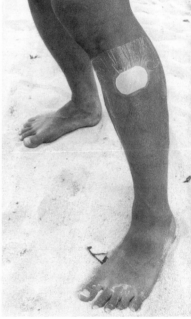

- Provide an excellent barrier against exogenous contamination by bacteria in seawater while sailing.
- Protect the wound against friction and pressure.
- Provide a moist environment that hastens re-epithelialization (i.e. the closure of the wound by epithelial or skin cells), and encourages the immune cells to clean up the wound.
- Reduce the pain that arises when the wound is stretched or touched.
- Do not have to be changed as frequently as the usual dry gauze dressing.

Contusions and other soft tissue injuries should be treated using the **R-I-C-E** formula to reduce swelling and pain:

- **R**est the injured area.
- **I**ce the area for 20-30 min, 4-6 hourly for the first two days to reduce pain and inflammation.
- **C**ompress with a crepe bandage to reduce swelling.
- **E**levate the injured area, if possible, to reduce swelling.

Fig 14.7 Occlusive dressing. 1) Clean the wound with sterile water (if available) or antiseptic wipes and remove any visible debris. 2) Clean (with an alcohol swab if available) and dry the surrounding area, taking care to remove sunscreen and grease, and shave if necessary so that the dressing will stay on firmly. 3) Cut and apply a piece of occlusive dressing (e.g. DuoDERM™) such that the dressing extends beyond the margin of the wound by about 3 cm. 4) To help the dressing withstand the rigours of sailing, apply a piece of transparent adhesive dressing (e.g. Tegaderm™) on top, ensuring that its edge extends beyond that of the occlusive dressing by another 3 cm.

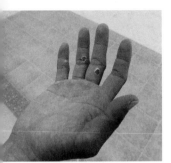
Fig 14.8 Blisters from sailing.

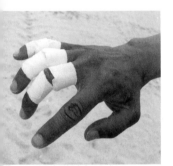
Fig 14.9 The fingers can be taped to prevent or to treat blisters. To improve grip and comfort, keep the fingers slightly bent while applying the tape, and avoid taping over the dorsal part of the joints. With good-quality zinc oxide tape, a 3-4 layer application should last the whole day.

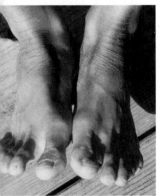
Fig 14.10 Thickening and pigmentation of the skin over the ankles of a Laser sailor. You can tell that this sailor has not been hiking from his toes!

Blisters and Calluses

Hands. Friction from the mainsheet can result in rope burns and blisters on the fingers (*fig. 14.8*). If a blister forms, pop it with a clean needle and dress with tape or a waterproof plaster to reduce pain and accelerate healing.

With time, calluses will form in high-friction areas of the hand, offering a natural protection. However, if you do not sail frequently enough, or if the winds are strong, then additional protection helps. Sailing gloves made of soft leather tend to be costly: a cheaper solution is to use rubber dishwashing gloves, with the fingertips cut off. They may not last as long, but they can be replaced easily. If you do not find wearing gloves comfortable, an alternative is to tape the fingers (*fig. 14.9*).

Calluses that get too thick can crack or a blister can form under the callus. Before this happens thin the calluses down with a pumice stone (sandpaper from your tool box is a cheaper alternative) or carefully pare them down with a sharp blade.

Feet. Some sailors prefer not to wear sailing boots to improve feel for the boat. The excessive friction against the hiking strap then causes thickening and pigmentation of the skin over the top of the feet and ankles (*fig. 14.10*). Small cracks in the skin may cause itchiness or pain. So to prevent them from forming, apply moisturizing cream daily over the affected areas.

MEDICAL CONSIDERATIONS AND CONDITIONS

Exposure to the Sun

Acute exposure to the sun leads to the all-too-familiar sunburn. Chronic exposure, especially with mother earth's thinning ozone layer, is associated with:

- An increased risk of skin cancer (e.g. melanoma, squamous cell carcinoma, and basal cell carcinoma).
- Photoaging, which consists of wrinkling, blotchiness, small dilated blood vessels on the skin (telangiectasia) , and a roughened, weather-beaten appearance.

- Pterygium, which is a triangular, greyish growth on the nasal side of the white of the eye, encroaching onto the cornea (*fig. 14.11*). It is associated with chronic eye irritation and visual impairment (if it creeps too far into the cornea). When the pterygium encroaches onto the visual axis, it can be removed surgically, but the condition may recur after the procedure.
- Increased formation of some types of cataracts.
- Damage to the back of the eyes (solar retinopathy) from looking directly at the sun.

Fig 14.11 A pterygium encroaching onto the cornea.

The culprit for all of these conditions is the ultraviolet component of the sun's rays. Ultraviolet light penetrates clouds and reflects off the water surface, so do not assume that you are safe just because the sky is cloudy or you are under a shade.

The Australian Anti-Cancer Council's "Slip, Slop, and Slap" slogan provides effective protection for the skin: Slip on a long-sleeved top, Slop on some sunscreen, and Slap on a peaked cap (*fig. 14.12*).

Sunscreens protect the skin by acting as a physical block that reflects ultraviolet rays (e.g. titanium dioxide and zinc oxide), or by acting as a chemical sunscreen that absorbs the radiation. They are formulated either as emulsions (creams and lotions) or oils. Water-resistant sunscreens retain their protective properties for 40 min in water; waterproof sunscreens remain protective for 80 min; whereas sweat-resistant sunscreens will remain active for at least 30 min of heavy perspiration. Even if they manage to stay on, sunscreens deteriorate in the presence of sweat, so they should be reapplied frequently. Sunscreens with a sun protection factor (SPF) of 15 or stronger are recommended.

Fig 14.12 To protect your skin against the sun, Slip on a long-sleeved top, Slop on some sunscreen, and Slap on a peaked cap. In addition sunglasses will reduce eye problems. A thin line tied to the life jacket keeps our model from losing his cap.

Protect your eyes with ultraviolet-proof sunglasses. Choose a pair that is light, extends well to the sides, and will not shatter in your eyes (e.g. polycarbonate). A peaked cap will help to further reduce the entry of light into the eyes. If you find it difficult to spot gusts with the sunglasses on, remove them while racing and replace them after the race.

In cold climates, sailors will naturally put on clothing to protect themselves from the cold, and this will effectively block out ultraviolet rays. It is in hot climates that sailors need to be convinced to put on a long-sleeved top to protect against the sun. Thin, loose-fitting, light-coloured, and open-weave garments will keep the sailor cool while blocking the sun's rays.

Exercising in the Heat

The 1996 Olympic Regatta was held in Savannah, where the heat index (i.e. the apparent temperature of exposed skin in air with a high moisture content) was 37-42 °C! The evaporation of sweat is by far the most important mechanism for dissipating heat and preventing body temperature increases. However, with increased sweat rates comes the risk of dehydration and heat related injuries. It has been estimated that dehydration of just 2 % body mass results in a 20 % decrement in endurance. Those who are acclimatized to the heat will sweat more, and thus they have higher fluid requirements. Strategies for ensuring adequate hydration are covered in *chapter 12*.

Wear thin, loose-fitting, light-coloured, and open-weave clothing to maximise the evaporation of sweat. Materials with high wicking properties (e.g. CoolMax®) are recommended, especially if skin-tight clothes are worn. Such materials draw sweat away from the skin to the surface of the material where it evaporates, cooling the body while providing barrier protection from the sun.

Performing in the Cold

To sail comfortably in cold climates, a range of clothing is available depending on how much insulation is needed. The range includes gloves and booties, thermal (polypropylene) tops and bottoms, wetsuits of varying length and thickness, spray jackets, dry steamers (one-piece neoprene suits with seals to prevent water from entering), and dry suits. Exercising in the cold requires a balance between the warmth from protective clothing and the heat generated during exercise. The solution is to dress in layers that can be removed or replaced as the ambient temperature or exercise intensity changes. For example, you can start with just a thermal top and progress to a thermal top plus spray top, a wetsuit alone, and a wetsuit plus spray top as the ambient temperature drops. When deciding on the clothing to bring with you to the course, do not forget to take into account the greater wind chill experienced on the water. In between races, there is a tendency to feel cold as less heat is generated when resting. It is therefore advisable to leave extra clothing with the support boat during training and racing.

Cold exposure causes an acute diuretic response (i.e. an increased urine production). Therefore, despite the inconvenience of voiding with full cold-weather gear on, fluid needs must not be ignored.

To maintain a constant body temperature in cold environments, heat has to be generated to compensate for the heat lost to the environment. Physical activity in itself generates large amounts of heat, so fit sailors who work hard tolerate cold racing conditions better than sailors who are unfit. Exercise and other heat-generating mechanisms that come with acclimatization to the cold are fuelled by carbohydrates and, to a lesser extent, fat. Indeed, a 3-4 °C decrease in body temperature has been suggested to cause a 588 % increase in carbohydrate oxidation and a 63 % increase in fat oxidation. This underlines the importance of a high carbohydrate intake when racing in cold climates.

Exposure to the cold increases muscle tone and stiffness. Sailors should therefore undergo a prolonged warm-up before the start of a race or training session. If the break between races is long, beat upwind and do a couple of tacks as a warm-up prior to the start of the next race.

Potential medical problems faced by sailors competing in cold climates include exercise-induced asthma (described below), respiratory infections, and an increased risk of cardiac incidents (in older sailors).

The Flu

Swimmers who overtrain have an increased risk of coming down with influenza (the flu), an upper respiratory tract infection caused by viruses. Likewise, sailors whose stress from high training volumes and intensities exceed that of their recovery processes run the risk of catching the flu.

Preventive Measures Against the Flu

- *Periodize your training and taper before major events, ensuring adequate rest and recovery*

- *Ensure adequate hydration and nutrition*

- *Limit exposure to physical (e.g. Sun, late nights) and psychological stress*

- *Wear adequate clothing when exposed to the cold*

- *Stay in well-ventilated areas*

- *Avoid exposure to infected persons and quarantine infected team members*

- *Observe good general hygiene practices*

Consult your doctor for an annual influenza vaccination during autumn if there is a high risk of catching the flu in winter, or for antivirals that may lower the risk of catching the flu or shorten its duration.

During a viral infection, the body's immune system will be busy warding off viruses. The sun as well as the physical stresses from training or competing taxes the body's immune system even further, tipping the scale in the virus' favour. If the virus spreads, serious complications like myocarditis (infection of the heart muscle) and pneumonia may follow.

Fever, headache, generalized body aches, and a high pulse rate indicate an active infection, so training and racing should be avoided at this time. During this period, the sailor under-performs, his training quality is compromised, and the risk of developing complications increases. Generally, when the fever has subsided and the resting pulse rate is within 10 beats of normal, training can be resumed. This usually takes about three days.

In deciding whether or not to race during a viral infection, you will have to weigh the risk of developing complications against the importance of the regatta in the context of your overall plan and targets. The expected sailing conditions (although sometimes hard to predict) should also be factored in when making the decision. If you do decide to race, ensure that you have a very good reason to do so. It is best to seek your physician's advice when making a decision.

Asthma

Asthma is a relatively common condition where narrowing of the airways in the lungs results in breathing difficulties. There are various triggers, including cold and dry air, an upper respiratory tract infection, and exercise. Medications are available to abort as well as to prevent asthmatic attacks.

In the event of an attack occurring while sailing, evacuation to a medical facility on shore may be difficult and delayed. Hence sailors suffering from asthma must take precautionary measures. These include ensuring that the asthma is optimally controlled under the guidance of a doctor and that the inhaler is kept close by at all times (e.g. in the pocket of the life jacket, or at least on the coach boat).

The use of beta-2 agonists (these are classified as stimulants) is permitted by inhalation only, in cases of proven asthma. Note that a written request, prior to an event, must be made by the competitor to the relevant medical authority (Member National Authority Medical Officer or ISAF Medical Commission). A certificate will be issued upon approval.

MEDICAL KIT

The common and annoying medical problems encountered when travelling include traveller's diarrhoea, upper respiratory tract infections, skin wounds, and rashes. Many minor conditions can be dealt with by carrying some basic medical supplies when racing or training overseas, where you will probably be less familiar with local pharmacies. A list of useful and easy-to-carry supplies for the traveller's medical kit is recommended in *table 14.2*. Most of the medications are available on prescription only, so before leaving for an overseas regatta, pay your doctor a visit and let him know what you need.

When travelling to some countries, prophylaxis against certain diseases like malaria and hepatitis is recommended. Your doctor will provide you with the updated recommendation for the country you are visiting, but do pay him a visit 2-6 weeks before leaving as some vaccinations have to be given early.

DOPING

Doping consists of the administration of substances belonging to the prohibited classes of pharmacological agents and / or the use of various prohibited methods (e.g. substituting your urine sample when called for a dope test). The prohibited classes of substances and prohibited methods are specified by the International Olympic Committee / International Sailing Federation.

The physical nature of Laser sailing might tempt sailors to administer anabolic steroids to increase muscle bulk and strength, drugs to numb the pain of hiking or a persistent injury, or stimulants to combat the accumulated fatigue of a long regatta. However, doping in this manner contravenes the ethics of medical science and contradicts the fundamental principles of racing the Laser. With doping, there is no level playing field. Furthermore, there is a heavy price to pay: doping can be harmful to one's health, and it has led to death in some cases. Let us also not forget that many of the "benefits" of doping can be attained safely through training.

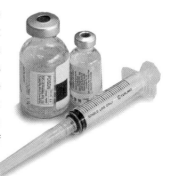

Table 14.2 Items for the traveller's medical kit.

ITEM	USE / INDICATIONS	QUANTITY*
Wound Care		
• Antiseptic wipes e.g. Elastoplast™	To clean open wounds	10 pieces
• Hydrocolloid dressing e.g. DuoDERM™	To dress open wounds including blisters	2 pieces
• Transparent adhesive dressing e.g. Tegaderm™	Holds the hydrocolloid dressing in place and seals the wound	6 pieces
• Compression stocking e.g. Tubigrip™	Provide compression as part of RICE	1 m
• Scissors		1 pair
• Plaster strips	Small cuts and blisters	5 pieces
• Zinc oxide tape e.g. Leuko Sportstape	Taping for fingers to prevent and protect existing blisters	2 rolls
Medications		
• Antipyretics e.g. paracetamol 500 mg	Fever	20 tablets
• Non-steroidal anti-inflammatories e.g. Voltaren®	For pain and to reduce inflammation	10 tablets
• Non-sedating antihistamine e.g. Clarityne™ 10 mg	Runny or blocked nose, allergies	10 tablets
• Lozenges e.g. Dequadin®	Sore throat	10 lozenges
• Anti-emetics e.g. Maxalon® 10 mg	Nausea, vomiting, motion sickness	10 tablets
• Antidiarrhoeals e.g. Smecta®	Diarrhoea	10 sachets
• Laxatives e.g. Dulcolax™ 5 mg enteric-coated tab	Constipation (e.g. due to change of environment)	10 tablets
• Sedatives e.g. Imovane® 7.5 mg	Difficulty falling asleep due to competition stress or a change of environment	5 tablets
• Betamethasone cream e.g. Betnovate® cream 0.1%	Rashes, skin allergies	1 tube
• Antiseptic cream e.g. Bactroban®	Small open wounds	1 tube
Skin Care		
• Sunscreen (SPF 15+, waterproof)	Protection from sun	1
• Lip balm	Protection from sun	1

* For medications, consult your doctor / pharmacist for the appropriate dosages and use.

All competitive sailors need to be aware of what they can and cannot take or do. The prohibited classes of pharmacological agents are listed in *table 14.3*. In addition to those listed, there are also classes of drugs whose use is allowed, but subject to certain restrictions. They include alcohol (alcohol is not tested for in yacht racing), cannabinoids (e.g. marijuana, hashish), local anaesthetics, glucocorticosteroids (a group of strong anti-inflammatory drugs), and beta-blockers (these reduce the heart rate and anxiety, and are banned for match racing helms).

Table 14.3. IOC / ISAF Prohibited classes of substances, issued on 1st April 2000.

PROHIBITED CLASSES	SOME EXAMPLES (THERE ARE MORE)	REASON FOR ABUSE
1. Stimulants	Amphetamines, cocaine, caffeine[1], ephedrine[1], pseudoephedrine[1], phenylpropanolamine[1], salbutamol [2] (e.g. Ventolin)	Perks the athlete up, giving him more drive and aggression
2. Narcotics	Morphine, pethidine	Dulls the senses
3. Anabolic agents	Includes anabolic steroids (e.g. stanozolol, nandrolone, androstenedione, DHEA, testosterone) and some beta-2 agonists (e.g. clenbuterol)	Increasing lean body mass and strength
4. Diuretics	Furosemide, acetazolamide	Weight loss (for weight-restricted sports), and to mask the presence of other drugs
5. Peptide hormones, mimetics, and analogues	Growth hormone, insulin, erythropoietin	Growth hormone and insulin increase body mass; erythropoietin increases blood haemoglobin

[1] *Drugs like caffeine, ephedrine, pseudoephedrine, phenylpropanolamine, and some others can be taken in small amounts, as long as levels in the urine do not exceed the upper limits specified by the IOC Medical Commission.*
[2] *Drugs like salbutamol are permissible if used in inhaler form to treat asthma. Written notification by the a respiratory or team physician is necessary.*

Inadvertent doping has occurred in the past. As a competitive sailor, you will need to take certain precautions to ensure that your urine sample will not turn up a positive result in the event that you are picked for a doping control test:

- Be on your guard as some prohibited drugs like ephedrines and pseudoephedrines are commonly found in medications that are used to treat headaches, coughs, and colds.

- When consulting a doctor for various ailments, let him know that you are a competitive sailor so that he will prescribe alternatives that are legal in sailing. Some medications require written notification from the doctor.

- The IOC / ISAF list of prohibited and restricted drugs is continually amended, with new drugs being added each time (and occasionally a few are removed from the list). Substances similar to the drugs already on the list, though not specifically included in the list, can also be illegal. If you are not sure if any substance you are taking or intend to take is legal or not, always consult your doctor, the local anti-doping in sport authority, or your National Olympic Committee. The updated list is also available on the ISAF and IOC websites.

- Herbal preparations and other mixtures are generally not guaranteed to be dope-free as it is difficult to get a complete analysis of what goes into the preparation. One batch might be dope-free, but another from the same source might not be. Athletes have failed tests before because of supposed herbal preparations they were taking, so do not risk it – if in doubt, leave it out!

- In some countries, banned substances are readily available in health food stores. Do not assume that any substance is legal simply because it can be easily purchased off the shelf.

There is also a list of prohibited methods that you should be aware of. Blood doping, which is the administration of blood, red blood cells, artificial oxygen carriers, and related blood products to an athlete, in order to enhance the blood's oxygen-carrying capacity, is understandably banned. In addition, pharmaceutical, chemical, and physical manipulation to alter the integrity and validity of urine samples in doping controls is prohibited.

Every year, many sailors are attracted to the Laser class because of the good, clean competition at all levels. Fortunately, doping is not prevalent in our sport, so let us keep it this way!

Chapter 15

Putting it All Together - Planning a Training Programme

content by **Ben Tan** *and* **Angela Calder**
reviewed by **Todd Vladich** *and* **Edgar Tham**

*W*hile the Laser is a relatively simple boat, the sport of Laser sailing is by no means simple. There is so much to know and so many skills to acquire. There is sail tuning, straight-line speed for various points of sail, boat handling skills, fitness, wind shift reading, tactics, strategy, and a whole lot more. Hence, the importance of a well-planned, systematic training programme.

While working hard to acquire sailing skills and fitness, we have to ensure that our bodies adapt to the training in order to reap the fruits of our labour. Recovery maximises this adaptation and reduces the risk of overtraining. In this final chapter, we will integrate all the various training elements, including recovery strategies, into a systematic and realistic training plan.

Water based training adds variation to your training programme.

YEARLY PLANNING INSTRUMENT

A good way to integrate all the training elements and avoid being overwhelmed is to have a systematic game plan. Here is a simple four-step formula:

1. Set your targets.
2. Devise a realistic plan on how you intend to get there.
3. Carry out your plan.
4. Monitor your progress, and identify and rectify inefficiencies and mistakes along the way.

After setting your targets, the best way to devise and monitor your plan is to use a yearly planning instrument (YPI) (*chart 15.1*). Putting it on paper gives you a good idea of how feasible and realistic your targets are, and helps you fit everything in. Furthermore, it is a reminder to keep the big picture in mind. With it, you are less likely to leave your training to the last minute.

Make an enlarged copy of the blank YPI found at the end of this chapter and fill it up. As changes will inevitably be made along the way, it is best to use a pencil. Here are a few explanatory notes on completing the YPI:

- *Year, month:* You may start from any month of the year. On top of the month "January," indicate the appropriate year.

- *Regatta:* List down all the races you intend to participate in. If you are not sure if you will be going for the race, put it in brackets. The race or races that are most important to you (i.e. the ones you are peaking for) should be highlighted.
- *Target:* For each race, write the position above which you realistically hope to finish. E.g. if your target is to finish in the top 10, then write "10" in the appropriate box.
- *Phase:* Periodize (see below) your training into preparatory, competition, and transition phases and mark out the period for each phase.
- *Training Hours per Week:* Indicate the intended total number of training hours per week for each period.
- *Testing:* Cross the box corresponding to the weeks where you will be performing your own fitness tests or the weeks where your coach or physiologist will be measuring your physiological parameters.
- *Exams / Work:* Indicate the periods when you have other commitments so that you can adjust and plan your training appropriately.
- *Speed, Boat Handling, Tactics / Strategy, Fitness:* Indicate when you intend to concentrate on each of these elements of sailing. Stretches that are not highlighted do not mean that you will not be working on those elements – it simply means that you are not focusing on them. Although 'recovery' is included under 'fitness,' psychological recovery strategies must not be neglected. Use the blank rows for additional elements that you may want to work on, e.g. match racing starts.
- *Prep:* Set aside time for boat preparation – to do repairs, replace worn-out lines, try out new systems and sailing gear, etc.
- *Mind:* This is where you set aside time to practice your mental skills (e.g. mental rehearsal, positive self-talk), read books related to sailing, browse through the accumulated sailing magazines, or review the sailing videos.

As the YPI gives an overview, it cannot be overly detailed. For detailed records and analyses, it is a good idea to keep a training logbook, where race details and training specifics are noted. Keep the YPI in your logbook so that you will constantly be reminded of the overall game plan.

Chart 15.1 Sample Yearly Planning Instrument.

Yearly Planning Instrument

Name: Mr Fast   Rig: Standard / Radial   Date: 1 Jan 2000

Season Planner

Year	2000	
Month	Jan, Feb, Mar, Apr, May, Jun, Jul, Aug, Sep, Oct, Nov, Dec	
Week	1 2 3 4 (per month)	
Regatta	Club series (Feb); Qualifiers (May); Sch Champ (Jun); Nationals (Jul); Inter-Club (Aug); Qualifiers (Sep); Invitational (Oct); (Asia Pac) (Nov)	
Target	5 / 5 / 5 / 5 (Club series); 5 (Qualifiers); 3 (Sch Champ); 9 (Nationals); 5 (Inter-Club); 5 (Qualifiers); 9 (Invitational); 30 (Asia Pac)	
Phase	Preparation — Competition — Transition (0)	
Training Hours per Week	15, 25, 8, 25, 8, 20, 5, 15, 5, 15, 5, 10, 4, 15, 30, 15	
Testing	X X X X	
Exams / Work	Exams	

Speed
- Upwind Speed
- Reaching Speed
- Downwind Speed

Boat Handling
- Tacking
- Gybing
- Mark Rounding
- 720° / 360° Turns
- Starts / Acceleration

Tactics / Strategy
- 1st 100 m
- Upwind Tactics
- Mark Approaches
- Wind Shift Reading
- Reaching Tactics
- Running Tactics

Fitness
- Target Weight — 82 kg, 80 kg, 78 kg
- Hypertrophy
- Maximum Strength
- Endurance Strength
- Aerobic Capacity
- Anaerobic Capacity
- Flexibility
- Nutrition
- Recovery

Prep
- Hull & Rig
- Sailing Gear

Mind
- Mental Skills
- Reading / Videos

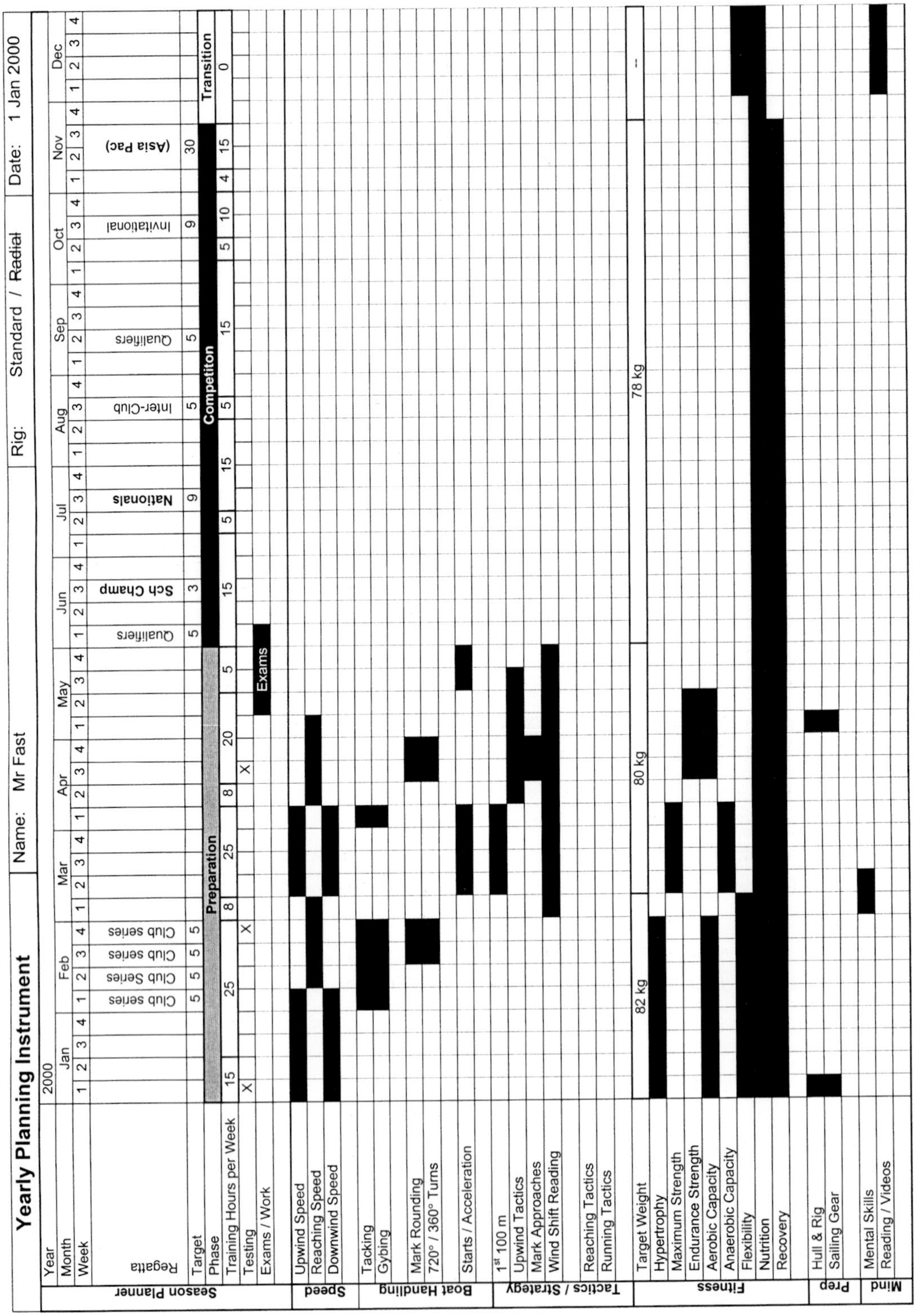

PERIODIZATION

Your training can be organized into cycles, within which the training volume and intensity are varied. This is called periodization. At the beginning of each cycle, the training intensity is typically low while the training volume is high. During the course of the cycle, the training volume is reduced while the intensity is stepped up (*fig. 15.1*). Periodization offers a few theoretical advantages:

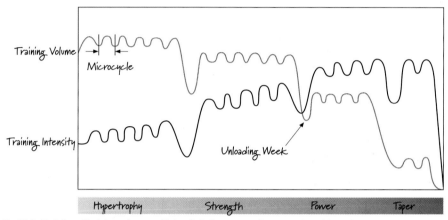

Fig 15.1. Variation of training volume and intensity in the course of a preparatory phase.

- Human performance is innately cyclical – it is impossible to remain in peak form throughout the year. Periodization varies the volume and intensity to conform to this innate cycle, such that the training is heavy when the athlete is fresh and light when the athlete is at risk of fatigue.
- The variations prevent staleness.
- The high-volume, low-intensity programme at the beginning of the cycle conditions the body for the high-intensity work later on.
- The low-volume, high-intensity workouts prior to the competition phase reduce the risk of overtraining and allow the sailor's form to peak.

In the sample YPI, the year's training programme was organised into one big cycle (macrocycle). If you come from a part of the world that is dominated by the Monsoons, you may opt to have, say two macrocycles a year, to accommodate the Northeast and Southwest Monsoon seasons. Each macrocycle is divided into mesocycles, each lasting 2-3 months. Each week is a microcycle. Note that at the beginning of the cycle, the programme is packed with many activities (e.g. beating, hypertrophy training in the gym, aerobic training) to raise the training volume. The high volume is also reflected in the relatively high number of training hours per week in the sample YPI shown.

Within each mesocycle, the training programme is further divided into:

- *Preparation phase.* During this phase, time is spent preparing for competition. Initially, the fundamentals like aerobic training, straight-line speed, and boat handling skills are practised. Towards the end of this phase, more complex skills like tactics and starts are mastered. In the last few days to two weeks of this phase, the training is tapered, whereby the training volume is drastically reduced (e.g. by 50%) to rejuvenate the body before the big race. As the preparation phase is tough, it is a good idea to intersperse it with an unloading week every 4-6 weeks to allow the adaptation process to "catch up" with the training load.
- *Competition phase.* The major races which you wish to peak for fall within this phase. The focus shifts from preparation to performance. Physical training takes a back seat, and only maintenance work is done in the gym.
- *Transition phase.* This is the rest phase, lasting approximately 2-6 weeks. Take a break from sailing and participate in other sports for a change (active rest). If the transition phase is long, continue your maintenance programme, but try something other than your usual gym routine (e.g. circuit weight training, water based training) so that you will not get stale when the next preparation phase starts.

RECOVERY

Hard work alone is not enough to produce the best results, for you also need time to adapt to training. The principle of recovery refers to that part of training where the benefits of the work done are maximised by employing practices to reduce residual fatigue:

Hard Work + Good Recovery = Optimal Performance

Good recovery strategies not only accelerate positive training adaptations (*fig. 15.2*), but they also enhance the sailor's capacity to undertake more work and minimises the risk of illness and injury.

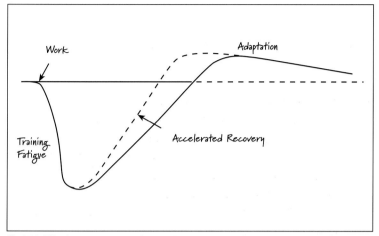

Fig 15.2 *Effective recovery strategies accelerate training adaptations and reduce training fatigue.*

Over-Reaching and Overtraining

A period of hard training is often followed by an acute decrement in performance. This is natural in the short term, as in over-reaching, where performance returns to normal or above normal after a short period of rest. However, with excessively high training volumes and intensities over a prolonged period, the overtraining syndrome results. Here, performance takes more than two weeks to return to baseline levels. It is therefore understandable that the overtraining syndrome is an anathema to be avoided by all athletes. Even when the training volume and intensity are low, athletes can succumb to the overtraining syndrome due to the additional stress from studies, work, and travelling (e.g. racing on the circuit).

With the pressure to perform, either from within or without, it is sometimes easy to make the mistake of overtraining to the point of diminishing returns. To avoid this mistake, sailors must be aware of and look out for the signs and symptoms of the overtraining syndrome. These include:

- Loss of motivation (burnout), feeling psychologically drained and fatigued, loss of appetite, mood changes.
- Sleep disturbances, especially insomnia (despite feeling tired).
- Elevated resting heart rate.

- Weight loss.
- Increased susceptibility to injuries.

Attempts have been made to identify markers in the blood that will help diagnose the overtraining syndrome in athletes, but none are as sensitive as the athlete's subjective feeling. Sailors must recognise and listen to the cues above.

Recovery Strategies

Recovery practices should be an integral part of training. Use them to enhance positive adaptation, even before the signs and symptoms of the overtraining syndrome start to creep in. The components of an effective recovery strategy include:

Replacement of Fluids and Calories. For positive training adaptations to occur, refuelling and rehydrating your muscles are essential. Take plenty of carbohydrate-rich foods and fluids soon after each race and training session to ensure that glycogen and fluid are available for positive adaptation processes like muscle-building. *Chapter 12* provides a more detailed dietary plan.

Stretches. These should be performed before and after training, and once more in the evening. Go through the whole range of stretches to relieve those sore and tired muscles.

Hydrotherapies. Contrasting hot and cold showers, or using a warm spa with a cold plunge pool or shower (*see boxed text*) increases the blood flow to the working muscles and accelerates the removal of lactic acid. Drink plenty of fluids before, during, and after treatments, as sweating tends to go unnoticed in hot and wet environments. It is also important to restrict the time in the spa, shower, or bath as lingering too long in a warm environment can lead to dehydration and neural fatigue. When used correctly, hydrotherapies should leave the sailor feeling relaxed but mentally alert, and not sleepy and lethargic.

Guidelines for Baths/Showers/Spa

1. *Rehydrate with water before, during, and after each session.*
2. *Clean skin with soap and shower off beforehand.*
3. *Alternate: Warm (37-39 °C) and Cold (10-16 °C)*
4. *Duration:*
   - *Shower: Warm: 1-2 min; Cold: 10-30 s (repeat process three times) or*
   - *Spa / Bath: Warm: 3-4 min; Cold: 30-60 s (repeat process three times)*
5. *Shower and rehydrate to finish.*

Sports Massage. This has two major physiological benefits. Firstly, massage increases local blood flow, and this enhances the delivery of oxygen and nutrients to tired muscles while removing metabolic by-products such as lactic acid. Secondly, the warming and stretching of soft tissues provides temporary flexibility gains. The psychological benefits include an improvement in mood states. Athletes feel less fatigued and more relaxed.

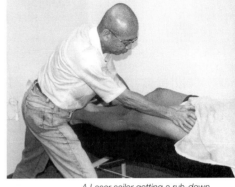

A Laser sailor getting a rub-down on his most valuable muscle.

Relaxation Techniques. Meditation, breathing exercises, music, tai-chi, relaxation massage, and flotation are frequently used techniques. They reduce the amount of stimulation to the brain to enable the athlete to calm down and relax. Apart from flotation, all these techniques can be practised daily without the need for any specialised equipment or facilities. An ideal time for using these strategies is immediately before going to bed, when learning how to 'switch-off' from the days' events will help to encourage a good night's sleep.

From the sample YPI, it can be seen that recovery is important almost throughout the training cycle. During the preparation phase, where training volume and intensity are high, recovery helps the sailor to cope with the training. During the taper, recovery strategies quickly rejuvenate the sailor for the big race. During the competition phase, exercise volume might not be as high, but exercise intensity and psychological stress are, so recovery is important here as well.

With a good training plan, progress can be made, and results will come. There is no need to hope for the right weather, a favourable shift, or luck. You will be well prepared for all situations.

Yearly Planning Instrument

Name: Rig: Standard / Radial   Date:

Season Planner	Year		
	Month		
	Week		
	Regatta		
	Target		
	Phase		
	Training Hours per Week		
	Testing		
	Exams / Work		
Speed	Upwind Speed		
	Reaching Speed		
	Downwind Speed		
Boat Handling	Tacking		
	Gybing		
	Mark Rounding		
	720° / 360° Turns		
	Starts / Acceleration		
Tactics / Strategy	1ˢᵗ 100 m		
	Upwind Tactics		
	Mark Approaches		
	Wind Shift Reading		
	Reaching Tactics		
	Running Tactics		
Fitness	Target Weight		
	Hypertrophy		
	Maximum Strength		
	Endurance Strength		
	Aerobic Capacity		
	Anaerobic Capacity		
	Flexibility		
	Nutrition		
	Recovery		
Prep	Hull & Rig		
	Sailing Gear		
Mind	Mental Skills		
	Reading / Videos		

The Complete Introduction to Laser Racing

INDEX

RECOMMENDED READING

Advanced Racing Tactics – Stuart H. Walker
W. W. Norton and Company, United States of America, 1992
To many sailors, this book is a bible for racing tactics. The in-depth and systematic discussion provides a comprehensive coverage of practically any tactical situation you might encounter. It is not exactly easy reading, but it is still must read for the tactical sailor. The author has also written other popular books on tactics like "Positioning: The Logic of Sailboat Racing" and "The Tactics of Small Boat Racing."

Championship Laser Racing – Glenn Bourke
Fernhurst Books, United Kingdom, 1998 Fax: +44 (0) 1903 882715
Triple World Champion Glenn Bourke's approach and attitude to competitive sailing are exemplary. In this book, he shares his thoughts and racing tips, providing the reader with not only valuable pointers, but also an insight into the mind of a true legend.

Concept2 Indoor Rower Website
http://www.concept2.co.uk/v4/index.html
Like sailing, rowing involves both the upper and lower body. This makes it a more sailing-specific aerobic training modality compared to running. Of the many rowing ergometers available, the Concept2 Indoor Rower is one of the most popular. In its UK website, sailors will find useful training programmes.

High Performance Sailing – Frank Bethwaite
International Marine, Great Britain, 1996
A scientifically in-depth book on the wind, water, sails, hull, and foils. The book has everything you need to know about the wind and the way if flows around your sail, plus much more. It is a tough read, but the insight gained makes it worth the effort.

LaserCoach 2000 – James O'Callaghan
SailCoach Associates Ltd., 1999
An interactive CD ROM with an excellent collection of video footage of top legends like Robert Scheidt and Ben Ainslie. Aerial shots taken during the 1996 Olympics and close-ups during training clearly demonstrate the advanced technique which few get a chance to see. Many of the clips complement this book and are worth viewing over and over again, until the technique sticks in the head. This is a must for those who want to be fast.

In Pursuit of Excellence: How to Win in Sport and Life Through Mental Training, 2nd edition –Terry Orlick
Human Kinetics, United States of America, 1990
This book is an all-time best seller in applied sport psychology written by one of the world's best sport psychologist. It will show you how to develop the positive outlook that turns "ordinary" people into winners in the performance arena and off. This book is a must for sailors and coaches who want to cultivate a winning strategy, and even for parents who want to better understand and help their children pursue excellence in sport, and balance in life.

Recovery Weekly Planner – Angela Calder
Australian Sports Commission, Canberra, 1992
A weekly planner designed with removable and reusable colour-coded stickers to help athletes manage their time and cope with their busy schedules. It includes a reminder about the various types of recovery with guidelines for stretching and hydrotherapy.

Sail Fitter: Sailing Fitness & Training, 2nd edition – Dr Michael Blackburn
Fitness Books, Australia, 2001
Michael Blackburn's systematic approach to training and racing has helped him evolve from club racer to international frontrunner. His PhD in the field of sports physiology and psychology, coupled with his experience as a world-class sailor makes his book a must-read for all competitive Laser sailors.

Survival for the Fittest – Australian Institute of Sport
Murdoch Magazines, Australia, 1999
This recipe book is sports nutrition in its most practical form. It is the definitive guide to getting organised at home and cooking great meals. Recipes are accompanied by nutritional analysis, easy cooking hints, and a selection of tips from athletes themselves. Quick, delicious, and foolproof, the recipes are designed to provide maximum energy and nutrition in a minimum space of time.

Tactics: Fleet Racing, Team Racing, Match Racing, 2nd edition – Rodney Pattisson
Fernhurst Books, United Kingdom, 1998 Fax: +44 (0) 1903 882715
This book gives a good overview of racing tactics, especially for those fleet racers who want an introduction to team and match racing.

Team Racing for Sailboats – Steve Tylecote
Fernhurst Books, United Kingdom, 1998 Fax: +44 (0) 1903 882715
For fleet racers, team racing is a good way to sharpen tactical skills and improve the knowledge and application of the racing rules. For information on team racing, Steve Tylecote's book is one of the best.

CREDITS

Cartoons: *Chew Eng Chong*

Photographs: *Peter Bentley:* pg 2, 5, 53, 72.
The Straits Times: front cover, fig 3.1.
Michael Blackburn, from Sail Fit: Sailing Fitness & Training, Fitness Books: pg 227. *Meteorological Service Singapore:* fig 7.6.
Wong Maye-E: back cover; pg 4, 25 (top), 36, 59, 126, 135, 146, 148, 154, 174, 231; fig 2.1, 2.3-2.16, 3.7, 3.8, 3.10, 3.11, 4.1-4.4, 4.6, 4.9-4.11, 5.1-5.3, 5.5, 6.2, 6.3, 7.9, 7.19, 7.21, 7.25, 8.6, 10.1-10.4, 10.6-10.11, 11.1-11.4, 11.12, 12.1-12.5, 14.1, 14.2, 14.4, 14.7-14.9, 14.11, 14.12.

Charts: *Meteorological Service Singapore:* fig 7.3.
Changilog: fig 8.1.

Drawings: *Josie Quak:* pg 91, 105; fig 2.2, 3.1, 3.8, 7.1, 7.2, 7.4, 7.5, 7.7, 7.8, 7.10-7.16, 7.18, 7.20, 7.22, 7.23, 8.2-8.5, 8.7, 11.5-11.11.

Quotes: *Michael Blackburn, from Sail Fit: Sailing Fitness & Training, Fitness Books (pg 5):* pg 199.
Glenn Bourke, from Championship Laser Racing, Fernhurst Books (pg 88): pg 124.
Glenn Bourke, from Championship Laser Racing, Fernhurst Books (pg 87): pg 129.
Dean Barker, from www.quokka.com: pg 171.
Steve Cockerill, from www.roostersailing.com: pg 49.

Sailor in Photograph: *Stanley Tan:* pg 36 (right), 174; fig 2.7, 4.3, 4.4, 4.6, 10.11 (right), 11.1-11.4, 11.12, 12.2, 14.1, 14.2, 14.4, 14.12.

Every effort has been made to contact the holders of copyright but in some cases without success. To these, the editor and publisher offer their apologies, trusting that they will accept the will for the deed.